TWENTY-FOUR | TIMES | A | SECOND

TWENTY-FOUR

New York | Evanston | and | London

| TIMES | A | SECOND

FILMS | AND | FILM-MAKERS

by William S. Pechter

HARPER | & | ROW | PUBLISHERS

To Eric Bentley

CONTENTS

CONTENTS

FOUR | **SPECTATORS**

FIVE | **THEORY**

FOREWORD AND ACKNOWLEDGMENTS

The pieces in this book were written at various times, indicated at the end of each, over the past ten years, and I hope they retain some topical sense of the occasions which gave rise to them. Though I have revised stylistically throughout, I've made no attempt to pretend to any infallible consistency of opinion, and have indicated afterthoughts and changes of mind in the form of occasional postscripts and footnotes which remain distinct from the original pieces; even where footnotes aren't dated, it should be clear when they have been added later.

I began writing film criticism in 1960, and have tried to capture, in the book's first piece, some sense of that period's bleak prospect for anyone who cared seriously about films. It was also in that dark time of CinemaScoped plays and rumors of a New Wave followed by films like *Black Orpheus* that I first read through the collected film criticism of James Agee, and I can recall how, reading it then, one wished to rise up from it and cry with him in anger and despair: The art of the film is dead! It's time to reinvent it! Soon after, that dead art was being reinvented by Antonioni and Godard—and most of this book was written in the light of their achievements—but I am no more prescient now than I was then. And so I think that past time may still be worth remembering.

Versions of some of these pieces first appeared in the following magazines: "Notes on Cant" and "For and Against Godard" in *Commentary;* "Satyajit Ray: An Appreciation" in *Commonweal;* "Two Movies and Their Critics," "The Closed Mind of Sergei Eisenstein," and the postscript on *The Virgin Spring* in *The Kenyon Review;* "Last Night at *Marienbad*" in *The Kenyon Review* and *Moviegoer;* "The Director Vanishes" in *Moviegoer;* "On Agee on Film" and "Trials" in *Sight and Sound;* "The Art of the Film (cont.)" in *The London Magazine* and *Contact;* " = Time²" in *Contact;* "The Light Is Dark Enough" in *Tulane Drama Review;* "American Madness" in *Kulchur;* "Parts of Some Time Spent with Abraham Polonsky" in *Film Quarterly;* and "Anti-Western" in *Film Comment.* Work on this book was made possible by a fellowship awarded by the Council of the Humanities of Princeton University, for which I am grateful.

Finally, I want to express my gratitude to my wife, Caroline, without whose help this book would not have been completed; and to Edward Pechter and Robert Chappetta for their invaluable criticism over the years of the pieces in it. In several instances, our arguing of the subjects of these essays has been so intense that I no longer feel able at some points to distinguish their ideas from mine, and I apologize to them for whatever unknowing plagiarism their insights may have tempted me to.

. . . All films are realistic in that they *show* things instead of suggesting them in words. What is seen is seen. Thereby it becomes *true* in the sense in which Goethe uses the word.—JEAN COCTEAU, *Cocteau on the Film*

Photography is truth . . . and the cinema is the truth twenty-four times a second.—BRUNO in Jean-Luc Godard's *Le Petit Soldat*

ONE | **PRACTICE**

PERIOD PIECE: HOLLYWOOD, 1960

I'd been prepared for vulgarity, and found it; yet it wasn't as it should have been. Alighting from a bus, I had asked the way to Hollywood only to discover I was in it. But where were the platinum pleasure domes, the screen-silvering studios? I'd expected the vulgarity of De Mille, and found instead the vulgarity of . . . Long Island City! Drab and uninteresting, a smog-laden, neutral gray façade of fortresslike factories and vast used-car lots; the pleasure domes—Grauman's Chinese, etc.—I later learned were elsewhere, while the factories were, in fact, the remaining movie studios. Nor does the resemblance to factories end, I was subsequently to discover, with the impassive granite exteriors. But, of course, factories are exactly what they are.

It's all too easy to sneer at Los Angeles; it is vulnerable. The architectural archetype of the city is unregenerately the hamburger stand, in all its splendid and elephantine variations; candybox modern the predominant style, "We Never Close" the motto. The fauna is often in actuality that loud, floral-hued booster one had thought, or hoped, to be the European's imaginary caricature of the American tourist. On the radio, I heard one of a group of foreign-exchange students ingenuously respond to the question of what he liked best about Los Angeles: "San Francisco!" The local newspapers recall the "Love Nest" days of the worst New York tabloids, each hawking its own matricide, uxoricide, infanticide; children's deaths by plastic bag seem most recently to have captured the public's imagination (do they preview them in Pasadena?). To a New Yorker, used to another style of sordidness, the customs of the country can be oddly disorienting. For there is also that curious underside to the city, not so readily understood or easily condescended to. The faintly disturbing spectacle of liquor being sold in drugstores; the hushed tableaux of shoppers in all-night supermarkets, coldly aglow in the blue fluorescence as you ride swiftly by: taken together, such things and others become vague hints of a kind of subterranean life, sinister and surreal, proceeding autonomously beneath the placid surface.

I had come to study film-making at UCLA. Perhaps it was because I was here on a tangent, so to speak, not wanting to make movies but only to learn how they are made, that the experience seemed to give rise to tangential questions. Is anyone engaged in the serious criticism of films really aware of the immense body of technical knowledge that goes into making them? Does Parker Tyler know the characteristics of integral bipack, the use of dimmer banks, the meaning of the lenticular process?[1] Meaningless questions, of course; more pertinent to wonder: how much of these things did Griffith know, does Chaplin? And where have the technological advances taken us? The crowning result of our mammoth mechanical sophistication seems inevitably to be an *Around the World in Eighty Days,* relentlessly pursued by an *Around the World with Nothing On,* a current British contribution to the nudist cycle.[2] And yet one cannot escape the fact that making films has become a complicated business; a visit to a studio, and one sees the massive, intractable machinery with which films are made, and the way the films are conceived so as best to accommodate the tools of their creation. And so we only dare imagine what we know the camera can do, as though the

1. Lest it seem I'm claiming here some technical expertise for myself as a critic, I hasten to add that, while I understood these things at the time I mentioned them, I haven't the slightest idea what they mean some ten years later.
2. In 1963, it was *55 Days at Peking* followed by *55 Ways of Peeking.*

camera might not do anything we imagine. And so our railroads ride upon us.

The ambiguous implications of this situation are reflected in the contradictions within the university's motion picture division. The division is affiliated with the theater arts department, and offers bachelor's and master's degrees, which are known to be both academically and professionally worthless. It intensely wishes to avoid identification as a mere trade school, yet its curriculum unavoidably veers toward vocational training. Meanwhile, the aesthetics of the film shrink further and further into specialized, not to say recondite, study, seemingly incapable of being effectively assimilated with the ponderous body of technology. And then there is that other unavoidable concern, money. One is constantly being reminded of the awesome costs of the necessary equipment; the making of even what are called low-budget movies can require prodigies of financing. And, perhaps, with the virtual regularity of a law, there is a certain point beyond which additional expenditure must bear an inverse ratio to artistic result; a point beyond which money determines the character of the event, beyond which film-making irretrievably becomes an industrial rather than an artistic occasion. Then money becomes, like aesthetic properties, one of the facts and limitations of the medium. One recalls the remark of Jean Cocteau: "Movies won't be an art until the materials are as inexpensive as paper and pencil." It is still one of the truest and most tragic things there is to say.

A lucky break: ROTC students were being recruited as extras for an anonymous major movie, and I managed to smuggle myself into the group. The studios turned out to be Universal-International, the film *Spartacus* with Sir Laurence Olivier, Kirk Douglas, and Charles Laughton, and the director Stanley Kubrick, White Hope model 1960, who, after making less than a handful of striking films independently, was trying his hand at Hollywood. Kubrick looked hopelessly out of place on the set, a dark and brooding New York type in a particularly somber tweed jacket amidst the bustle of a sun-tanned, short-sleeved local crew. Actually, the scene, in which a throng of Roman soldiers hail the accession of a new ruler and march around a plaster coliseum, was to be handled by the second-unit director as such great crowd scenes usually are, presumably according to Kubrick's instructions. The students were the praetorian Guard, with marching directed by ROTC officers and brown body paint applied by epicene old men: "Now hold your leg up, honey!" The scene will probably last several minutes on the screen, took over eight hours to film, and probably cost in itself as much as several of Kubrick's previous films in their entirety. The only line was spoken by Olivier, but Laughton managed to steal the show with a magnificently obscene, ad-libbed gesture directed at the massed extras when, late in the day, they began to grow unruly. Unfortunately, no one was photographing at the time; so much the worse for *Spartacus*.

Walt Disney was presenting an exhibit of "The Art of Animation" at the art museum in Exposition Park. It was not very surprising that the art of animation had become more or less synonymous with the art of Walt Disney; still, one had to admire the sheer nerve by which Disney displays his own "Squirrel Descending a Tree" alongside Duchamp's "Nude Descending a Staircase" and Balla's "Dog on a Leash" as an illustration of the attempt of modern artists to create the illusion of motion in painting. Both arts, however, merged finally into the higher one of merchandising the Master's latest artifact, *Sleeping Beauty*, being presented as the culmination of the animation art (if not all art; one whole panel is devoted to an enthusiastic depiction of the process by which a Brueghel canvas was modified and adapted to a *Sleeping Beauty* background). Cartoons now look like real people; animation has been perfected to the point at which it has become as dull as live action. Since it is known that Disney himself carefully supervised the content and presentation of the exhibit, it is interesting to note that, in order to publicize the later Disney, he is not averse to patronizing the earlier one. Early drawings of Minnie Mouse are compared to the anonymous realism of Sleeping Beauty, the latter labeled a superior example of "character development" and utterly devoid of the vitality of imagination to be found in the stylized simplicity of the former. And a sequence from *Steamboat Willie,* shown as an introduction to the exhibit, was curiously analogous in its effect to that of Méliès' *A Trip to the Moon* shown as a prologue to *Around the World in Eighty Days*. Ostensibly, in both cases, the early works are there to demonstrate how far we have come; in fact, they establish a level of originality and invention which the later works simply cannot match.

The motion picture division was issued invitations to a mysterious preview at MGM. The film was to be *The World, the Flesh and the Devil,* which, it was later discovered, had already opened in other parts of the country. There was no one on the lot to greet us on the evening of the screening but a perplexed guard who hesitantly directed us to a plush projection room. When the small theater had filled, the lights went down and the picture was shown. Afterward, there were no cards to be filled out, no polling of opinions; even the guard had disappeared, and we were left to find our own way out of the darkened studio. Later, it was generally agreed that the purpose of the preview that was not even a preview was to gain the word-of-mouth support of "college intellectuals" for a film that made a tentative pass at being serious. About as close as it comes to that mark is to lift bodily, from *Potemkin,* Eisenstein's famous montage of three stone lions edited into an illusion of movement, only expanded in number to five and extended in size to fill the wide screen. That these amplifications actually seem to be an improvement may well be the most telling comment which can be made on the quality of the original. Though the idea of progress in the arts may be a myth, we do at least make progress in gimmicks.

The division seems to have fallen into a certain fixated contemplation of *Gidget,* a polished attempt to resuscitate the Andy Hardy myth of teen-age innocence against the current strain of violence, whose fascination resides both in its pristine mediocrity and in its being so skillfully made by a youngish director having his first commercial success and thus perforce being also one illustration of how-to-do-it.[3] Like rape, you can even enjoy it if you're willing to relax a little. What would be the most vapid trash on the printed page is given a certain solid, fleshly reality

3. So skillfully made but not *too* skillfully made, or as Bosley Crowther reports of Louis B. Mayer in *Hollywood Rajah* (New York, Holt, 1960), "Along about the fifth Hardy picture Mayer passed the unbelievable word: 'Don't try to make these films any better. Just keep them the way they are.' And to the logical suggestion that the series might be improved by a stronger director than Seitz, he made the curious rejoinder, 'If you had a stronger director the films wouldn't be as good.'"

on the screen—pretty people, pretty scenery—as it runs smoothly along tracks leading inevitably to a fade-out on that Hollywood-hallowed solipsistic kiss.

Yet none of this seems adequately to explain the attention the film receives, which is rather that commanded by an all too powerful adversary. *Gidget* draws the crowds in Westwood Village; meanwhile, George Stevens' *The Diary of Anne Frank* (or *I Remember Mama* plus history) dies a quiet death on Hollywood Boulevard despite advertisements designed to make you feel like a war criminal if you don't patronize it. No matter that the Stevens film isn't very good, it seems to stand for a certain level of seriousness and conviction; and, as the jaundiced screen writer says in *Sunset Boulevard*, "Who wants true? Who wants moving?" *Gidget* is an epitome of the kind of commodity entertainment that the students will eventually have to come to terms with; already, they compete for UCLA apprenticeships to the production of such half-hour filmed television series as *Dennis the Menace*. Once, new talent had a chance of introduction through low-budget films which might allow some individuality. Now, the small black-and-white film has degenerated to the rock-bottom level of *Dragstrip Queen* and *I Was a Teen-age This-or-That*, and, at the other extreme, there is the three-hour blockbuster; often there is more life and vigor in the crudity of the former than in all the gloss of the latter. But a *Porgy and Bess* is simply too expensive a property to be entrusted to an unproven hand (instead, it is entrusted to a proven hack[4]). And Stanley Kubrick, whose last two films (*The Killing*, especially), both made independently of Hollywood, have been among the few recent American films worth caring about, seems less likely to alter Hollywood than be altered by it. The pattern is too well established; even mavericks can get ridden down if they step into a stampede.[5]

4. Albeit a renaissance hack in Otto Preminger, of whom one might say (borrowing Professor Irwin Corey's comment on Sammy Davis, Jr.) that "versatility is the cloak behind which mediocrity hides."
5. I was wrong here, of course; Kubrick's subsequent work, whatever one might think of it, is not merely an instance of this. But I thought then that I saw distressing parallels to the case of John Huston, White Hope model 1941–50, whose latter career, in its breath-taking downward spiral from *The Asphalt Jungle* through *Moby Dick* to *The Roots of Heaven*, might be interred under the epitaph: "White Hope: White Whale: White Elephant."

From *Time* magazine, we learn there is an American New Wave, even before we've had more than a glimpse of the French one. *Shadows* was made on location in New York by John Cassavetes with a cast of semiprofessionals improvising a story about a Negro family. Perhaps as a consequence of its spontaneous nature, *Shadows* comes closer at times to being that elusive entity, a true slice of life, than almost anything else I can think of which claims the name.[6] There is, in effect, no beginning or end to the film—just middle—and the three central characters are not really significantly different when the film stops than they were when it started; not really, with the slight exception of the older brother, any closer to anything like self-knowledge. All this tends to give *Shadows,* especially in comparison with other films concerned with Negroes, the air, if not of art, at least of resolute honesty; without a point, what need polemics? But this very asset, insofar as it is one, is also the film's key liability. In *Shadows,* things just happen; the film makes no attempt to discriminate or differentiate between the several qualities of experience it describes. This isn't to say that the film fails to interpret this experience, only that nowhere in *Shadows* does one see any evidence of the recognition that, perhaps, at some level, experience may be susceptible to some understanding, to some mental apprehension.

Yet I don't so much object to *Shadows'* mindlessness as to its formlessness, regardless of the practical excuses that may be advanced for the film's rambling incoherence. (In fact, the motion picture's ability to give embodiment to an uninterpreted action is one of the most interesting and least explored aspects of the medium, some ramifications of which are touched upon in a brilliant piece on *Paisan* by Robert Warshow and a brief piece on film by Nicola Chiaromonte in the March 1960 *Encounter,* though the latter seems to believe further that this ability signals the only valid direction for the medium to follow.[7]) It's not the lack of conventional shaping in *Shadows* that I object to; after

6. This quality was increasingly lost in subsequent versions of the film that Cassavetes edited as the material was pressed into successively more conventional molds.
7. A position later taken by Chiaromonte to its fanatical extremes in *Encounter* of January 1963.

all, since the film is intended as an assault on certain artistic
conventions, why not an assault on conventional notions of form
as well? Some of Lionel Abel's remarks on *The Connection* seem
to apply to *Shadows* with equal justice. Much of the film is
cruelly, almost unendurably boring, and its implied challenge
seems to be that since it is purporting to depict life itself, un-
fettered by the intrusion of art, you, the audience, are free to
leave any time you become convinced that your own life is this
interesting and this sensitively observed. I was on the verge of
leaving countless times, but what, I believe, finally held me to
the end was so conventional an element as suspense: how will
it all turn out? As the film meanders to a close, one may, in fact,
observe a few other conventionalities as well: a dreadfully Victorian scene of postseduction *tristesse* ("I never knew it could
be so awful") and a heavily moralizing example of a Negro-hater
getting his just deserts, among them. The great mistake of *Shadows* is, it seems to me, to fail to realize that fresh ways of seeing[8]
are useless, or, at best, merely diverting, unless they are allied
with fresh modes of perception.[9]

Pull My Daisy, "starring" Allen Ginsberg, Gregory Corso,
Larry Rivers and friends, with an improvised narration by Jack
Kerouac, was made by Robert Frank and Alfred Leslie, and is
probably, with John Rechy's story, "The Fabulous Wedding of
Miss Destiny," the best Beat creation to date. The "plot" is
bafflingly simple.

It is morning in a loft on New York's Lower East Side. The

8. An example of this: During one scene, there is a playful chase in Central
Park, the two young lovers being pursued by the boy's middle-aged rival.
The lovers elude the older man, and, as they progressively outdistance him,
are seen to run between two park benches, set up so as to divide the screen
symmetrically. Thereafter, the camera holds on the two deserted benches,
while the audience laughs at the amount of time it is taking the pursuer to
reach the spot. The audience waits for his arrival as a punch line to the
visual gag, but he never comes, and the scene fades out on the empty benches.
Thus the educated expectations of the audience for the obvious are left
frustrated, and the spectator's eye is forcibly wrenched from the anticipated
visual cliché.
9. These remarks apply a fortiori to *Faces*, with the exceptions that even
the visual aspect of the earlier film has gone stale, and, in its absence, or that
of any sympathetic response to the characters, "suspense" didn't suffice; I
walked out. I seem to be alone in having found the first half of *Too Late Blues*
easily Cassavetes' most intelligent work in films.

lady of the house awakens, does some desultory straightening up, and attempts to get her little boy off to school. He objects: will he never cease having to eat bowls of farina? Meanwhile, Allen Ginsberg and Gregory Corso arrive with cans of beer and much cheerfulness; the mother shuttles her child out. There follows a brief hiatus in this tight-knit action, wherein the poets smoke what appears to be pot and react accordingly, gamboling about the room. Then the woman is back, and soon her husband Milo, a railroad brakeman, returns home, accompanied by a companion in a peaked woolen cap named Peter the Saint. "Is he really a saint?" one of the poets asks; and, of course, he is.

Milo's wife is much upset. The Bishop is coming with his mother and sister to pay a call; will their other guests behave? The Bishop arrives, and, while Milo's wife runs downstairs to greet him, Milo breaks into a sly little dance. The Bishop and his entourage are brought upstairs, with formal introductions all around. Aside from a tendency to sit in chairs already occupied, the Beats observe proprieties. About this time, an unidentified girl in racy dress appears upon a bed, where she remains reading a book, unremarked, until the movie's end.

The occasion's sobriety is somewhat shaken by the noisy entrance of Mezz McGillicudy, who promptly retires to the toilet, whence he emerges to shake each person's hand. The poets begin to involve the Bishop in nonsensical theological disputation; finally, one of them asks a question: Bishop, is the American flag holy? There follows a brief hiatus in this tight-knit action, during which we find ourselves out on the street where the Bishop is addressing a straggling assemblage of local housewives; to the accompaniment of some exceptionally poignant background music by David Amram, an American flag continues impiously to be blown into his face. Then we are back in Milo's apartment for a bout of pensive silence, broken finally by a brief spat between Milo and his wife; why did he invite all these terrible people just at the time the Bishop was to come? She slaps him.

Again there is silence, during which the camera begins a frantic inventory of the apartment's contents: a table top, a sink, a stove, cockroaches, coffee cockroaches, beer cockroaches, peanut butter cockroaches; a myriad catalogue of cockroaches. Then the poets are at the Bishop once again. Is poets holy? Is baseball holy? Is girls holy? Is holy holy? Is the organ of man holy? This last apparently serves as music cue for the Bishop's mother, and she sails into a rousing hymn on a pump organ that happens to be in the apartment. But, about this time, Mezz McGillicudy walks out of the toilet with a French horn, Milo appears with his tenor sax, a few other instruments arrive and attach themselves to people, and the boys begin to jam; even Milo's child emerges sleepily from the bedroom, rubs his eyes, grabs a horn, and joins in. At this point, the Bishop and his ladies decide to defer to the competition, and make their apologetic departure. Milo's wife is furious. Why did all of Milo's unpleasant friends have to be there to spoil her day? Duly offended, the Beats prepare to leave. Milo's wife begins to cry. The Beats implore Milo to join them. What is she crying for? Milo doesn't know, but "I certainly *do* know what there is to cry about, and it hasn't anything to do with what's happening right now!" So Milo leaves, as the omniscient voice on the sound track assures us, "She'll get over it." Milo dances gaily down the stairs to join his friends. Exeunt, having a ball.

All of this is lovingly but ironically observed through the fuzzy diffusion of Lower East Side light by a camera eye that is, without pomp or pretension, thoroughly poetic; light verse, to be sure, but with a beautiful poise about being this. Events succeed one another in batty disorder, but not really. *Pull My Daisy* isn't a dramatic film; like *Zero for Conduct,* which it in no other way resembles, it moves by metaphor through a field of verbal and visual imagery. Actually, were one to seek out antecedents for the film, one needn't look to other cultures; it is so obviously, as is so much else of Beat creation, a wild fantasia on the theme of *Huckleberry Finn.* Again, as less successfully in *On the Road,* one sees, filtered through a haze of ingenuous, boyish euphoria, the riotous encounter of the unspoilt, natural child with the agents of "sivilization," culminating in the cathartic freedom of the final flight: the boys light out for the territory. Nothing permanent, you understand; for perhaps the truest criticism one can make of the Beat movement is that its territory never really seems much further than the corner bar. But, even in this, *Pull My Daisy* is without guile.

I decide to light out for the territory: San Francisco. I haven't learned how to make movies at UCLA, though I think I've picked up some new ideas on how not to make them. I could pursue this, but I think I won't. Some kinds of knowledge may be corrupting.

I could stay and study film criticism, of course, but fortunately UCLA doesn't teach it. It does teach film theory, armed with Arnheim and Spottiswoode, but here again I think I'd rather not. Perhaps someday from one such course a theorist will emerge with proof that the art of the film exists, and the news can be rushed to the set of *Dennis the Menace*. He will, however, have made a mistake, which is this.

Theory is of value only insofar as it illuminates how actual works of art work; the enemy insofar as it legislates rules for works to follow and be measured by. (So good-bye to Arnheim, Spottiswoode, and virtually everyone except Bazin.)

That the film is an art cannot finally be proven, only demonstrated. No argument can improve on the fact of a *City Lights*.

Yet perhaps a justification for film criticism can be found in just these limits of theory. The fact of *City Lights* exists, and there must be someone to care about such facts, and to insist on them.

(1960)

TWO | **FILMS**

=TIME²

We took the camera in our hands in order to move fast.—GODARD on method

Breathless, according to my trustworthy copy of *Cue,* is supposed to have a running time of eighty-nine minutes; yet I saw it more than twice in less than half that time. The reason? *Breathless* time is like no other movie time. It leaps and whirls, swoops and staggers; above all, it is animate; always active, always *seen.*

But this is, after all, not so very difficult to see, or to say; easier to say it than to know what it means. In the review of the film which appeared in *Time* magazine, all the right words and phrases managed to get said—"cubistic thriller . . . jaggedly abstract piece of visual music . . . heart-stopping energy . . . eye-opening originality . . . crazy humor . . . anarchic beauty"— but, like some jaggedly abstract piece of critical music, they remain unrelated in such a way that no one can really tell what it all adds up to. The trouble with *Breathless* is that, with all its unnervingly original and elliptical quality, it leaves one with the lurking suspicion that the whole thing may be, finally, just one terribly esoteric joke; it was, perhaps, in deference to those American critics who prefer their seriousness straight that the

17

film's American distributors eliminated its prefatory dedication, "To Monogram Pictures." (Other, less obvious jokes have been allowed to remain unexpurgated. Jean-Luc Godard, the film's director, served his apprenticeship as critic for the French film periodical, *Cahiers du Cinéma,* and several scenes are shot against posters advertising some of that odd magazine's odd enthusiasms: *The Harder They Fall* and *Ten Seconds to Hell.* Godard begins one scene with an iris-in, and ends another with an iris-out, employing two of the movies' most archaic technical devices in this most modern of films. Ten minutes after *Breathless* begins, a shaggy girl approaches Michel, the film's hero, on the street, vending a copy of *Cahiers du Cinéma,* which he declines indifferently. "Have you got anything against youth?" she asks belligerently. "Sure, I prefer old people," he replies.[1]) But if the film is only a joke, then those who take it seriously tend to look slightly foolish; if it is serious, then, in dismissing it, one may have failed to champion a Worthy Cause: such are the dilemmas with which Bosley Crowther must daily make his peace.

Probably the best way to cope with a dilemma is to attempt to make the most of what you know. A dilemma *Breathless* certainly is. What, then, do we know?

The film opens on a screen filled by the comics section of a newspaper; pause. A line is thought, or spoken: "After all, I'm no good. If you have to, you have to." And the paper lowers to reveal the face of its reader, Michel; that battered, ugly face so scorned by the reviewers, that battered, handsome face no movie star slickness could ever hope to match. The thumb brushes across the lips in classic, reflective gesture. *"Il faut!"*

Michel steals a car. He races it to Paris, singing and shouting at the sun, even firing a gun into its afternoon blaze. A cop chases, and catches up to him. The gun; in meticulous detail, we see it appear, cock, aim, and kill. The cop, collapsing. Michel, running

---

1. Still further items for the erudition hound. The film's hero occasionally operates under the alias of "Laszlo Kovacs," the name of the character which Belmondo played in *A Double Tour,* an earlier film by Claude Chabrol, and really an embryonic version of Michel. The role of the celebrity who is interviewed in *Breathless* is taken by Jean-Pierre Melville, director of an interesting film of Cocteau's *Les Enfants Terribles,* and regarded by some as a spiritual father of the *Nouvelle Vague.* Finally, Godard himself appears briefly in the role of an informer.

across a dark, open field; through apparently endless space, running.

Michel arrives in Paris, makes a few assorted telephone calls, scans several newspapers, visits the flat of a casual girl friend to cadge some money which he ends up stealing. In her mirror, he mugs at his reflection: his mouth stretched open to a ferocious "O," distended into a grin-grimace, compressed into a pout, and, finally, relaxing as his thumb brushes reflectively across his lips; the sequence of face-making is repeated at intervals throughout the film, like a leitmotif. In block letters, across the girl's wall is written, POURQUOI. It's just a word, she tells him.

On the Champs Élysées, Michel finds Patricia Franchini, his American girl friend, selling Paris *Herald Tribunes*. He wants her to accompany him on a trip to Italy. He wants to sleep with her again. Why? she asks. Because "It's nice to wake up next to a girl." He continues his persuasion, but her only response is in the form of a detached, factual curiosity about those words which he uses that she does not know; *"Qu'est-ce que c'est"* this, and *"Qu'est-ce que c'est"* that? Kiddingly, she tries to sell him a paper; he declines; there's no horoscope. *"Qu'est-ce que c'est horoscope?"* "The future," he explains. "I'm very interested in it."

They part, to meet later. Michel passes a movie theater, its posters screaming: TO LIVE DANGEROUSLY TO THE END! As a man crosses a street, he is struck by an automobile and killed. Michel crosses himself in mock piety, and walks on. It is only death. He visits a friend at a travel agency, in an attempt to raise some money. Unsuccessful. Minutes after he leaves, the police arrive, and, learning Michel has just been there, they frantically pursue him. He disappears down a Metro kiosk; moments later, the cops go down after him. The camera swings leisurely across the broad avenue, holding for a moment in stiff, center frame on a picture-postcard view of the Arc de Triomphe, and then resumes its movement to the adjoining kiosk on the opposite side of the street as Michel casually exits. He passes a theater playing *The Harder They Fall*, and stops to blow cigarette smoke reverently across a screen-filling still of the late Humphrey Bogart.

The screen goes to blackness. "I saw a man die today," Michel's voice says. Patricia's voice: "Are you taking me to dinner?" Iris-in on the couple walking down the street together. Still she will not consent to sleep with him. He tells her an anecdote of a bus driver who, in order to win the woman he loved, stole some money, and posed as a tycoon; when the money ran out, and his imposture was revealed, the woman remained with the bus driver anyway: she loved him also. Patricia remembers she has a date with a journalist who is getting her a chance to cover a story for his newspaper. Disgustedly, Michel drives her to her rendezvous, continuing in his coaxing her to sleep with him: "I like lying next to you." Still unsuccessful, he mockingly derides her as they speed through the city. "Here I am in love with a girl . . . beautiful breast . . . lovely face . . . pretty forehead . . . But she's a coward!" Finally, they arrive at her destination. "Good-bye, you little bitch,[2] you."

Inside the café to which she has come, Patricia finds her journalist at a table. She is a different person, fawning on her vacuous companion. An exchange of sophistication, and callow *Weltschmerz;* Patricia says, "I don't know if I'm unhappy because I'm not free, or not free because I'm unhappy." Then time dwindles away as the journalist becomes involved in an interminable, self-glorifying anecdote which seems to occupy the entire afternoon. Michel follows the couple after they leave, and into the evening, until, seeing them kiss in the journalist's car, he turns away in utter disgust. Scenic views of the Tour Eiffel and Arc de Triomphe give way to Patricia as she hops childishly across paving stones on her way home early the next morning.

Inside her apartment, Patricia finds Michel where he has spent the night, in her bed. He smokes, jokes, cajoles her to join him. He follows her about in his shorts, casually applying his hands, in vain continuing his persuasion. Patricia brushes her hair, and studies her reflection in the mirror; Michel makes his faces at her, and she mimics them. He makes advances.

"Let me alone. I'm thinking."

"What about?"

"I don't know."

"I know."

"Nobody knows. I think of nothing. I'd like to think of something, but I can't."

She moves away. "What are you looking at?" she asks.

"I'm just looking at you."

They sit together on her bed. She plays idly with a Teddy bear; he rummages in her pocketbook, thumbs through magazines. They play games. He puts his hands around her throat, and tells her he will count to eight, then strangle her unless she smiles. "You're such a coward, I'll bet you smile." He counts. She smiles. She fumbles in lighting a cigarette, and he tells her that she does so because she is afraid. He lights a cigarette with poise.

2. *Dégueulasse.*

He asks her, "Do you ever think about dying? I do all the time."
"Say something nice," she replies.
"What?"
"I don't know what."
"Well, neither do I."
Then:
"I've something nice to say."
"What?"
"I want to sleep with you because you're pretty."
She parries his conversation disingenuously. She makes a joking reference to Romeo and Juliet, and the camera cuts to a print of Picasso's *The Lovers*. "You're a liar," he tells her; the camera cuts instantaneously to a print of a face and mask. "There's no need to lie. It's like poker, the truth is best. The others think you're bluffing, and you win."
They engage in a staring contest. She loses. She tells him she is pregnant. He berates her for having been careless. He tells her a joke: a condemned man, climbing the scaffold stairs, trips, and says, "I'm in the future!"
He muses, "What a nutty idea—a baby!"
"I wondered how you'd feel," she says. Staring wide-eyed at her reflection in the mirror, she raises her fingers, and counts to nine.
"Tell *me* something nice," he says.
"I don't know what to say." Then: "You said I was scared. I am scared. I want you to love me, and, at the same time, I don't want you to."
He tells her that he knows what she is thinking.
"You don't know what I think. It's impossible!" She turns on him. "I want to see what's behind that mask of yours. I watched you for ten minutes, and saw nothing, nothing!"
But, abruptly, she changes the subject. Has he read William Faulkner? What does he think of the last sentence of *The Wild Palms*? She reads to him, " 'Between grief and nothing I will take grief.' "
"Which would you choose?" she asks.
"Grief's a waste of time. I'd choose nothing. Grief's only a compromise. And you've got to have all or nothing.
"Looking into each other's eyes, we get nowhere," he tells her. They slip under the sheets, and make love. There, entirely under covers, she says, "It's strange. I see myself in your eyes."
"We're improving Franco-American relations," he assures her.
Later, as they prepare to leave the apartment, the radio babbles

senselessly in the background about De Gaulle, and the Arc de Triomphe. "I feel tired," Michel says, disinterestedly. "I'm going to die."

They go out. Panoramic aerial views of Versailles, and Notre Dame. He steals a car in order to drive her to the airport, where she is to cover her newspaper assignment. In the car, she tells him that she is afraid of growing old.

"You're stupid," he tells her. "You should never be afraid of anything."

They stop for a moment at her newspaper's office, where a man reading a newspaper on the street recognizes Michel from a photograph, and informs a passing cop. But too late; they have already driven away. At the airport, a celebrated writer is being interviewed, questions flying from the press with characteristic inanity.

"Do you believe in love?"

"It's the only thing one can believe in."

"Rilke once said man and woman would grow apart in modern life."

"Rilke was a great poet. He must be right."

"Are women sentimental?"

"Do French and American women have the same love life?"

"*Aimez-vous Brahms?*"

Into this barrage of absurd interrogation and like response, Patricia intrudes her single question: "What is your greatest ambition?"; it goes unheard. Finally, she succeeds in attracting the writer's attention with an acceptably fatuous question about the woman's role in modern society.

"What is your greatest ambition?" she repeats.

He looks at her carefully. "To become immortal, and then to die," he says. The interview fades out on Patricia's face, lost in ambiguous understanding.

Minutes after, she is in a taxi with Michel, rushing to her newspaper's office. On a side street, they jump out to cut through a tunneled passageway which Michel knows. There, in the shadows, Patricia remembers Michel's story about the bus driver, and his lover; what was it about the woman that Michel admired? "She seemed normal, and that's rare," he answers.

Patricia enters the office; Michel waits outside. While she is there, the police arrive to question her. Does she know this man? She is shown Michel's picture. No, she doesn't believe so. She was seen with him earlier that day. Oh, yes, now she remembers; it is a bad picture. No, she doesn't know where Michel is; they met just by accident that morning; yes, he may get in touch with her again to make a date. The police give her a telephone number to call in case Michel should contact her, and warn her against abetting him. She leaves the office, obviously being followed.

Outside, she signals to Michel across the street to indicate that a cop is following her. He follows the cop, and, as they parade thus farcically through the streets, they meet another parade, no more ceremonious, for some foreign dignitary (Eisenhower?); an official parade of state. In the confusion, she ducks into a movie theater; the cop follows her, but not into the ladies' room. She leaps from a low window, and rejoins Michel in the street.

They spend the remainder of the afternoon in another movie theater, watching a Western, kissing. When they leave, it is already night; they go to meet Antonio, the friend from whom Michel hopes to get enough money to take him and Patricia to Italy, driving through the neon-streaked streets in still another one of Michel's stolen cars.

"The cops are after me, and I'm one of the few who likes cops."

"I love you very much," she says to him, for the first time.

"Some jerk must have squealed," he says. Patricia tells him that she hates informers. "It's normal," he answers. "Squealers squeal, burglars burgle, killers kill, lovers love."

He decides to change the car, and drives into a garage. They select a Cadillac, and drive out, Patricia at the wheel, waving good night to the guard at the door as they pass.

"Are you a coward, Pat?" Michel asks.

"It's too late for that now," she replies.

In the neon-lit night, a *New York Times* Building-like illuminated sign flashes news of the imminent arrest of Michel, trailing off: OUI, MAIS . . .

At a sidewalk café, they meet Michel's friends, one of whom he introduces as "My spiritual adviser, Karl Zumbach."

"You're wearing silk socks with tweeds," his spiritual adviser reproaches him.

"I like the feel of silk," Michel explains.

"Then don't wear tweeds."

Patricia sights her journalist at one of the tables. He motions to her to join him, and she goes, but continues to wave and throw kisses to Michel as he makes arrangements with his friends. Antonio is to bring the money to Michel in the morning; he and Patricia are to spend the night in an apartment belonging to one of Zumbach's girls.

Once there, Patricia grows thoughtful.

"I've an idea," she says.

"What?"

"I'm undecided."

"About what?"

"If I knew, I wouldn't be undecided."

He puts the Mozart clarinet concerto on the phonograph. He picks up a novel at random, and scans the quotation from the *NRF* on its cover; the eye seems directed to a word: *mort*. Patricia says she thought he hated music, and he tells her that his father played the clarinet.

"It's sad to fall asleep," she says. "Sleep separates people. Even when you're 'sleeping together,' you're all alone."

The next morning, she gazes at him with loving affection. She goes out to get coffee, telephones the police, and turns him in.

She returns to the apartment, and tells Michel what she has done. She asks him if he will not run. He neither runs nor grows excited, but begins a sort of monologue which she, in turn, takes up; an aria-like dual monologue, sentence overlapping sentence, thought upon thought.

He: "I talked about myself. You talked about yourself. We should have talked about each other."

She: "I don't want to be in love with you. That's why I telephoned the police. I stayed to find out whether or not I was in love with you. And because I'm mean to you, it proves I don't love you."

He: "There is no happy love, they say. That's not true. There is no *unhappy* love."

She: "I wish people would leave me alone." And: "Maybe you love me, and I don't love you. That's why I turned you in."

He: "I'm superior to you." Then: "I don't give a damn. I feel like going to prison."

He goes out into the street. A car pulls up: Antonio with the money. Michel tells Antonio that the police are coming. Antonio tries to convince Michel to get away. He refuses. "I'm beat anyway, and I just want to sleep." Another car turns down the street: the police. Antonio tries to give Michel a gun; he refuses. Antonio tosses the gun into the street, and drives away. Michel picks up the gun, disinterestedly, and begins to trot dully off in the direction Antonio has taken. The police stop their car, leap out, take careful aim, and fire. Michel is wounded in the small of his back; still he continues to run, weaving, staggering, a bloodstain beginning to darken his shirt as he continues his grotesque *Todtentanz* down the length of the street. At the end of the street, as it opens into an expansive avenue, he collapses.

The police reach him as he rolls over on his back, eyes squinting up into the morning sun, dying. Patricia catches up with them. Michel exhales his last breath of cigarette smoke, looks at Patricia, makes his faces: an "O," a grin-grimace, a mocking pout. He whispers, almost inaudibly, and dies.

Patricia asks them what he said.

A cop answers, "He said, 'You are really . . . a little bitch.' "

She looks at them with apparent incomprehension. "A little what? . . . I don't understand."[3] As she speaks, she gestures to complete the sequence of Michel's faces, brushing her thumb across her lips. She turns away.

What, then, do we know? I have made so detailed a summary of the film simply because there seemed no other way adequately even to begin to talk about it. Unlike a play, or novel, there is no written text to which to refer. All is motion, flux; everything happens for an instant on the screen, passes, and is gone; one even wonders, did it really happen? And, if it happened, was it serious? It is difficult enough to prove *Breathless* is serious, no less that it is profound; it *is* profound, yet it resolutely refuses to admit even to being serious. The serious and the comic in the film are fused so inextricably that anyone who tries, at any given moment, to speak of the one without the other is telling only part of the truth, and, to that extent, partially lies. In *Breathless,* everything is serious with meaning, and everything is outrageously funny, and both at the same time. To attempt, for purposes of discussion, to separate the seriousness from its comedy leaves one not only misrepresenting the work, but looking slightly foolish as well, for *Breathless* is never itself so naïvely single. This mixture in *Breathless* is the peculiarly contemporary one, and the achievement of the film's contemporaneity is one which ought not to be underestimated. Offhand, I can think of no other film which has caught with such exact accuracy the look and feel of the present moment—the urgency of the *now!*

3. MICHEL: *C'est vraiment dégueulasse!*
   PATRICIA: *Qu'est-ce qu'il a dit?*
   INSPECTEUR: *Il a dit: vous êtes vraiment une dégueulasse.*
   PATRICIA: *Qu'est-ce que c'est: dégueulasse?*

To capture merely the complex surface of life at a time when that surface has grown unprecedentedly complex is, in itself, an enormous accomplishment. Arguably, it has never before been more important for a work of art to be contemporary than at the present moment; unarguably, the fact remains that *Breathless* does exist unmistakably, and with a shock of recognition in that complex present.

It has been suggested by the press, to the point of being conspiratorially misleading, that *Breathless* is about the empty life and meaningless death of a young French hoodlum; even intelligent admirers of the film have largely been satisfied to accept it on the level of sociological and/or psychological document of the alienation and moral nullity of the present generation, a reading which tends to say more about the admirers than about the work; by their needs, know them. And yet it is true that *Breathless* may be apprehended, in some part, at this level. Much, for example, of what is worst in Patricia may be succinctly enough ascribed to one readily identifiable phenomenon: American college girl in Paris. And Godard occasionally does seem to be describing merely a specimen of familiar bitch; the short-haired, Culture-conscious, whim-ridden, castrating American female. It is this Patricia who, at one point, dons Michel's hat, who is constantly brushing out her no-hair, who counts to nine in a play at pregnancy; indeed, Godard even grants this bitch in Patricia her question during the interview: "What is the role of woman . . . ?" But, finally, this is not enough, and is inadequate to understanding that in Patricia which runs deeper: that lethal female ruthlessness which extends beyond this time, or that place. *Breathless* is best seen without reference to any sociological or psychological context, although either might be provisionally invoked. Patricia's American-ness seems, finally, a direct and efficient way of establishing her estrangement from Michel, and, of course, vice versa; much as the imaginary foreign settings in the plays of Brecht serve immediately to put the events at a certain remove. One gets sufficient sense of the unique difficulties of Michel's relationship with Patricia from the contrast of the brief scene between Michel and the French girl friend from whom he steals some money; everything there is casual, comfortable, and easy. With Patricia, the established forms for circumventing the pain of human contact simply will not do. Everything has to be learned from the beginning, the rules made up as the game moves ceaselessly on.

Yet it is slightly misleading (even as one has the sense that anything one can *say* about *Breathless,* that is, anything short of the actual experience of seeing it, must be at least *slightly* misleading) to speak of Michel's and Patricia's "relationship," with the now unavoidable halation of benign adjustment psychology that has come to blur that term. The characters in *Breathless* exist without psychology, or sociology, even without history; certainly no other modern hero has come to us with so little biography as does Michel. Aside from what we actually see of Michel and Patricia, aside from their concrete actions and elusive words, we know nothing. To discover, at the last minute, that Michel's father played the clarinet is not to be granted any revelation; rather, this fragmentary scrap of information only serves again to emphasize how little of what does not take place directly before our eyes do we actually know.

To the extent that *Breathless* is *about* alienation and communication, that it is *about* a particular human relationship, it is pertinent, and even necessary, to note that the relationship in which its characters exist is a significantly flawed one. Their conversation often sounds like conclusive data from an experimental laboratory in the breakdown of human speech and feeling. He tells her that he saw a man die, and she asks him if he is taking her to dinner; and such data continue to file in. "It's nice to wake up *next to* a girl. . . . I like lying *next to* you. . . . Even when you're 'sleeping together,' you're all alone." Everywhere is the pervasive sense of alienation; people are *next to,* never *with,* one another. Everywhere is the sense of contact not made, failed communion. "We should have talked about each other." "Say something nice" is the recurrent, unanswered plea; "You don't know what I think!" the cry of defiance. But, in fact, "I think of nothing. I'd like to think of something, but I can't."

But the curious fact is that one's final sense of their relationship is of something fully realized, and ultimately truthful. I think this is because they participate in that relationship, conflict and combine, not as psychological vessels, but as moral agents, even divergent life principles. The characters in *Breathless* have

wrenched themselves utterly free from public morality; everything moves too fast; the facts of this life have irrevocably out-
distanced the kind of judgments we have been accustomed to
make on them. Suddenly, we see Michel shoot the cop; suddenly,
we are somewhere else, in the middle of further action. There
simply isn't time to undergo the conventional moral revulsion;
the event exists remorselessly independent of it.

Yet, while *Breathless* takes for granted the death of public
morality, it is misleading and, finally, meaningless to speak of
the film as being "immoral," or "amoral." The important fact
is that, in the midst of their world's chaotically accelerated action,
the characters in *Breathless* have created their own private ethics,
and it is the conflict of these that lies at the heart of the film's
central tension. Both are committed wholly to life, both in
divergent ways. For Patricia, life is boredom, the condition, at
all costs, to be avoided; she must constantly "make it new,"
and yet it is never really new, hardly even different. The life
which constitutes that boredom she accepts as something socially
given: it is the life of the world in which one plays at love, drops
the name of Dylan Thomas, flatters journalists; in short, sells
and deceives oneself in perpetuity. Her single truth, as Michel
perceives, is in her viciousness, in her being really a little bitch,
and in her unwillingness to accept this truth lies what Michel
throughout names as her "cowardice."

For Michel, life is action; in action he finds life's source, and
even its joy. Michel exists in perpetual motion, constantly engaged in action, constantly engaged. To say the last is, in some
sense, to give away the game, for Michel has much of the look
of the existential hero, *l'homme engagé*. And *Breathless* is a fascinating illustration of the progress of existentialism, from the vis-
ceral nonreflectiveness of a Hemingway through the professional
philosophers, and back again, creatively embodied, into the work
of art; impure, but bristling with ideas. But Michel seems, in
the end, as free from the orthodoxies of existentialism as from
any other codified image of Man; he is, finally, simply *a man,*
possessing himself, and bound to nobody's code; after all, he
wears silk socks with tweeds!

If it is in action that Michel discovers himself, one must finally
observe that his moral discrimination does not end at this. Action

has value for him only as it conforms to an individual's truth, and he declares his own simple truth from the very beginning. "After all, I'm no good. If you have to, you have to." Michel's image of himself is neither immoral nor amoral; it is simply normal, and, in this, essentially moral. Michel never seeks to justify himself; he does not sanction but only accepts his sense of what he is: "... I'm no good" ... But: "*Il faut!*"

Throughout, Michel maintains faith with his truth, which is normality. "It's normal. Squealers squeal, burglars burgle, killers kill, lovers love ... and I'm one of the few who like cops." And again, of the woman who remained with her lover, "She seemed normal, and that's rare." All this could easily degenerate into some mere attitudinizing, or specious Noble Savagery, but it never does. Michel is no primitive. His truth is a simple one, but his ethic subtly refined, and it is this: Evil is a fact which can never be civilized out of existence; and: Better to be no good, alive, and in action, than be self-deceived, and morally dead.

To be alive! It is this which informs all of Michel's action; and such a commitment ineluctably involves a commitment to freedom. The act is never gratuitous; it is always a blow struck for liberation. In Michel's every gesture, from physical violence to nuance of speech, he frees and defines and fulfills that in himself which society wishes not to exist; against its animosity, he continuously asserts his own image. On this point, there can be no moderation, no compromise, no grief. "I don't know if I'm unhappy because I'm not free, or not free because I'm unhappy." The question is only unintentionally with meaning, but, indirectly, it gets its answer. "Grief's a waste of time ... only a compromise. And you've got to have all or nothing."

From the joyous ride through the countryside to the final, staggering collapse, Michel is constantly in motion, inventing himself in motion. He is a man caught inventing his own life as it happens, making it up as he goes along. Here one sees the point of an intended appearance of casual spontaneity in a work so obviously and absolutely controlled;[4] for it mirrors Michel's own aesthetic: life as improvisation; a continuous improvised inven-

---

4. Godard on method: "As a director, I improvise at the last minute, but from material that is intensely worked over. . . . The actors do not improvise; all dialogue is written for them, on the spot."

tion on the theme of self. But at the end is always freedom. For while Michel, in some sense, accepts the fittingness of his end, he still cannot but also rebel against it. When last seen, running; away from death, toward an unfolding expanse of open space.

One of the most disturbing of perplexities in this continually disturbing and perplexing film is the relation of Godard, the film's author, to his hero. Throughout, Godard appears to maintain a cool detachment from all he depicts; even Patricia provokes not scorn but only an increasingly incisive interest. Michel is manifestly not the trivial hoodlum of the newspaper reviews; he is, on the contrary, one of the few heroically imagined figures to be found in a contemporary work of art. But is he *the* hero, Godard's image of the best of human possibilities? This Godard cannot be made to say; his one discernible predilection is for vitality, for the state of being alive, and of this predilection Michel is the superb exemplar. Against the furious energy and vitality of his hero, Godard constantly plays off the deadness of the official life. In the most *outré* of circumstances, we are presented with frozen, Fitzpatrick-like travelogue views of public monuments, and state parades; as we lean forward intently to catch every word that passes between Patricia and Michel, automobile horns and sirens blare through the open window, and, in the background, the radio chatters ridiculously of De Gaulle. Which sphere, public or private, is the meaningful one, as they strive desperately to cancel each other out? Against the life of continuous action which Michel creates *ex nihilo,* the beautiful views of the Arc de Triomphe and Notre Dame seem only like so many picture postcards arrived from limbo.

It is in this role as principle of life and freedom that Godard has Michel confront Patricia, principle of evasion and self-deceit. Despite the outcome of this confrontation in terms of plot, it is never in doubt who holds the balance of power in their relationship. Throughout, Michel leads Patricia, pulls and pushes her, despite every resistance she can offer, toward his kind of commitment. In this respect, *Breathless* is virtually unique among current serious films (cf. Bergman, Fellini, etc.): it is supremely a film of hard sensibility, in which the male principle does not abdicate its force in succumbing to the superior wisdom of feminine nonintellect, but triumphs over it. The terms of Michel's engagement frighten Patricia; they demand an end to the comfortable cowardice which is her self-deception. Throughout the film, Michel is constantly inventing ritual tests of courage which she is unable to pass. "I am scared. I want you to love me, and, at the same time, I don't want you to." But in the contest of their encounter she really has no chance; no choice but to submit to the excitement of his kind of daring. In the speeded-up world through which Michel travels, one can't afford the excess baggage of a lie. "Are you a coward, Pat?" he asks her, near the end. "It's too late for that now," she replies.

She turns him in. In part, the reviewers are right: this is merely the way in which a particularly malignant girl disposes of a lover who has become a burden to her; it is, in being that, Patricia's last attempt to cling to that protective cowardice which Michel threatens. But never is it merely this, never is it *merely* any single thing: it is the act which constitutes the film's crucial paradox. "I don't want to be in love with you. That's why I telephoned the police." But, even as Patricia struggles to rid herself of Michel, she capitulates to him. If only he would run, she might pretend to be free of him, but he stays and mocks. "I'm superior to you." He has forced her to a gesture of self-revelation; only in the act of betraying him does she realize that in herself which is her own unique truth. Only in the act of turning him in does she truly kill boredom; she telephones the police not in apathy, but with an undercurrent of nervous excitement like nothing so much as the anticipatory thrill of . . . first love. She comes alive. "You are really . . . a little bitch."

Yet the paradox continues to open inward, a box within a box within another. For Patricia kills Michel not after having grown tired of his attentions, but at that moment—following their last afternoon, night and morning together—when she seems manifestly to have come to love him. And she turns him in. The two facts exist inescapably side by side, and in seemingly absolute contradiction. One scrutinizes the text for some key to their resolution, for some usable idea. "I've an idea," she says. And in the curious way that *Breathless* has of sounding echoes, the screen is resonant with other lines. In *Breathless*, everything is over in a flash, yet all seems coexistent, and contemporaneous. With her love for Michel at its most intense, and his escape from danger imminent, she grants him death. *"To become immortal, and then to die."*

To become immortal . . . yet, certainly, it is a peculiar kind of immortality. For the writer who unleashes the aphorism which so impresses Patricia, immortality is simply fulfillment, if it is anything. For a writer, immortality consists simply in performing as truthfully as one can in the hope that out of this one will be able finally to define one's identity, and stamp its image on the gray blur of the commonplace. To define one's identity, and to fulfill that identity; this is the immortality of a mortal world. And for Michel, for the killer, this means simply to kill, and to be killed . . . by a police bullet. His trip to Italy with Patricia has no place in this identity, and so, even, one might say, as a love offering, she cancels it.

Still the paradox opens, for Michel is not only a killer, he is a very special kind of killer: a killer in a movie. Even as Godard jokes about his own role as artist by appearing in the film as an informer, so Michel stops reverently before a still of Humphrey Bogart, killer and killed a thousand times, and solemnly removes his dark glasses, the gesture of ultimate respect. The moment is an absurd one, yet it is also curiously moving. Above all, it is serene; the only point at which *Breathless* comes completely to rest. For the movie killer, there is only one conclusion, his fate fixed in an eternal return; there are no idyllic trips. And as Michel's dying body careens crazily down the street, the screen reverberates with echoes of inevitability. "The future. I'm very interested in it. . . . Do you ever think about dying? I do all the time. . . . I feel tired. I'm going to die." Climbing the scaffold stairs, the condemned man slips, and says, "I'm in the future!"; the eye falls on a random word: *mort*. All along, Michel saw the end, and named it; not with any gestures of romantic fatalism, but simply by way of keeping faith with the simple, single truth of his existence. "It's like poker, the truth is best. The others think you're bluffing, and you win."

"There is no happy love, they say. That's not true. There is no *unhappy* love." Even as Michel scornfully rejects that in Patricia's final act which springs from weakness, so does he accept, almost gratefully, that which lies locked in the innermost box . . . a genuine gift: the only immortality which can properly belong to him—death by violence. And, in return, he leaves her with a gift of his own: his own kind of truthful courage to accept one's identity. Stripped of masks, she has a face. "You are really . . . a little bitch," he says, and shows his faces; the gesture she completes. And in her identity is still again his immortality.

And there is the music. To discuss *Breathless* textually in this way is a little like treating *Don Giovanni* solely as drama; it can be done, but there *is* the music. The music of *Breathless* is its incessant movement, and the startlingly altered time through which that movement hurls; time orchestrated, and radically rearranged. The reference by *Time* to cubism might be good enough, if a better one did not suggest itself: *Breathless* as the consummate work of futurism, an art of space in motion; and an art which has probably never produced its masterpiece until now. How does the film achieve its extraordinary effects? To begin with, it is important to note that every shot is illuminated only by available light. This is no concession to any imitative fallacy, and the effect of the illumination is to make everything seem suddenly new, rather than comfortably familiar. This, our eyes tell us, is our contemporary world, and, if we are taken quite by surprise, it is because, on the screen, it *is* new, startlingly unfamiliar.

In addition, in *Breathless* Godard has flagrantly perpetrated endless variations on what, in Hollywood, is regarded as a technical error, the jump cut. It is a textbook rule of professional filmmaking that, when one cuts on an action, one cuts to a point exactly contiguous with the action in the previous shot; for example, if a man is raising his arm in medium shot, and we cut to long shot, we expect to find the arm continuing in its motion from the exact point in the air at which we last saw it in the medium shot. Another rule is that one never cuts to the same shot of the same subject; for instance, from a close-up of Patricia to a close-up of Patricia. These rules and others Godard violates throughout his film, and the effect, both individually and in aggregate, is extraordinary. Whereas the purpose of such rules, in the Hollywood film, is that all should appear to be smooth and continuous, their violation creates, in *Breathless,* the sensation of extreme disjointedness and angularity. *Breathless* thrusts us into a world where none of the conventions to which our eye has been accustomed can be taken for granted, in which we can depend no longer on the fulfillment of our old expectations. Everything has been disrupted.

Specifically: Michel drives Patricia to her meeting with the journalist; as they speed along and he berates her, the camera cuts a number of times, but remains in close-up of her face. The effect of these elisions in the image is to accelerate time astonishingly; with Michel, time is constantly plunging forward at a breathtaking pace. With the journalist, the camera cuts on Patricia in a variety of changing positions, while, on the sound track, her escort drones a single sentence; the effect is of time drastically slowed down, and, as the light fades in the background, even of time brought to a stop. Time and again, in the film, we see someone walking to a door or sitting at a table only to be, in seemingly that very instant, in a car, speeding through the streets, or miles away in the midst of some new action. All the film's action takes place, in a sense, *in medias res.* In the first minute after Michel's arrival in Paris, we see him driving a car, making telephone calls, reading a newspaper, having breakfast, washing up, all in different surroundings, all in virtually the same instant of time as it receives the shock of exploding space. All time is made relative, and made visual; visually represented in terms of moving space.

In the middle of all this spatial play on time, Michel remains the constant point of reference, appropriately enough, the norm. He is the film's center in every way. It is perhaps germane to observe that, while the film is, textually, amazingly tight and intricate, it is, structurally, extraordinarily loose and free. I know of nothing in *Breathless* that could be eliminated without some loss, and yet, one suspects, there is much that could be harmlessly rearranged. It would not be excessive to say that Michel provides the film's form, and its structure: indeed, he *is* that form and structure. But in this one sees only an extension of that mode of the picaresque to which *Breathless* owes so great an allegiance.

And although *Breathless* is, in this way, episodic, and despite the way in which the film's elliptical sequence of events tends to create a sense of the fragmentation of experience, it remains to be said that the total impression left by *Breathless* is one of exceptional integrity. Nothing is wasted, and everything counts. Outside of the work of Buñuel, I know of no other film in which the details work so precisely with and contribute so much meaning to the whole. All elements of the film are made animate, galvanized, perhaps, by Michel's electric presence. Prints and paintings, marquee titles, posters, stills, all objects become thoroughly alive, and charged with meaning. *"Pourquoi"* whispers from a wall; *"mort"* beckons from a book. The camera responds to every nuance of its world, and its world exists in infinitely shifting, kaleidoscopic nuance.

Breathless is, in fact, so good a film that one is tempted foolishly to venture estimates of its importance; after all, it is the film that Sartre has described as "beautiful," and Cocteau called "a miracle." Being already fool in its behalf, I might as well compound my folly by admitting that I think *Breathless* one of the genuine masterpieces of art in the twentieth century, to be compared with *A Portrait of the Artist as a Young Man* and *Les Demoiselles d'Avignon* (not exactly to choose names at random) in its vitalizing impact on its medium. Make no mistake: it is not another Film Classic; no *Potemkin* or *The Passion of Joan of Arc*. It is rather an authentic work of art in the film medium, by which I mean only that it will never be elected to the Ten Best List in the Cinema Hall of Fame when the experts next convene to cast their ballots. And that, too, is an aspect of its achievement.

And it is new, truly new and truly revolutionary. Unlike such a film as *Hiroshima, Mon Amour*, which, in its *rigor artis* (to steal a phrase from James Agee), seems like the end of an old way, *Breathless*, in its boundless life and energy, really does seem like the beginning of a new. I do not mean that, in any direct sense, one might expect to see more films like *Breathless*; it is too much a case of a style invented to suit a subject. *Breathless* has the effect of a violent assault on every narcotizing convention to which our eye has become habituated; we resist it as we resist any breaking of our habits. But with its hand-held camera moving ceaselessly, its flood of natural light awakening our eye, it comes as a tremendous gesture of freedom, an act of liberation; the kind of work which opens up whole new areas of possibility. *Breathless* comes to us unarmed by theory; it exists supremely, inalterably, in the realm of accomplished fact. But, finally, the very fact of its existence seems the most important kind of argument that can be offered in behalf of the art of film: *Breathless* exists. *Breathless* exists that the Siegfried Kracauers of this world might save their breath. *Breathless* exists!

(1961)

TWO MOVIES AND THEIR CRITICS

There is not really much similarity between *La Dolce Vita* and *L'Avventura*. Both were made at about the same time, and in the same country; if anything, they only show how big, artistically, one country can be. But the films have, in fact, been brought together by a rather arbitrary event: the publishing of twin encomia to them in the pages of the Autumn 1961 issue of *The Hudson Review*. In his analysis of the Fellini film, Norman N. Holland makes mention of *Time* magazine, which, "following its current mythy bent," argues that *La Dolce Vita* is, in fact, a monumental allegory of the Book of Revelations and the Second Coming. Well, as they used to say around my block, it takes one to know one. Holland pursues the *Time* suggestion to its most detailed and elaborate and doctrinaire extremes; no doubt, he rates a cover. No names are "not without significance," which is true enough; that is the function of names: they signify. When Anita Ekberg is offered a huge pizza, she is "ritually . . . offered the fruits of the Roman fields." In the sequence in which Marcello, the film's nonhero, is visited by his father, a night club suggests to Holland a place where "the walls glitter like a temple's and everywhere there are statues of women." But is not a night club precisely a place where the walls glitter like a night club's, and everywhere there are women? Please don't ask. For we are in the presence of Myth.

Why pick on Norman Holland, certainly not the greatest offender when it comes to the abuse of film criticism? And, certainly, as both Parker Tyler and Manny Farber have many times shown us, there are many ways of not writing film criticism while allegedly writing film criticism. Now between the relentless Myth Hunting of *The Hudson Review* and the dogged Popular Culturism of *Commentary,* I will take the latter, for, while both approaches seem to me fundamentally antithetical and even hostile to art, the latter, at least, allows implicitly the possibility of some supplementary, if not alternative, way of getting at the subject. I have nothing against the elucidation of myth per se. Indeed, I thought the original intent of such a method was to reveal how the individual work of art transforms the myth, how it adapts and uses it for its own particular ends. Instead, we are now treated to a painstaking annotation of a work's mythic elements, and then . . . but that is all—the end! The elements are articulated (often impressively; I, for one, am impressed by Holland's learning, if not his accomplishment), and the case rests proven, Q.E.D.; but the commentator has, in fact, proven—what? That the presence of myth is one with the presence of art? That the presence of myth is art's chief fulfillment? The comments of *Time* have, at least, the power of suggestion. Tentatively, they open the discussion; dogmatically, Holland closes it. Here, one last time, is the voice of the critic speaking: "Man is impotent, helpless. Marcello's dying father or Steiner, with his sounds and language, frozen, turned into stone by the fixity of his life. (Indeed, sacred to Cybele was a small meteoric stone *acus,* supposed to have fallen from the heavens.)" Q.E.D.

Now let me state, this close to the outset, that I have nothing personally against Holland, that I don't, personally, know him; he is, for me, a figure of symbolic, if you will, mythic, significance. His record, as alternate regular film critic for *The Hudson Review,* is an impressive one. There is a certain truth in that disparagement of criticism which maintains that, finally, it is all an elaborate wrapping by which to clothe the simple propositions of "I like it" or "I don't." Well, in the course of having occasional genuine insights into the films, Holland has *liked The Lovers,* has *liked Room at the Top,* has *liked Black Orpheus,* has gone bobbysox for Bergman, has beat the drum for *Hiroshima, Mon Amour;* he has been, in short, a fancy-dress publicist for all the winds of fashion which blow so noisily through our so-called art houses. I have nothing against publicity. Like myth, it has its place.

In no other area have we been harassed by so many assorted incompetents and pamphleteers and idiosyncratic causemongers as in the writing of high-brow film criticism; certainly, in no other areas have the otherwise intelligent editors of otherwise intelligent periodicals displayed such credulity. But faith can be misplaced, and I happen to believe that one can learn more about the so-called art of the film, not its unique techniques but its over-all artistic affects and poetics, from Aristotle than from Arnheim and company. I happen to believe that the art of the film, if it exists (disingenuousness here, for I *know* that it does), exists in the domain common to all art; only its techniques, its particular combination of affects and effects, its *means* of moving toward art's traditional ends, are different; and, even in this, not entirely, not uniquely, different. I believe that when a first-rate film criticism comes to be written (as the work of Robert Warshow decisively shows), it will be based not on a cultivated technical sophistication, but on the incorporation of such special knowledge within the basic framework of a first-rate criticism of any of the arts. It will not come from the verbal graphs and charts of *Commentary.* It will not come from the recent pages of *The Hudson Review.*

Well, as they also used to say around my block, put up or shut up.

I

It might reasonably be complained, were one to surrender to an unsophisticated, unmythic frankness, that Fellini's film is just too long; but *La Dolce Vita* is not so much long as redundant. Scene duplicates scene; and scene after scene is protracted long after its every point has been unmistakably made. The trouble would seem to be that the film is *conceived* on a grand scale, but *imagined* only within rather narrow limitations. Fellini almost invariably extends all his scenes beyond every interest save the visual; he seems to find no end of sheer delight in the exercise of his enormous virtuosity in juggling crowds and moving his camera; a negative compensation in all of this is in the proof it offers that the film is definitely *more* than a visual medium. One cannot help but wonder if Fellini's position, his moral predicament, in assuming this kind of relation to his material is not really analogous to Marcello's, the film's nonhero journalist, who early claims exemption from the general depravity because he is only there to observe and describe it, but who inevitably ends up as merely another symptom of the world he would portray. For all Fellini's splendid command of his medium, he is not so much the master as the slave of his material: he simply cannot tear himself away from it.

As it is the method of *La Dolce Vita* to pile detail upon detail, moving quantitatively from the particulars to the generality, it is, perhaps, not unfairly dealt with in terms of certain generalities, and I intend to do so; in any case, the particulars of the film have been made well enough known through its publicity. *La Dolce Vita* is a pageant of decadence; against its mammoth canvas, we watch Marcello, the disinterested journalist, in his inescapable progress from observer of to participant in that titanic world of disorder and decay. Or is it inescapable? The question is not illegitimately put; it is raised by Fellini. At one point, Marcello's mistress, helpless and compassionate and ultimately corrupted with Marcello in his headlong rush toward his own fall, turns to him, and says, "Don't you understand you've found the most important thing in life, a woman who really loves you. . . ."

Now there is reason to believe we are meant to take this seriously. Up to that point, the mistress is the one character in the film treated with something like sympathy, accorded a certain measure of pathos. In addition, she is made to enunciate one of the two ideas which informed Fellini's earlier *La Strada*, and one of the two obsessive, so-called themes of contemporary dramatic art (*vide* Bergman *et al.*); the other being that we are no longer capable of communicating with one another, which is the second informing idea of *La Strada*. But, in fact, Marcello's mistress is not his savior. His savior is yet to come.

Of course, the role of the artist is to ask the questions, not provide the answers; and we judge his worth by the relevance, and, indeed, the unanswerableness, of the questions which he chooses to ask. It would not trouble me that Fellini did not provide the answers to his questions if he did not appear, and, in fact, try to appear, to be doing so. About midway through the course of the film, Marcello meets a golden-haired young girl at a seaside café where he has gone for the quiet to complete his destined-never-to-be-finished novel. The girl, out of her beautiful innocence, makes an unstated appeal to Marcello to abandon his life of depravity, his sweet life, for one of peace, of innocence and beauty; Marcello is attracted to, but, at the last minute, distracted from, her claims; it is his sweet life, beckoning to him from the telephone. And that is all; except for that moment, during the last sequence, when Marcello, by this time immersed irrevocably in *la dolce vita,* watches as the famous monster fish is hauled up from the sea. Then, from a distant shore, a figure waves to him, waves and beckons. It is the girl, the golden angel, making again her mute appeal for him to join her. But it is too late, too late. Marcello shrugs his shoulders, smiles apologetically; he cannot hear her. Then he turns away. And then, in the film's final shot, we see the angel in gigantic close-up as slowly, very slowly, she turns her head from that point off-screen that was Marcello, and looks at us; fixes on us that gaze of innocence, and that silent claim.

The moment is an impressive one; one of those disturbing instances of the screen's ability to affect us emotionally by what we know is bad; and it *is* bad. Fellini has made his bid to have us both ways, in fact, all ways. Instead, he stands revealed before us; desperately pressing his resources; utterly unable to conceive of any alternative to *la dolce vita in reality.* "Innocence!" he says to us. "Choose innocence!" But really, gang, I know it's terribly ungrateful to ask after you've spent such a lot of time and money just to save our souls, but really: *after such knowledge . . . what forgiveness?*

And one thought more, no doubt a captious one. In the café, we see Marcello look the angel over; there is no doubt, he is interested; there is no doubt, she is interested; there is no doubt, he is giving her the eye. A nagging thought then, at the end:

considering the seemingly irresistible progress of Marcello's degradation, does he, in his final act, renounce salvation, or, instead, decline to seduce his savior? Previously, after all, he had made a pretty good, aborted try.

In a sense, the whole of *La Dolce Vita,* following its famous prologue, is redundant: it tells us nothing not contained, embryonically and by implication, in the image of the statue of Christ being flown by helicopter over the city. Christ flying above modern Rome: those images, I submit, exist as poetry, both beautiful and grand, and losing nothing of their grandeur for being so well publicized; and poetry, in the film as elsewhere, depends for its particular power on concentration and compression, not elaboration, on metaphor, not documentation. There is nothing more beautiful or more terrible in *La Dolce Vita* than what is suggested by, and contained by implication in, its opening. It is a metaphor charged with meaning that the rest of the film strives in vain to equal.

Fellini seems unable, but is more likely unwilling, to accept this. Time and again, he achieves his best effects in the film (and it is a film of some very splendid moments) with his most modest means; the sequence in which Marcello is visited by the aging, virtual stranger who is his father is, in its small but profound way, especially moving. But when Fellini goes after the Big One, he brings back the bulk of *La Dolce Vita* and *La Strada.* Where, as in that earlier film, all else gives way to allegory and abstraction, there must at least, by way of justification, be some compensating profundity and complexity of ideas. In *La Strada,* we are deprived of all the density of life and lifelike art, and, in its place, served up one simple, huge abstraction; you know it: Love. And in *La Dolce Vita*: Innocence. *Reductio ad abstractum;* the operative word is *reduction.* Rumors from the press would have it that Fellini's next film will be his attempt to elucidate the main point of *La Dolce Vita.* The ironies here are too abundant for me to attempt to name them.

It would be a mistake to judge Fellini by *La Dolce Vita,* or *La Strada.* His masterpiece (and it *is* a masterpiece) is *I Vitelloni,* but there are beautiful things in both *The White Sheik* and *Nights of Cabiria.* The highest reach of his imagination seems to be a kind

of all-encompassing, oceanic compassion; a profound identification with the defeated. One had hoped, from the advance word
of *La Dolce Vita,* that Fellini had found a subject in which he
might, at last, transcend himself; reach into that area where the
compassionate and the moral imagination become inseparable.
Until he does so, he may give us (as he has) fine works, but never
great ones. Fellini *is* a fine artist; he might be a great one. *La
Dolce Vita* is, I think, a failure, but not, I believe, a disreputable
one. Fellini has failed before, but never disreputably. Of how
many other artists can we say as much?

II

About the *Hudson*izing of *L'Avventura,* I have little to say. It
exemplifies the reason why I keep no notebook: for fear I might
begin believing things just because I put them there. Its author
is not a regular film reviewer for the magazine, and so lacks that
mythic character of Norman Holland, making each alternate
quarter his eternal return. Its author is, in fact, a *Hudson* editor,
and his greatest guilt is of self-indulgence, accepting for publication a fragmentary compilation of would-be *aperçus* because they
happen to be his. Technically speaking, is this nepotism?
    In New York, *L'Avventura* tended to be rather eclipsed by the
success of *La Dolce Vita* as the season's big hit of the art-house
circuit; indeed, Fellini's film rated all the apparatus of the hard
sell: "legitimate" theater, reserved seats, intermission, etc. *L'Avventura* was dropped from memory so quickly that, about a
month after its disappearance, the movie editor of a local weekly
could refer to it as that previous film by the director of *Rocco and
His Brothers* so as to compare it unfavorably to that wretched
work, in the apparent spirit of "All wops look alike to me."
While still held in the memory of the press, Antonioni's film was
dismissed as obscurantist; slow, so slow, and impossible to understand. It *is* a slow film, as it properly should be, but one never
feels impatiently its sheer *length,* as one does of *La Dolce Vita.*
Adagio may be as valid as allegro, but for Bosley Crowther, having to catch that train or whatever, you've got to keep things
really moving.
    There is a difference between complexity and obscurity. *L'Av-*

ventura may not be easy to understand, but is never difficult to follow; which is only another way of saying that, like any other richly textured work of art, it exists on many levels. *L'Avventura* came to us with its press notices howling "Obscurity!"; naturally, then, it was thought of as obscure, both by all of those who stayed away and by those intransigent few who like their art obscure. Yet the most salient quality of the film is its manifest simplicity. A girl disappears; her friend and fiancé search for her. The narrative has all the immediate appeal of a good mystery, evoking, quite properly, all of the mystery's appropriate questions: Where is she? Will she be found? Only by the most unobtrusive subtlety does this immediate mystery gradually extend and complicate itself until one realizes, at the end, that these questions have been answered . . . by more urgent and important questions. The film ends as it begins, in mystery. But mystery on that level where it admits no longer of solutions.

Antonioni has somewhere remarked on his particular admiration for Conrad, and the predilection seems to me an illuminating one. Like Conrad, Antonioni possesses an almost archetypically novelistic imagination; he has a virtually insatiable appetite for reality—the reality of man in society—as it reveals itself in exemplary action through significant nuance and detail. Of that action—the plot—I intend to make no extensive summary here: the film has already been synopsized well enough in both *Sight and Sound* of Winter 1960-61, and *Film Quarterly* of Summer 1961; and, in a sense, its plot is most faithfully suggested by the simplest description: a girl disappears; her friend and fiancé search for her. It is some sense of *L'Avventura*'s nuance and detail which I wish, with no pretense at exhaustiveness, to describe at present; detail so apt and lucid that the very naming of it becomes an exegesis.

There is to be a yachting party. Anna and her friend, Claudia, go to pick up Sandro, Anna's fiancé, an architect who has become a commercial contractor, at his apartment; there, while Claudia waits outside, Anna and Sandro make love. It is Anna who initiates the love-making, yet, one feels, she also resists it; resists Sandro's ability to arouse her. As she accepts his embrace, she regards him with an unmistakable expression of loathing. She has earlier told Claudia that she has begun to tire of Sandro, and yet he continues in his ability to arouse her, to obliterate her. They make love, and she hates him for it.

On the yacht, a group of bored and idle pleasure-seekers. Partners are coupled incompatibly, and seem constantly on the verge of shifting casually into new combinations, no less incompatible: the varieties of erotic experience. A man viciously mocks his wife's banality; another wife remains faithful to her absent husband because of "laziness." The boat threads an aimless course through promontory islands of barren rock; extinct volcanoes, we are told, with cities buried under them. An invisible boat sounds its melancholy horn. "Those islands depress me," says one of the company. "The poor things look so abandoned."

On the yacht, boredom and dissatisfaction. One of the party works a jigsaw puzzle of a great cathedral. Below deck, Anna jokes ironically with Claudia, and gives her one of her blouses to wear, smiling in some secret understanding. Minutes later, Anna has dived from the yacht to swim toward one of the deserted islands.

Sandro and some others swin after her, and the yacht follows to the island. Ashore, the party breaks up into smaller, disparate groups, the same only in that the people in them characteristically face away from one another; all wander off in separate directions. Time elapses, and, when the party is ready to leave, as a distant boat sounds mournfully in the background, Anna is discovered to be missing. The island is combed without success. The police are summoned. Anna's belongings are searched, among them copies of the Bible and *Tender Is the Night;* the latter, taken by some to be of much symbolic significance, surely a conceit, and a witty one, and reminder that only works of the most masterly confidence and control (cf. *Breathless*) can afford so to joke at their own expense. During their investigation, one of the police divers discovers an ancient vase, relic of that time when volcanoes could erupt and cities were inhabited. He gives it to one of the party, who handles it, drops it, smashes it. "What a pity," he shrugs. "It can't be helped." By designation of the police, Anna becomes, officially, a "missing person."

Once returned to the mainland, the members of the party go their separate ways. Sandro is to pursue the search for Anna, and tries to persuade Claudia to join him, but already she is aware of his incipient sexual interest in her, and, appalled and frightened by the situation, she declines. Sandro's investigations take him about the countryside; at one town, he finds an excited crowd parading its lechery behind a publicity-seeking whore; but he meets with no success. He returns to the villa of the yacht's owner, where the party has been reassembled, dissonant as ever, scarcely changed by the loss of one of its members. "In Italy, forty thousand people disappear each year," says one. "They'd fill a stadium."

While they dress for dinner, one of the women playfully offers Claudia, who is blond, a wig the dark color of Anna's hair. Claudia accepts it and puts it on, as she has accepted and worn Anna's blouse. "You look like someone else," laughs the other. Later, Claudia assents to Sandro's desire that she join him, and together they resume the search, their adventure.

It takes them to a small, country pharmacy where they interview a couple who have told the police they believe they have seen Anna. The pharmacist and his wife bicker with each other in some ruthless mutual excoriation that seems as involuntary as a tropism; like the spouses in Strindberg and Bergman's hitchhiking couple in *Wild Strawberries,* the two suggest a paradigm of unsuccessful union. The adventure takes Sandro and Claudia on to a deserted structure of aggressively modern design, an immaculate array of geometrical buildings presided over by the severe spire of a dead church; an echo-filled ghost town, as extinct as the volcanoes, as uninhabited as the buried cities. It is the city of the present, abandoned. "These buildings are madness," says Sandro. "It's not a town, it's a cemetery." As they prepare to leave, the camera watches at a distance from one of the narrow, empty streets; as they drive off, the camera moves through the street after them, but they are gone. The effect, difficult to explain, inescapable to experience, is of a silent presence, mysterious and frightening, reaching out toward them. Is this where Anna disappeared?

They go to another town. By this time they are lovers, and their adventure has become a more complicated, ambiguous one: still compelled to pursue the search for Anna, they now nevertheless fear the consequences of actually finding her (and, later, Antonioni, in one quiet, brilliant touch, momentarily deceives both Claudia and the audience into thinking that they have, in fact, done so). Claudia waits for Sandro in the town square while he checks a clue. Gradually, we become aware of a growing undertone of sound from off-screen, and the camera pulls slowly back from Claudia to reveal her surrounded by a crowd of whispering men, thronging about her in unconcealed lechery as, earlier, a similar mob flocked about the whore; to them it is all pretty much the same, all "trade," no matter what you call it. Our awareness of the men and of the meaning of them is typical of the unobtrusive, masterly way in which Antonioni has built his work: at first, we know their presence only by their buzz; then, as one gradually becomes aware that the ground on which one stands is alive with insects, we see them swarm. Metaphor moves quietly into the realm of meaning.

Claudia and Sandro take a room in a hotel. They make love. Sandro goes out into the piazza; he tries to visit a church, but it is closed. He finds an easel with a sketch of some of the rich, ornamental detail which decorates the façade of a nearby baroque structure; the artist is off speaking to someone a short distance away. Deliberately, Sandro spills ink on the sketch, and derisively restrains the angry artist: "When I was twenty-three, I used to look for fights—and I looked harder than you." He returns to the hotel room, and attempts, in a virtual frenzy, to take Claudia by force. The sudden, desperate quality of his need frightens her, as does the realization that he doesn't need *her,* and she weeps.

Abandoning the search, they return to a huge, luxurious hotel, where several members of the original party are now gathered, among them Sandro's employer. Sandro has decided with Claudia that he will refuse any further work in contracting, and return to the practice of architecture. The adventure seems to be at an end; Anna is gone, and now they have become lovers. "Everything has become so terribly simple. Even getting over a tragedy." They have arrived in time for a celebration, but Claudia, exhausted by their adventure, retires early for the night. Sandro moves disinterestedly through the party, from one room to another, succumbing again to the familiar rhythms of his life. The contracting job is offered to him, and he accepts it. He begins to look over the women. Early the next morning, he has still not returned to Claudia's room, and she goes down to look for him. She finds him, making love to the whore we have seen earlier; as, after his pre-

vious weakness, he needed Claudia, so, in his present one, he
turns to whatever happens to be available; in either case, annihilating self through sex. Claudia runs from the room, anguish-
stricken by the betrayal. Sandro, horrified by his guilt and weakness, runs after her. In the bleak dawn, he follows her out onto an
open terrace, sits alone, and weeps. Then, in a moment, Claudia
joins him, places a hand upon his head as she stands beside him
on the terrace, under a skeletal bell tower, both facing into the
cruelly empty dawn, toward the drone of the surf and the distant
sight of Mount Etna, monumental and dormant; to the eye, extinct. Sandro cries; he is weak, and Claudia acquiesces in his weakness. A mysterious boat sounds and signals in the distance. It is a
moment where Fellini characteristically ends, and where
Antonioni begins—a moment of great pity and compassion, but
not merely that. For this is the final meaning of their adventure:
that, in weakness, everything is the same, all differences obliter-
ated. A mysterious boat sounds and signals in the distance. And
Claudia, too, has become a "missing person."

In *The Hudson Review,* after the opening announcement that
(here we go again) "this film is about the impossibility of communication between human beings," *L'Avventura* is hailed as the
greatest existent example of "the *cinéma pur,*" a film existing absolutely, without reference to any meaning; and, at the festival at
Cannes, where it was jeered and hooted, *L'Avventura* won a
special prize for something like (and I quote from memory) "the
unusual beauty of its images in its development of a new cinematic language." Both responses, in their way, affirm the first
principle of film unappreciation: when you don't know what it all
means, praise the photography. And yet the film is manifestly
neither without conscious, deliberate meaning nor new, in any
experimental sense; certainly, it is one of the films I would wish
least to single out for the beauty of its imagery, that imagery,
beautiful as it is, being so inseparably allied to the film's meaning.
What is new in *L'Avventura* is not the language but the voice;
the voice of an artist in absolute control of his medium, and in
pursuit of meaning; and this in the medium which most lends
itself to the illusion of its creative autonomy, its impersonal
independence of any individual artist. That this voice and the

imagination which informs it are so fundamentally, so traditionally, novelistic ones is what is unusual, and what is extraordinary is the extent to which the medium responds to such a voice and imagination. *L'Avventura* has been called an abstract film, yet it abounds with concrete, realistic observation. The love affair between Claudia and Sandro, for example, obviously regarded by Antonioni as a moral failure, is nevertheless depicted with great fidelity to the detail of its natural development, even with humor and charm. But *L'Avventura* does move always from its accumulation of particular, often minute detail toward some integrity of abstract idea, some general truth; it is the movement, I believe, of every true novel, from *Emma* to *The Victim*.

To the extent that Antonioni's imagination is novelistic, he sees all his characters in their individual differences. Whereas Fellini, in *La Dolce Vita,* editorializes every individual he presents, assigning each his relative order of merit, Antonioni is without contempt for even the most contemptible of his characters; like Dickens, he seems to love even his "villains," although, unlike Dickens, there are no villains, only cripples. Having incorporated all his feeling into the deepest substance of his work, Antonioni, unlike Fellini, has no need to flaunt it on the surface. But to the extent that Antonioni's imagination is a moral one, and this moral imagination is, I think, his defining quality as an artist, he sees all his characters as the same, lost in their similarity. The self-conscious cynics and sybarites are, finally, not much different from the "decent" few who gather about their fringe; the whore, finally, not dissimilar to the lover; the initially confident, nonchalant Sandro and the initially lively, independent Claudia end alike in their shared, mutual weakness. All are united in this common weakness, all made anonymous; all missing persons. This weakness, for Antonioni, is not the grounds for some final surge of redemptive compassion, for forgiveness, but the mark of culpability, of moral failure. For we might be strong, we might be responsible. Claudia, acquiescing to Sandro, abdicates her self. Antonioni's vision, clearly though complexly, is of the loss of self in a society preoccupied with self. And one can only marvel at the utter rightness of the action, the sustained metaphor, he has invented to embody and contain the meaning of this.

In his discussion of the vogue of Ingmar Bergman which appeared in a recent *Commentary*, Harris Dienstfrey concludes by remarking that all discussion of Bergman, both pro and con, has really centered on

> the old argument of whether or not film—which is to say, really, movies in general—can be taken seriously and not merely as a sociological bellwether. But is this question . . . a meaningful one? I doubt if it is. The truth seems to be rather that Bergman's popularity and the widespread discussion of his films are only the most obvious signs of a larger and more general phenomenon: the increasing relevance and force films have in portraying the way we live today. The important question concerning film now is not whether it speaks significantly but, indeed, whether as a medium, it does not speak more significantly than fiction.

It is a question which was inevitably to be asked, as the general intellectual audience comes inevitably to acknowledge the film as an artistic medium beyond its any specialized interest; that the question should be put in *Commentary*, bastion of the sociological bellwether, lends it, indeed, the stamp of an historic occasion. It is not my intention to conclude here with any authoritative speculations on the questionable death of the novel. What I do wish to say, in the most personal voice I can summon, and for someone else, possibly you, to draw conclusions, is that the best new novel I have encountered in the past few years is *L'Avventura*. And it is a film.

At this point, I would like again to be able to say Q.E.D. I find myself unable to do so. I have written, at no great length, about two vastly different works, one "I don't like," and one "I do." About the former, I find I have said just about all I would wish to say; about the latter, I find I have said only what I feel myself, at this time, imperfectly capable of saying. I have seen *L'Avventura* twice. Once is enough fully to experience it; twice not enough fully to understand the experience.

But I did not mean to pretend to be having the last word on the subject. I wished only to *open* the discussion.

(1961)

FROTH IN A WIDENING CONTEXT

Perhaps the best way for me to approach Philippe de Broca's disturbing little film, *The Five-Day Lover,* is chronologically, and, in its case, the chronology extends back prior to the time I actually saw it. To begin with, there was de Broca's first film: *The Love Game,* which came to us publicized in the advertisements as the New Wave's first comedy, and lauded in the reviews as the work of an authentic comic poet; a film which I found dreary and depressing in almost every way, dreary and depressing as only a work of labored charm and willed spontaneity can be; a kind of René Clair by fiat. When de Broca's second film, *The Joker,* arrived here, I decided to make it very much my business to stay away, and I did. By the time his third film made its appearance, I was still determined to miss it at all costs, but was urged personally to see *The Five-Day Lover* by someone whose taste in these matters I generally respect, and urged so repeatedly that any failure to comply might be taken as an affront. I indulge in this inconsequential bit of autobiography only that one might allow for it; a person, not a critic, sees a given movie, and sees it in a particular context, not Olympian detachment. My last thought upon entering the theater on the final night of the film's engagement, as I was separated from some ridiculously excessive amount of money in order to see it, was, "This is a movie I'm going to hate."

Such were the expectations I brought to *The Five-Day Lover*, but, almost at once, I was made to realize that they simply wouldn't do, that they were inadequate to the occasion. *The Five-Day Lover* wastes no time in getting off the ground, and, from the very beginning, it becomes immediately apparent that de Broca's third film exceeds his first in sheer verve and comic invention; minutes from its start, we find ourselves already helplessly engrossed in a farcical tangle of irreconcilable amatory complications. One obvious asset in this early part of the film is Jean-Pierre Cassel, de Broca's leading man and discovery, who, with no difficulty, takes charge of the beginning of the film, and makes it his. In the context of *The Love Game*, Cassel had seemed to me only to partake of the general listlessness, his antics all deliberate, and spiritless, and rather more those of an acrobat than an actor. Cassel commands an impressive repertoire of funny and, occasionally, even beautiful bits of business, yet they all seem to have somewhat less to do with creating a character and a comic situation than with displaying an impressive repertoire of funny and beautiful bits of business. One is not so aware of this in *The Five-Day Lover* as in *The Love Game*, where the flimsiness of the script's invention left more of the character for the actor to create. In *The Five-Day Lover*, Cassel has a certain written role to play; one can imagine him taking some further instruction from the script beyond a desperate *plus de charme!* Given a role, Cassel seems willing to meet it, at least halfway, and, close as he occasionally comes to going wrong, in the end he manages always to go right.

Still things are wrong. *The Five-Day Lover* is a farce in the manner of the silent film classics, a genre of great delicacy and fragile charm. Yet in those silent films this delicacy and fragility is all on the surface; underneath is the constant hum of powerful machinery, and a foundation of rock-hard strength. It is perhaps a curious but I think not so curious fact that, for years, my recollection of *The Gold Rush*, which I first saw as a child and which was one of the first films I remembered distinctly of those I did see, was of a work of epic realism; yes, it was hilari-

ously funny, but funny in a world of concrete substance and
solidity, a frightening world of cruel cold and limitless expanses
of an absolute and inhuman white. *The Five-Day Lover* has all
the superficial delicacy of this kind of comedy without any of
its underlying strength; it looks fragile and it *is* fragile; it looks
fragile *because* it is fragile.

Although *The Five-Day Lover* veers occasionally toward a
comedy of sentiment—I don't mean sentimentality—throughout
most of its length, its aspirations clearly are more decidedly in the
direction of farce. Now the world of farce is a world analogous
to but independent of our own; one with its own internal laws
and logic. Were one for a moment to mistake the world of, say,
The Italian Straw Hat (and I am thinking of the farces of Labiche
and Feydeau rather than our theater's current artifacts) for our
own, the effect would be, not of comedy, but of suffering and
madness. We do recognize in it an image of our own world, but
our world in a new creation, an image of our world reflected by
some grotesquely distorting mirror: this is farce, and we ascribe
the madness to the manner. The trouble with *The Five-Day Lover*
is that there is too much of the real world left out, and not enough
of any other put in; which is perhaps better said as too much of
the real world left out and still too much of it left in. The world
of *The Five-Day Lover* is neither quite any recreation of the real
world nor any other imaginative creation of its own. The film
shifts incessantly back and forth from one to another of the
available alternatives without ever establishing any satisfactory
tension, not to say balance, between them.

One is never quite so aware of this lack of a world, that is to
say, a context, in the film as when its characters go out into the
street: for the streets in this film, as in *The Love Game,* are always
empty. The effect is always of streets seen in a dream, and all of de
Broca's characters exist in a curious, dreamlike isolation, as if, in
fact, only they have an existence; the four characters in *The Five-
Day Lover* relate only to one another as, in *The Love Game,* the
trio was similarly self-contained. In one scene, to be sure, all four
are seen at a crowded party, but the others present are related
to them only as a backdrop before which the principals move in
high relief. What one sees in such a work as *The Italian Straw Hat*
is a world which is dense and complexly interconnected, a society;

and even in so trivial a current work as *Pocketful of Miracles,* Capra manages to people his film with a multitude of particularized characters and orchestrate their various interactions. But in the films of de Broca there is none of this. In *The Five-Day Lover,* the guests at the party come in, perform their amusing but irrelevant little comic arias, and recede fixedly into the background until de Broca is ready to dispense with even this much of them; and then, as if on cue, the whole company suddenly departs. In fact, they have not been people all along, but only props; props in the form of people.

But the fact is that de Broca *requires* this kind of extreme isolation; he *has* to lock the real world out; for only in a work of this rarefied atmosphere can characters and a comedy of such frailty be said to exist. As if to compensate for this absence of any exterior world, de Broca has crammed his interiors with a clutter of bric-a-brac—vases, flowers, assorted *objets d'art*; all inanimate objects. To fill his vacancies, de Broca has hired a marvelous quartet of actors, but even they cannot entirely disguise the fact that what we have in the women are two characters from stock (without any of the several legitimate justifications for their being stock), and, in the husband, a variation on the cuckold as a man who perceives his own pathetic foolishness, a conception which only the impeccable control of François Périer keeps from lapsing into sentimentality—and I don't mean sentiment. Only the role of Cassel—Don Juan as impotent—seems to contain some inherent reality and to offer some promise of interesting implications, but scarcely are these suggested when they are abruptly dropped; in any case, the model was not likely to have surpassed its most recent original, in *Knave of Hearts,* when he was called M. Ripois and played by Gérard Philippe. When one tries to recall the characters of *The Five-Day Lover,* one comes back always to the image of four gifted actors performing with unexceptionable skill, whereas M. Ripois has a certain, definite existence, even without Gérard Philippe.

Well, so what? *The Five-Day Lover* is a light comedy of no great consequence, and to write at all about such a film is a bit like doing an annotated monograph, MLA style sheet, on the delights of whipped cream; to write of it adversely, a bit merely like com-

plaining that the cream is not sufficiently rich. Yet this is the
light, inconsequential film of which *Time* magazine was able to
conclude that "the context of the comedy widens and the laughter
dies in the spectator's belly as he perceives that the froth is bub-
bling from the lips of a corpse, from the sores of a rotting civilization." Something strange is certainly at work here, and I must
reluctantly admit that the strangeness is not *Time's*. Initially, I
described *The Five-Day Lover* as a disturbing little film; it *is*
little; it is also disturbing. For the disturbing fact is that, after
laboring for approximately one hour to create a lighthearted
work in the manner of vintage René Clair, de Broca abruptly
abandons this film for quite another of his own: one about
infidelity and forgiveness and the ineffable sadness of life. I speak
of two distinct and different works because the two films do not,
in fact, coexist, nor does one grow organically out of the other.
This schizophrenia, showing itself occasionally during the earlier
parts of the film but generally obscured by the mechanics of the
farce, suddenly erupts unmistakably in the sequence of the party,
which begins as that obligatory scene in farce where all the
hidden complications will finally be revealed, and come climacti-
cally into collision. This is how it begins and how it progresses,
the comedy of it culminating in the business of the cuckold and
the lover solicitously adjusting each other's hopelessly recalcitrant
ties and collars until the two have become locked in a virtual embrace; the moment manages to be wonderfully funny and wonderfully suggestive at the same time. But de Broca is not able to
sustain this kind of complexity and the moment is also approximately that at which the business of comedy is permanently
terminated, and the scene which began as the crescendo of farce
ends in a diminuendo of pathos; the lovers contrite, the husband
forgiving, and the person who had intended mutually to humiliate
them herself humiliated. The scene which began as farce ends
with a distant image of the husband engaged in a stately dance
with the rejected lover of the man who has cuckolded him, his
wife and her lover wordlessly watching, as we glimpse it through
a window to the sad sound of softly falling rain. Thereafter, this
poignancy is the sole mood which prevails. When the husband
appears, in the next scene, in nightdress, we have moved so far
from farce that the hat which he has forgetfully allowed to re-

main on his head becomes an emblem, not of his ridiculousness, but of his pathos, his humanity. Our last, brief glimpse of Cassel, the five-day lover who had been the source of all vitality throughout the first part of the film, is of him immobilized on his bed, gazing out dazedly from behind the bars of an iron railing: visibly caged. He has been rejected by both women, and speaks his own epitaph: "I wish I were George"—the cuckolded husband! The film closes with the sense that, in love, all must end sadly, and the suggestion that this inseparable sequence, love and sadness, is destined to repeat itself endlessly over again.

How is one to reconcile these two films: the gay little farce out of René Clair, the elegy to love's perpetual sadness; neither one working with the other, each going off in its different direction? The fact is that de Broca seems to realize that the Clair world is no longer viable, and that sex now has serious, which is to say noncomic, overtones and ramifications; he may begin with charm and gaiety, but he must end in wistful sadness, in noncomedy. It is simply false to the fact of *The Five-Day Lover* to say that it ends in another kind of comedy, that its "context . . . widens"; its funny moments are all farcical, and there is really nothing funny, nor intended to be so, in all of the final part of the film. De Broca's temperament leads inevitably away from comedy; what bothered me fundamentally about *The Love Game* was his unwillingness to admit to this; in *The Five-Day Lover,* he does, however belatedly. De Broca's subject is sex, and it is not a subject he finds funny, although Cassel obviously finds it hilarious; but, by the film's end, Cassel has virtually vanished—like the guests at his party, de Broca has exhausted his use for and summarily disposed of him—and *The Five-Day Lover* is no longer even pretending to be comedy. It was somewhere in the middle of that party that I was brought to the curious realization that, never having seen a photograph of de Broca, I had previously tended to think of him in the image of Cassel, literally looking like his leading actor; which I recognized as only the reverse of my sense of Cassel as the films' director. Certainly, in their first film, the intention of both had seemed so nearly one, and even the first part of de Broca's third film is equally Cassel's; the camera merely trains on him, and records his movement; all the film's movement is his. But, by the end of *The Five-Day Lover,* there can be no mistake about de Broca's distinct and separate identity. And he's not funny.

I don't know that this figure who finally emerges from the rift of *The Five-Day Lover* is, in himself, a very interesting director; what is interesting is the question he raises with him. What is interesting is to see someone preoccupied alternately with sex and comedy, but, to reverse the Lawrentian diagnosis, having not sex but comedy in the head. Cassel is a comic actor; not a Chaplin but, at least, a Danny Kaye, whom, by the way, he extraordinarily resembles. De Broca is not a comic director—one need merely observe how hard he works at what, for a Capra, comes by nature —but a director who wants to make comedy. In our present dearth, the ambition alone seems to have qualified him as our most gifted director of comedy for a number of people. We all know that tragedy is dead from endless scholarly lucubrations and symposia. And comedy? Capra ransacks the past for some suitable subject, and de Broca is hailed as messiah for want of any original and creative comic talent. And, although I have restricted my observations to the movies, it seems to me that similar conclusions might arise with equal force from the situation of our current fiction, where one may see a Bernard Malamud deliberately larding his latest work with scenes of low slapstick which, however successful in themselves, remain extraneous to the quite serious meaning of the novel. Or take the spectacle of this week's messiah for the comic novel, out of Mack Sennett via Max Shulman, *Catch-22* by Joseph Heller, a tract in defense of Life which manages somehow to be completely lifeless, the apologetics on behalf of which have usually run that the jokes are bad but come with such speed and in such quantity—the argument we are given for *One, Two, Three,* and one I am unable to dissociate from the old advertising swindle about losing money on each item but making it up in volume. Before it appears that I am distorting particulars to fit them to the shape of some general thesis, I wish to say that I had been troubled by *A New Life* and *Catch-22* before seeing *The Five-Day Lover;* but it took *The Five-Day Lover* to make me see a context common to all these separate failures.

Something is lacking, and, tentatively, I suggest this: that comedy, whatever its impulse toward anarchy, requires a certain stable and cohesive social structure to sustain its existence.[1] In the meantime, tragedy dead and comedy absent, some form we have yet properly to name and understand has been doing much of the work of both; certainly, the funniest new film I saw during the past year was also the most terrible: Buñuel's *Viridiana;* and then there is *Breathless.* The question which occurs to me in the situation, the most interesting question I find arising from the work of de Broca, is that of whether comedy, at least a comedy of sex, is any longer a viable form. Which is really to ask the question: is comedy still possible?

(1962)

---

1. And it is interesting to note, in this connection, that the situation I am describing is one which in England would seem largely not to obtain, in that one could see there the recent emergence of a novelist as gifted as Kingsley Amis, whose chief talent is a traditionally comic one and whose comedy is chiefly dependent upon the actualities of a given social structure.

LAST NIGHT AT MARIENBAD

Last night, or was it last year, at the theater where I saw *Last Year at Marienbad,* they were—truthfully—selling a "pocket edition of 192 'Marienbad' games" for a dollar in the lobby. The item was, frankly, not without a certain fascination for me, but, as I advanced on the concession after seeing the movie to inquire, I suddenly broke out into a sweat at the thought of what I might discover, and fled the premises instead. Yet, even as I ran, I had to admit to the perfect reasonableness of the thing. Indeed, why not a do-it-yourself *Marienbad* kit, including a *Marienbad* hat among other things? Certainly, I had neither the right nor desire to deny such to others even though nothing I had just seen had made me wish to change my recently acquired *La Notte* hat (and *Viridiana* suit), the first articles I had found really to fit me since my *L'Avventura-Breathless* ensemble—already, I'm afraid, beginning to look a bit *démodé.* Yet I'd hardly wish to make my style into someone else's uniform. So why not?

The games did not simply happen to be in the lobby last night. At the conclusion of the film, they were advertised, on screen, via a trailer, which also announced the availability of the scenario in book form, introduced by its author, and a special issue of the

New York Film Bulletin devoted to the film, including the film-makers' statements of their intentions, adding of the latter, "It may help." This is interesting; the thoroughness of the merchandising points unmistakably to the fact that there is now a small *Marienbad* industry in existence, only in part directed toward the usual campaign to get you inside the theater. Its main concern is explaining what has happened to you inside the theater once you have left. Although this explaining starts even before you see the film. Last night or last year, at the theater where I saw *Last Year at Marienbad,* the movie was also preceded by a filmed announcement, this explaining that what you were about to see, despite the fact you might think you didn't understand it, was, nonetheless, indisputably great. Like Ring Lardner: "Shut up," he explained.

Well, why not, why not? I've nothing against free enterprise, and, in any case, one cannot fairly blame the movie for any such commerce as has adventitiously become attached to it. Why not this form for the work of art of the future; beginning with its own review, culminating in a bibliography; an encumbrance at both ends? I repeat: I am not attempting to credit these accessories to Alain Robbe-Grillet who wrote and Alain Resnais who directed this film; they are hardly responsible. Rather, I wonder if it is any longer possible to have an immediate, unmediated response to *any* work of art in *any* medium; the recent television production of Stravinsky's *The Flood* emphatically suggests that this format of the judgmental prelude and explanatory coda is equally serviceable to a piece of music; indeed, when you removed the Stravinsky from its setting, you found the latter exceeded the former on a ratio of roughly one and one-half to one. It is the ultimate in audience flattery; the producers have spared no expense to save you the trouble of having independently to decide what to think. And so with *Last Year at Marienbad*: even before we see the film, we are provided with the appropriate adjective to be applied to it. The future with a vengeance, one might say; only it is the present.

Am I only being deceived by nostalgia when I recollect once having been able innocently to come upon a book, become interested in it, and begin reading, knowing of it only what I discovered in that reading? Now I am unable so much as to pick up a book without ten reviews instantly getting between me and it. Why does one read the damned things? And, then again, how does one avoid them? In any case, I became aware of the steadily increasing body of literature on *Last Year at Marienbad* being accumulated in my desk drawers months before I had any opportunity to see the film, and early resolved not to read a word on the subject until I had seen it. Even so, there were two *Marienbad* radio symposia, one from New York, the other from San Francisco, with participants ranging from James Broughton to Dwight Macdonald, which, unlike books and magazines, could not be filed for the future; to have missed them at the time of their broadcast was to miss them permanently, and this, frankly, I didn't wish to do. Listening, I tried, as much as is humanly possible, to transmit the material directly to the back of my mind without thinking about it. Unavoidably, I had heard from the first word of it that *Last Year at Marienbad* was to be a singularly unconventional work, and I was determined that this time nothing extraneous would get in the way of my immediate response to it. My response!—how then shall I describe my response to it; how can I describe that response? Neither bored nor interested, neither in comprehension nor in confusion, neither liking nor disliking, I sat before the film in what can perhaps best be understood as a kind of impassive, numb neutrality. Was I capable any longer of an unaided response? In something like a panic, I fled from the theater, and headed for my desk drawers.

It is not that *Last Year at Marienbad* is a "difficult" work in the sense that one ordinarily speaks of a work of art being difficult. As its admirers themselves have declared, the film is "not half as difficult as it has been made to sound"; is, on the contrary, "remarkably easy to take." That characteristic sense of bewilderment and disorientation, of *disturbance,* which one commonly experiences before the obscurity of modern art is almost totally absent while watching *Last Year at Marienbad.* One feels no compulsion to understand the film, no need to know what it means; at least, one feels the film itself does not demand these things. It is positively *relaxing;* as relaxing, anyway, as such a thing can be.

This is not to say there isn't an undeniable temptation to

interpret the film, to pursue its correspondence to all manner of meanings. Of the two radio discussions I heard, it was the one from San Francisco which audaciously took up this hazardous pursuit: the film was a retelling of *Sleeping Beauty,* it was an allegory of man's quest for his soul; the mysterious suitor rescued the heroine from a kind of death to awaken her to Life, he stole her from life to claim her for Death. The New York panel, on the other hand, not to be caught looking so naïve, played it relatively safe by sticking sophisticatedly to the details: the game of matchsticks, progenitor, I assume, of the 192 variations; the technical devices borrowed from earlier experimental films; the alleged parodistic elements derived from Hollywood. Doubtless, these questions are valid enough, yet even to reach complete agreement on all such details still leaves one with the unresolved problems of Life, Death, and man in search of his soul. They remain, prey to be pursued, for anyone with the audacity, with the naïveté; for it is a quarry which maintains a constant distance no matter what attempt to overtake it, and all suggestions as to which trail to follow are equal. What must be said is that it is not the film, which rigorously refuses to pursue any such suggestion, but the film's *action*—the action itself—which constantly lends itself to allegory. *Last Year at Marienbad* is as technically awesome a film as any I have ever seen, and yet all the equipment of cinema has been marshaled to what end? But there is no end, and that is the point, or the nonpoint. As we were told to begin with, it *is* great, and "The great thing about the images of *Marienbad* is that they are completely *disponible.* In themselves they mean nothing, but they can carry any meaning with which one chooses to endow them."[1] The suitor in *Last Year at Marienbad* is equally the incarnation of Death and of Life; the trio of characters, denoted in the scenario only by the letters X, A and M, I have seen as convincingly "read" as id-ego-superego and algebraic quantities, and they might as well be, and probably have been, taken to correspond as convincingly to anything in between. To me, the interesting question is not what X, A and M mean, but, if one may grant that X, A and M equal such and such, what

1. I quote from a brilliantly reasoned little piece on *Last Year at Marienbad* by Geoffrey Nowell-Smith which appeared in the January-April 1962 number of *New Left Review.*

then? What is the difference? Which is to ask again: to what end?—when clearly there is none. Can you permanently defer the question? If so, *Last Year at Marienbad* is for you. For the fact is that the film has been provided with a pattern of relationships and an action, almost, one might say, a machine, capable of *bearing* any amount of meaning with which one charges it, and yet *revealing* none. All is Becoming, nothing is Being; all is in the process. This is not to say that *Last Year at Marienbad* means everything, which would be something different. It is to say that, like an inkblot, the film, in itself, means nothing in particular. Which is to say that it means nothing.

And yet this is exactly as the film's makers would have it. "I'd like anyone who sees it to interpret it in terms of its meaning to him," Resnais has said. "It's not a 'fixed' work of art. I'd like to make films which can be approached from all kinds of angles, as one looks at sculpture." And, in an article which appeared in *Sight and Sound* and serves as his introduction to the published scenario, Robbe-Grillet has made a theoretical defense of the anticonventional convention which gives the film this multifaceted, sculptural quality.

> What happens when two people meet and exchange ideas? Take this little dialogue . . .
> "What if we both went to the beach? A wide, empty beach where we could be warm in the sun . . ."
> "With the weather the way it is! We'd spend the whole day indoors, waiting for the rain to stop."
> "Then we could make a wood fire in the big fireplace . . ." etc.
> The actual room or street where they're talking will have gone from their minds, replaced by the images they're suggesting to each other. It really is an *exchange of views* between them: the long stretch of sand, the rain trickling down the windows, the glancing flames. And the spectator in the cinema would undoubtedly be prepared to see neither street nor room, but in its place, and while listening to the dialogue, to see the couple stretched out in the sun on a beach, then as the rain begins to see them taking shelter in a house, then to see one of them beginning to stack the logs in a big country fireplace. . . .
> . . . The cinema audience, then, seemed to us largely prepared for this kind of film, through its acceptance of such devices as the flashback. It might be said, though, that the spectator is likely to

lose his footing if he isn't from time to time given "explanations" which will let him place each scene chronologically and according to its degree of objective reality. But we've decided to trust the spectator and to leave him from start to finish with subjective images only. Two attitudes then become possible. He can try to reconstruct some "Cartesian" scheme of things, as rational and straightforward as he can make it; and he will undoubtedly find the film difficult and quite possibly incomprehensible. Or he can let himself be carried along by the remarkable images in front of him, by the actors' voices, by the sounds, the music, the rhythm of the cutting, by the hero's passion . . . and if he does this the film will seem as easy as anything he has seen: a film which addresses itself directly to his sensibility, to his faculties of looking, listening, responding and allowing himself to be moved. The story it tells will seem to him more realistic, more true, will correspond more closely to his ordinary life as he feels it, from the moment he agrees to get rid of all those preconceived ideas, psychological analyses, more or less vulgar schemes of interpretation, which bad novels and bad films repeat to him *ad nauseam,* and which are themselves the worst of abstractions.[2]

In *Last Year at Marienbad,* we are shown the thoughts of A, X and, possibly, M in images equally as emphatic as those of objective, physical reality, if any images in the film are to be taken as corresponding to an objective reality. I say "possibly" M because, in addition to usually not being able with certainty to place the image which happens at a given time to be on the screen in any verifiable past, present, or future, it is frequently impossible to discern whose thoughts constitute the image we see at any particular moment. And it may well be that *all* the images we see on the screen are those of a subjective reality; not what the character sees but what he thinks he sees, which may be as much a distortion in the present as in past or future. There does, in fact, seem to be some schematic range of exposures in the film, some shots overexposed and others underexposed, which may correspond to the truth or falsity or, at least, the tense of the image, but since we are *never* certain we are witnessing objective reality, this may be guessed at but cannot finally be determined. Resnais has spoken of images in the film whose "degree of reality is doubtful" and "images whose false-

2. Alain Robbe-Grillet, *"L'Année Dernière à Marienbad," Sight and Sound,* Autumn 1961.

ness is much cleaner and lying images which in my opinion are completely evident." He singles out a scene in which the heroine takes three hundred identical photographs of herself from a drawer as one in which "we are probably in the presence of a more 'doubtful' image . . . more mental than objective." This seems like something which can readily be agreed upon; yet what is the "degree of reality" in the image? Granted it is unlikely though not impossible that the heroine should possess three hundred identical photographs of herself: does she possess one? . . . Or a half dozen? . . . Does she, in fact, possess any, and, if so, did she ever, as we see her in the image, remove them from her drawer and arrange them in a symmetrical pattern—the pattern, as it happens, of the game of matchsticks—on the floor? Are we seeing a fantasy of the future, or a distorted recollection of the past, or a hallucinated image of the present? In any case, *whose* fantasy or recollection or hallucination, since it is not necessarily the heroine's? Or are we meant finally to understand that it makes no difference; that it is all the same, all equal? But this is not merely to play with objective reality within the boundaries of the film; it is, by inescapable implication, to question the concept of objective reality per se.

And what is, perhaps, most remarkable about this is that it is presented to us, in Resnais's words, as "a victory for realism." It is, we are to understand, not only a new or higher realism in art, at least the art of the film, but a faithful rendering of psychological reality as well. In the interview published in the *New York Film Bulletin,* Robbe-Grillet speaks condescendingly of the old-fashioned movie device of presenting a flashback framed by a "halo" which occasionally lasted for the length of the sequence; what he has attempted to demonstrate by the few lines of imaginary dialogue I have previously quoted is that we think by way of images which all exist equally in the present. Do we? Now all thought and communication are based on some convention, and, in a sense, we do tend to see the past in a "halo"; at least, the movie halo accurately represents the nature of mental process. We don't "see" mental and physical reality as equal and indistinguishable, or the past, present, and future as contemporaneous. Not so to discriminate, not to make distinctions, not to see certain things within a "halo," is the "reality" of a madman. Actually, the curious effect of *Last Year at Marienbad*'s extremely aestheticized version of total contemporaneity, its sense of having been absolutely ordered down to the tiniest detail, is that the entire film exists more firmly in the past tense than any other that I know. And Robbe-Grillet's adduced bit of dialogue is really an instance of dealing from a stacked deck of cards. A conversation about the seashore such as the one he has invented might indeed evoke the images he describes, but there are whole areas of discourse which exist without the evocation of any such corresponding visual imagery. A sentence such as the one I have just written, for example, or most of those Robbe-Grillet uses to argue his position, evokes not a visual but a conceptual correspondence; indeed, it is common for this kind of conceptual thinking to be accompanied by the loss of image, even exterior image, as when one stares blankly into space, eyes focused out on some inanimate object; in such a mental state, visual images operate only on the level of distraction.

But beyond all this is the claim that, if one relinquishes any attempt to understand a given flow of images, the experiencing of them (and since, in a given context, these images constitute our experience, experience itself) will become immediately easy, "as easy as anything he has seen." If only one will not attempt to "reconstruct some . . . scheme of things"; if only one will "get rid of all those preconceived ideas, psychological analyses . . . vulgar schemes of interpretation"; if only one will just "let himself be carried along . . ." Surely, Jonas Mekas cannot be very far away. From this point of view, really all schemes of interpretation become "more or less" vulgar; the paramount belief is that we could respond fully to our experience if only we would cease trying to understand it. It is a notion which contradicts not simply art but nature. It is true we have inherited enough formularized, conventionalized, clichéd, if you will, "vulgar," schemes of interpretation from bad novels and bad films and bad everything; stale habits of thinking which serve only to blunt and frustrate our ability to respond wholly to our experience. It is true we may never understand that experience, it may always remain "difficult" and, ultimately, "incomprehensible." But to give up that attempt to interpret and to understand, categorically to forgo such understanding—this is not *easy*,

granting even it is possible. It is, rather, the most difficult thing
to do: not to attempt to understand one's experience. There is
no more natural thing in the world than to try to understand it.

At this point, I would like to say a few things about the case of
Alain Resnais; for whatever interest *Last Year at Marienbad* may
have in itself is at least equaled by what it reveals of its director
precisely thus: as a case. Such observations as may be made are,
it should be said, all quite conjectural. Resnais has made, as I
write, only two feature-length films; although these were preceded by a number of shorter films, I have not seen them; and
I intend to involve myself in a number of suspect generalizations,
suspect in that any generalization is suspect which relies on so
limited a quantity of particulars: the danger is always that one
will treat mere coincidence as if it were necessity. In addition, it
is always problematical to fix individual responsibility and speak
assuredly of the work of a director in an enterprise as variously
collaborative as the making of a film. One tends, for example,
to speak of the films of De Sica, yet De Sica without Cesare
Zavattini might be a vastly different kind of artist; and, for
another, a director such as William Wyler, one now sees, can
scarcely be said to exist apart from his earlier collaborators. It
may be that, when one speaks on anything less than extensive
evidence of the work of a particular director, one is necessarily
speaking provisionally and symbolically, as a matter of convenience; quite possibly using a single name to signify what may, in
fact, be a complex of diversely authored contributions. Moreover,
the case of Resnais has been complicated by the involvement, in
both his long films, of two exceptionally assertive collaborators:
Marguerite Duras and Alain Robbe-Grillet; and, although *Hiroshima, Mon Amour* occasionally betrays a decided dissonance of
sensibilities which enables one to make credible guesses as to
what in that film owes to Duras and what to Resnais, the collaboration between Resnais and Robbe-Grillet is so close and
so entirely simpatico that at one time the two had intended to
"sign" the film jointly, without making any distinction between
the writing and the direction. Yet there is this much to work
with: *Hiroshima, Mon Amour* and *Last Year at Marienbad,* although, in a number of respects, dissimilar works, possess several

large, essential qualities in common. And it is to these fundamental similarities that I wish now to address myself.

Alain Resnais has given us two films about persuasion.[3] In
both, there is the same obstacle to be surmounted: something
which is resisted by the person subjected to the persuasion, and
must be established over the protest of this resistance. To effect
this persuasion, the participants in it, in both films, assume a
relationship which I am not the first to describe as that of patient
and analyst. It is not the psychoanalytical implications of this
which I wish to stress, however, but the structural ones. This
relationship between the characters might as well be likened
to that of attorney and witness; the interesting point remains
that, for Resnais, the typical, or, at least, a typical, relationship
between people is that in which one is, in a sense, objectified
by the other, one in which the characteristic form of communication is not conversational exchange but monologue and interrogation. We see the characters during a time at which they are, in
a sense, out of action, a time at which they are suspended; during
a time before which some crucial action has or may have taken
place, and after which—once the facts of the earlier action have
been established—another may follow. As in the psychoanalytical
or legal relationship, the participants have ceased temporarily
to be subjects, that is, protagonists of an action, but have instead
become objects, vehicles through which we are directed to something else; something which takes precedence over them, and
must first be established before they once again can act.

What must be established in both films is the reality of a significant human situation, a dramatic action, over before the films
begin; in *Hiroshima, Mon Amour,* the heroine's experience with
the German soldier, the repressed memory of which is re-
awakened by her affair with the Japanese; in *Last Year at*

3. I refer those who believe *Hiroshima, Mon Amour* to be *about* Hiroshima,
and peace, and the Bomb—and most of those who have objected to the film
have assumed it was about these things, and dishonestly so—to the quotation
from a conversation with Resnais to follow. I think the film is clearly not
about these things despite their invocation, and that the suffering of
Hiroshima is intended to serve as a poetic analogue to the individual suffering
of the heroine; they are things, however, which, once invoked, carry in themselves too great a force to be successfully contained. Resnais's attempt to use
them analogically does not strike me as an instance of immoral exploitation
as it has others; only as being impossibly mistaken.

Marienbad, the meeting last year which may or may not have taken place. *Hiroshima, Mon Amour* is about a persuasion which seems to fail. In an attempt to know and thus possess her, to define their relationship as more than merely a casual affair, the Japanese elicits the painful secret of the heroine's past: he probes, and probes, and exults triumphantly when he discovers that she has at last told him what she has never told anyone else. But, finally, he is baffled; in the end, he seems unable to persuade her to abandon her husband, and remain with him in Hiroshima. I say "seems" because both Resnais and Marguerite Duras have stated in various obiter dicta that the heroine and the Japanese may have remained together for a day or perhaps longer after the point at which the film concludes. "Certain spectators of the film thought she 'ended up' staying at Hiroshima. It's possible." Thus writes Duras in a footnote to the synopsis of the film which appears along with the published edition of its scenario, although, in another context, she has rejected all such speculations. In *Last Year at Marienbad,* the persuasion appears to succeed; as much as one can state anything about the film with any certainty, it ends with the heroine leaving the man "who is perhaps her husband" for the sake of a love affair with a man she hardly knows although she may have known him last year at Marienbad. Did they actually meet last year? In a literal sense, the question probably does not matter, yet the "reality" of that meeting is the man's irresistible claim on the heroine; if they did not meet, than all his persuasion amounts to no more than a high-toned pickup, his line only a variant on the clichéd "Haven't we met somewhere before?" In both films, however, the persuasions essentially are seductions, although, in the latter film, to the extent that the man persists despite the heroine's extreme resistance, seduction verges occasionally on rape; indeed, one of the most striking images of *Last Year at Marienbad* is that of the attempted rape of the heroine, although it is an instance when, to use Resnais's words, "we are probably in the presence of a more 'doubtful' image." But the ends of the persuasion are the same in both films. In both, the heroine is asked to relinquish the claims of knowledge and authority, the absent husband and the man "who may be the husband," and to succumb to incomprehensible passion, to her capacity for allowing herself to be moved; to reject intellect for sensibility, understanding for feeling, conscious decision for impulsive response; in fact, to "be carried along. . . ."

And, of course, beyond all such similarities are those of the particular formal qualities, that extraordinary refinement and deployment of technique, which mark both films as unmistakably the work of a single artist. There is not a frame in either film which does not bear the stamp of this exceptional precision with respect to all the techniques of the medium, this absolute technical control. In this respect, I know of no one to whom Resnais may be compared since Eisenstein; even a director as exacting as Antonioni positively rambles by comparison; and, indeed, in their equal inclinations toward a cinema of total control, a comparison with Eisenstein seems inescapable. It is not their individual techniques which are similar, but the rigor of their commitment to technique per se; it is their general cast of intellect and temperament in which one sees a resemblance. It is a resemblance, however, which can extend to details. Anyone who has read the theoretical writings of Eisenstein is familiar with his penchant for charts and diagrams; reproduced in the special *Marienbad* issue of the *New York Film Bulletin* is a graph by Resnais of that film's chronological sequence of such astounding complexity that it must be seen to be believed; even then it cannot entirely be believed. When Resnais discusses technical questions, he is authoritative and unimpeachable, and it is something of a feat to discuss *Last Year at Marienbad* apart from questions of technique. But it is less difficult to imagine the subject, that is to say, the dramatic action, of *Hiroshima, Mon Amour* apart from the particular ways in which it is treated. Here are the makers of that film on the question of their subject.

> *Let me ask you one last question. It seems clear to me at the end of* Hiroshima *that the two are separating for ever, and yet I read an interview with Resnais in which he says that they stay together for a few days, and then separate.*
>
> I don't know why Resnais goes on about their sticking together. That's not the way I wrote it, and it's not the way we planned it. I'll have to talk to him about that. . . .[4]

4. "Conversation with Marguerite Duras" by Richard Roud, *Sight and Sound,* Winter 1959–60.

. . . I went on to ask about *Hiroshima*: what, to his mind, is the meaning of the juxtaposition of the two main story-themes in that film? He had obviously been asked that question before, but I did not feel that I was getting a stock answer when he told me, very simply, that for him these themes had no rigorous relationship at all. He had chosen them quite intuitively, *"the way a composer might choose two chords."* "There are things in everyday life which arrest one's attention, which seem to go together, the way words rhyme in a poem." . . . When I asked him what the film's last line meant— "You are Nevers, I am Hiroshima"—he was even more vague; for him it was merely a way of conveying the nostalgia of two lovers destined to be separated. "But then of course Marguerite may have had something else in mind." When I suggested that here and elsewhere in the film there was an atmosphere of "significance" which seemed to bely this simplicity, he allowed I might be right and implied he had heard the criticism before.[5]

In some respects, the most entertaining way of seeing *Last Year at Marienbad* is that of looking *through* the dazzling array of its surface, the intricacies of technique and the chronological rearrangement, so as never to lose sight of what is going on as a possible dramatic reality, as we traditionally think of human beings and their relations with one another in anything from *Little Dorrit* to *Breathless;* to keep your eye, in other words, on *what* is happening, not *how*. It's true; this is entertaining; it is also more than that. The displacement of chronological sequence acts as a diversion in both *Hiroshima, Mon Amour* and *Last Year at Marienbad;* especially with the latter, so great an effort must be made merely to follow what is happening that one is left all but unable to consider the happenings in themselves. This deliberate fragmentation of event into a kind of jigsaw puzzle is surely part of both films' fascination, and I think one might even legitimately say that *Last Year at Marienbad* is the more fascinating of the two simply because the "reality" of that film is so much more recondite; in fact, finally unknowable; certainly, once the "puzzle" has been solved, the mystery exhausted, in *Hiroshima, Mon Amour,* and we are left with only the straightforward dramatic situation—the walk through the neon-lit streets—the film appears quite commonplace, and drags

5. "A Conversation with Alain Resnais" by Noel Burch, *Film Quarterly,* Spring 1960.

interminably. In both films, the interest is not in the action itself, but all in the rearrangement; all is in the process. Once you piece the action back together, you arrive, in *Hiroshima, Mon Amour,* at a disgraced daughter being turned out in the middle of the night by her parents, and, in *Last Year at Marienbad,* at the dark, handsome stranger who comes to sweep the heroine away; you arrive at banality.

But the trouble lies deeper than this. For the fact is that the "reality" of *Last Year at Marienbad,* when one makes the effort to apprehend that reality beneath its infinitely shifting appearances, does not, as a reality, even begin to exist. There is scarcely a situation in the film that is not literally incredible; scarcely a line of dialogue that one can imagine being spoken. The characters *are* involved in situations, they *do* speak lines of dialogue; all these things which are the signs of both human and artistic existence and yet not that existence itself are granted to them. To a degree, one might say the same of most of *Hiroshima, Mon Amour,* but there, at least, the early scenes of the love affair seem genuinely felt and truly observed, and the extraordinary performance of Emmanuelle Riva, with its nervous intensity bordering occasionally on hysteria, constantly asserts a reality beyond the boundaries of her role. In *Last Year at Marienbad,* the camera, like a living being, prowls ceaselessly around the people, and yet they will not live; indeed, it is one of Resnais's most ingenious devices to "freeze" the actors while moving only the camera about them. The actors become props; inanimate objects there to serve the beauty of the image. They are statues. They speak, but the language itself, for all its rhetoric, is curi- ously without resonance; it serves only to lead one back to the accompanying image, or summon the next one. Statues; and one recalls that the most celebrated part of *Hiroshima, Mon Amour* was that opening sequence in which the screen is an abstract tangle of limbs, limbs "covered successively with the ashes, the dew, of atomic death—and the sweat of love fulfilled": statues. The sequence is, I've no doubt, a brilliant success, and both *Hiroshima, Mon Amour* and *Last Year at Marienbad* have their brilliant successes. I think particularly, in the latter film, of the opening; that long, labyrinthine, gliding tour along the walls, ceilings, and moldings; and of the final distant image of the hotel, a few windows gleaming starlike in the mysterious, moonlit night, as the voice of X intones: "It seemed, at first glance, impossible to get lost here . . . at first glance . . . where you were now already getting lost, forever, in the calm night, alone with me." The beauty of these moments is entirely self-contained; significantly, I think, they are moments made up of music, language, and an image without people. Resnais can wondrously transform people into inanimate objects, but it is with inanimate objects themselves that he is truly magnificent. It really is so that "the furniture is more alive than the people," as J. G. Weightman observed, borrowing George Orwell's remark on Charles Morgan, in his study of Robbe-Grillet published in *Encounter;* and it is perhaps some kind of tribute to the closeness of Resnais's collaboration with Robbe-Grillet that what Weightman writes of the latter seems to apply with equal force to the former: "objects are apprehended with an unusual, almost mad intensity," but the final effect is of "the same numb, mysterious center, linked to an abnormally sensitive eye." Perhaps nothing is more kinetically exciting in all of *Last Year at Marienbad* than an actual statue, not in itself a good statue, but one set up and angled about in such breathtaking perspectives that it becomes the most dynamic object in the film. There is a wonderful irony here, but it is Resnais's, not mine; he has said that he wishes to make films like statues, and he has made a film *like* a statue in which the dynamic center *is* a statue. One thing you must say for him: he has adopted an aesthetic consonant with his limitations.

But there is this one final, insurmountable difficulty: Resnais wishes his statues to breathe, wishes to persuade us that these statues live. Perhaps there is a certain truth in the solipsistic idea I have heard suggested that an artist makes, of his own artistic weakness, his subject; a truth, at least, for minor artists; thus Tennessee Williams writes about mendacity, and Alain Resnais has given us two films about persuasion, twice trying to persuade us that a reality which is described genuinely does exist. Resnais wishes us to achieve an understanding of the heroine of *Hiroshima, Mon Amour,* to allow ourselves to be moved by the love story of *Last Year at Marienbad.* Time and again, in the latter film, one *does* wish to respond so to the characters, if only because of those stray, unaccountable expressions which occasionally cross their faces, there if for no other reason than that the roles are filled by real human beings who will unaccountably be expressive. But one's response is always frustrated, blocked by the machinery with which they are surrounded; they remain caught fast in an aesthetic trap from which it is impossible to rescue them, equally impossible not to try.

Yet when the camera draws back from the sculptured limbs in *Hiroshima, Mon Amour,* the female figure manifests itself as a person, an independent human being at the film's very center, and this fact alone Alain Resnais, master of the arts of cinema and graph-maker extraordinary, is unable to control. Technique itself is not enough. Nor is it precisely that Resnais's technique gets between him and his subject, as, say, an Orson Welles' increasing preoccupation with the ever more elaborate choreography of the camera has gradually crowded out his interest in anything else. Resnais is, if anything, too intimate with his subject; nothing is allowed to interpose itself between them. We enter so deeply into the characters' interior that we become incapable of dissociating our discriminations from theirs, their consciousness becomes ours; we see the fantasies of the characters in *Last Year at Marienbad* as vividly as we see the film's "reality," and the heroine's obsessions, in *Hiroshima, Mon Amour,* are finally less illuminated than shared. What is lacking, above all, is distance, that aesthetic distance through which an artist endows his work with the means by which we may understand it; which is to say that what is lacking is control. Resnais cannot tell us what those charged last lines of *Hiroshima, Mon Amour* mean, but he will invent for his heroine a life which extends beyond the end of the film, beyond the limits of the work of art. But do we need to know anything of an Emma Bovary that is not in the novel? What Resnais gives us in these extraneous extensions of his heroine's existence are the simulacra of understanding and control, but they are substitutes which only emphasize the absence of the real thing. It is this combination of an almost obscene intimacy with the subject and a lack of understanding or control of it which gives the film that obsessed, neurotic quality in which lies its very real fascination, and its peculiar hold on its audience; what is really neurotic in the film is not the heroine— no work of art is ever "sick" by virtue of its subject—but the relationship between the artist and his subject. The film does fascinate its audience: people do not simply go to see *Hiroshima, Mon Amour;* they return to it compulsively, think it the greatest picture ever made, and cannot exactly tell you why. I have spoken several times now of both films' fascination: both have the rather remarkable capacity for being fascinating while not really being interesting, like a woman who is dazzling but dull. The fascination of both films is in the paradox, imperfectly embodied in *Hiroshima, Mon Amour,* perfected in *Last Year at Marienbad,* that the deeper we probe into the characters' consciousness, the less we know and understand of them. But this is to say the films' fascination is in their failure.

And Resnais seems, on some level, to be aware of this failure. Everywhere, in both films, technical control is imposed almost madly, as though to compensate for that critical kind of control which is missing. In that same interview in which he tells us that the themes of *Hiroshima, Mon Amour* were chosen intuitively and have no rigorous relationship at all, he goes on to speak of "a macrocosm and microcosm" of suffering, a "funnel-shaped structure, moving from the infinitely vast to the infinitely small"; and, after disposing of the question of the film's last line, he advances his theory of language as music, or words being used not for their literal meaning but rather as "emotional notes." When he speaks in this vocabulary—the vocabulary of funnel-shaped structures and emotional notes—his assurance is nothing less than masterly; and then there is that graph. It is not the graph itself but the need behind it that I find disturbing. Out of the obsession to possess his subject, the material, comes this obsession with technique; but the material remains recalcitrant. Although both Resnais and Robbe-Grillet have claimed they do not wish their work to be "understood" in the sense we conventionally speak of understanding, the failure of *Last Year at Marienbad,* as of *Hiroshima, Mon Amour,* is actually one of understanding, the artist's understanding, by which means alone can he fully possess and control his material; and, for the artist, the failure of understanding is not so much one of intellect as of imagination: this is the numbness at the center. For this failure, technique is made to serve as a form of therapy, but it is a kind of failure which no end of technique can serve to remedy. For all their technique, for

all their artistry, the films of Resnais remain art without understanding, art insufficiently imagined; they are art only half-
realized.

At the conclusion of the aforementioned piece in *New Left Review*, the author writes: "Faced with a choice between . . .
L'Année Dernière à Marienbad and . . . *L'Avventura*, I know I
would choose *L'Avventura*, but unwillingly. I would feel I was
opting for an intelligible world against an irredeemably opaque
one, for cruel sense against beautiful nonsense. But I would also
feel I was opting against the cinema."

So it comes again to this: to the idea of pure cinema; a cinema
of beautiful images without meaning.

It comes really to the old question of whether art ultimately
serves beauty or knowledge. I would say this: that, where the subject of art is the human being, at least, the human being as protagonist of an action, the end must, of internal necessity, be that
of knowledge. Where, as in nonobjective painting, or absolute
music—and this may be the source of music's supremacy among
the arts—there is no concern with human representation, the end
may well be beauty alone; and this is true of the film as well
when the use of the medium is not representational. It is not
true of *Last Year at Marienbad;* endlessly posing questions which
are not to be answered, the film provides an almost paradigmatic
instance of artistic self-defeat. And in this, I think, is its ultimate
value.

(1962)

8½ TIMES TWO

"There weren't any problems in *8½*; it was a film to amuse." I remember then, that when he began shooting *8½*, he took a little piece of brown paper tape and stuck it near the viewer of the camera. Written on it was REMEMBER THAT THIS IS A COMIC FILM.—EUGENE WALTER quoting Fellini, "Dinner with Fellini," *The Transatlantic Review*, Autumn 1964

The first time I saw *8½* I liked it, but I didn't think it consistently good. What was good was very, very good, but it didn't seem to me of a piece as *Eclipse* or *Last Year at Marienbad*, whether one loves or loathes them, are decidedly all of a piece; rather, it seemed very much a film of parts. Things appeared to go now this way and then that, while other things were left hanging, and, occasionally, there were moments when my interest simply flagged. What seemed to be chiefly lacking in this film so concerned with states of mind was just that—mind; the kind of central and omnipresent intelligence which one encounters in a film by Antonioni. I found myself thinking of Antonioni more than once in the course of first seeing *8½*, not because Fellini's new film really resembles those of Antonioni—except in that there was Mastroianni once again portraying the alienated artist as he had done in *La Notte* (although a different kind of artist, and

portrayed differently)—but mainly because of the extreme differences in temperament of the two film-makers.

8½ is about a crisis in the life of a film-maker, both as a man
and artist, at the point at which he seems to have exhausted his
resources both for living and for art, and there were moments,
seeing it for the first time, when I wondered if the director *of*
the film, faced with *his* several crises, had not simply abdicated
his controlling role, not only to his several collaborators but to
the machinery of cinema itself—throwing things together merely
because they looked visually effective—much as the director *in*
the film, who both is and is not Fellini, might in his desperation
do. But, although, along the way, the kind of sentimental salvation which is served up in *La Dolce Vita* is very pointedly rejected,
the conclusion of *8½* struck me as weak in a way characteristically Fellini's. I shall not seek salvations and Big Answers,
says Fellini's director; rather, turning toward the characters of
both his life and art, I shall accept you; and so, as the film
within the film finally gets under way, Guido, the director in the
film, joins his characters in a sprawling, all-inclusive dance, and
8½ closes. To plunge thus into the stuff of his experience may
indeed be a resolution of the crisis for the artist, and, in one of
the film's most unambiguously autobiographical strokes, it reveals for us directly Fellini and his imagined director as one at
the point at which they were able to begin to create a work like
8½. And there can be no mistaking, even on first encounter, that
8½ constitutes an emphatic triumph wrested from the wreckage
of Fellini's two[1] previous films. But what of the man? What does
it mean to turn finally to the people whom you have used and
failed and lied to, and tell them you accept them? Anyway, can
you not accept them? The conclusion of *8½* creates the impression that a man has finally chosen no longer to evade but to
confront an urgent personal crisis. But does he any longer even
have that choice?

So much for *8½*, I thought, and yet the several incoherent (I
thought) bits and pieces of it managed to remain in my mind with
surprising intensity, and with a persistence which finally drew me

1. Or is it one and one-half? I mean *La Dolce Vita*, and Fellini's contribution to the omnibus film *Boccaccio '70*, a short work which is undoubtedly
his nadir.

back to see the film again. What happened upon my return is
something which has happened very rarely in my experience of
movie-going, for I am now not at all convinced that *8½* is not a
masterpiece. Where were those things going in different directions, those threads left hanging, those moments of flagging interest? I could not find them. It is not primarily the content of *8½*
which is illuminated on seeing the film a second time for, in fact,
this possesses, from the first, an exceptional, pellucid clarity; the
revelation of my twice seeing *8½* was rather of its form, of structure and unity. The pieces fit together beautifully, and they
cohere; the fabric is whole. I gather that *8½* has been linked by
the reviewers to the "difficult" or "experimental" cinema of such
as Resnais, but the comparison is a palpably false one. What
strikes one as most unusual (but not difficult) in first seeing the
film is the way in which what constitutes in it a representation of
"reality" is merged with memories, hallucinations, dreams, and
fantasies; all these things mixed up in turn with the film within
a film, not for the purposes of paradox and enigma, but to the
end of a direct expression of the way in which the "fiction" and
the "reality," art and life, interpenetrate, and draw for their
sustenance upon one another. But, unlike *Last Year at Marienbad,* it is not that one is unable to distinguish the one level from
the other; only that the precise point at which one leads into
another is often not quite to be grasped. Yet, rather than confus-
ing or stalemating our response, this blurring of boundaries has
the effect of heightening our awareness of both the rational content of dream and fantasy and the fantastic element in what we
call reality. It is sensitizing.

The fabric is whole, and how surely all the threads are spun
out to the end. Had I really not noticed the first time that the
hilarious harem sequence is set in the same place in which is
enacted earlier an extraordinarily moving scene recollected from
the director's childhood, lending to the later sequence, an almost
self-contained bit of first-rate comedy, a special undertone of
poignancy which one senses even if not conscious of its source?
The theme of the director's fixation on his childhood permeates
the film, embodied in such recurrent figures as his mother, his
dead father, and the grotesquely voluptuous whore from whom he
took his sexual education in defiance of his authorized educators,

the ubiquitous priests. At the moment when his elaborately expensive, latest film project is collapsing about him, Guido is remembering the magic words told to him as a child by a little girl named Claudia, which, spoken when the moon is right, will bring a treasure. It is a treasure, an answer and salvation, which he has not stopped seeking, the object of his work and life, and it forms a theme which works intimately and pervasively with that of his pursuit of another girl named Claudia, the girl in white.

"Of all the symbols in which your work abounds, this girl in white is by far the worst." But this, which Guido is told by the obnoxious writer-intellectual who is to be his collaborator on the film in preparation, Guido knows, and still the girl in white returns to him in all her Purity and Innocence, now offering him salvation in a glass of mineral water, now putting the disarray of his hotel room into order. No more escapist ideas of purity and innocence, he vows, and still he is unable to relinquish them. Perhaps he can work her into his film as the daughter of a curate who has grown up in seclusion, surrounded by objects of art and culture, protected from the contamination of this world. The girl leafs through his script and laughs at the transparency of these self-deceptions. And still she, in her turn, is reluctant to break with him: "I bring you cleanliness," she entices. "I bring you order." Yet out of the seeming chaos of images with which the director is assailed by both his mind and eye, those images which constitute the stuff of 8½, he does find himself capable at last of breaking with his work's worst symbol and his life's dream of innocence. As he sits watching the hopeless screen tests for his floundering film, an autobiographical work including impersonations of the various characters of 8½ but everywhere compromised by lies, Claudia arrives to play her role. She retains her old attraction for him, but, although he sees her in another vision of proffered salvation, her promise of comfort is no longer powerful enough to cope with the recalcitrance of his material nor avert the urgency of its demands on him. She has become a weak image in a film crowded with forceful ones. "No woman can be a man's salvation," he tells her. "No. There's no part for you in this picture."

His rejection of Claudia is followed by a comic fantasy of suicide; he kills in her something of himself, but it is the worst part, and, in rejecting her, he becomes free to accept something better. Having destroyed the old director, he destroys the film that director was planning to make, a film emblematized by a gigantic, extravagantly expensive, artificial rocket platform constructed for its set, a construction as bloated as the image of Anita Ekberg in Fellini's section of *Boccaccio '70* for a film as bloated as *La Dolce Vita*. "Aren't you tired of films where nothing happens? Well, in this film everything happens. I put in everything," the director says at one point of his unmade film, later confessing, "I've nothing to say. But I want to say it, anyway." But, just as Fellini is never wholly to be identified with the director he has created, so do neither of these descriptions really fit the film that is *8½*, no matter how much, at moments, that film may seem to resemble the one or the other. In the end, Fellini and his director do have something to say, neither everything nor nothing, nor is that something the weak statement I had at first imagined—for, inevitably, one's understanding of the film's meaning is altered by an apprehension of its form. "I have no answers. All I can do is question and search. . . . I accept you," Guido addresses his characters; which is to say, by force of all that has gone before, No longer will I impose my meanings on you and imprison you within my constructions upon reality; I accept you for what intrinsically you are. And, having said this, he has his last vision of Claudia, now waving good-bye as she moves away toward the seashore, and then he is suddenly free to see that all his characters wear white, that what he had been seeking as an ultimate and absolute is to be found everywhere about him, in forms as various and imperfect as the forms of other people. "I'm not sure that's right, but we'll see," Guido's wife says to him in her voice of cool intelligence. And Guido, directing the dance of his characters through a megaphone, takes her hand and joins them, to the musical accompaniment of three circus clowns and a little boy in school uniform beating a drum. One by one, the lights go out until only the boy, who is Guido himself as a child, remains. And slowly that last light, and the music, also die away.

The meaning of this, as of all that has preceded it, is not, perhaps, extraordinarily complex, or profound, nor is it even new; what is extraordinary about *8½* is the richness with which it has all been imagined. From first to last, the film proliferates with incident and detail, and the wonder is how thoroughly this

profuse invention has been integrated to the whole. How firmly
all the pieces fit together: Guido's ambivalent attraction to and
repulsion by the sexuality of the women who surround him (they
are always displaying themselves to him in vulgar ways, but he
is always watching); and, with this, his sexual attraction toward
his mother, who kisses him passionately on the lips in a dream
and, as her younger self, also appears in Guido's harem fantasy,
a fantasy of sexual conquest without sexual consummation. En-
twined through all is Guido's girl in white, his invented symbol
of purity, who, although only the property of his imagination,
nevertheless refuses to remain unsexual; and, bound up with
these sexual conflicts, Guido's deep involvement with the Catholic background he has rejected (still seeking the Church's paternal
sanction and yet finding no answers in the words it has for him).
Echoing that to his faulted parent, the Church, is his failed relationship with his own dead father; and, with it, the failing
relationships of Guido to all those who revolve about him, the
close and the hangers-on, pressing their claims on his time, his
talent, his emotions: the parts interweave much as *8½* itself inter-
weaves with all of Fellini's previous films. Who is Claudia if not
the billboard goddess of *Boccaccio '70* and the beckoning angel
of *La Dolce Vita,* waving good-bye to Mastroianni from another
seashore, in their turn badly imagined versions of the blind girl
in *Il Bidone,* the waif of *La Strada,* and the prostitute Cabiria.
Indeed, Guido's father is enacted by the same man who was
the visiting father in *La Dolce Vita,* in one of that film's best
and most moving scenes. And the circus clowns (*La Strada? The
White Sheik?*), and the seedy night club telepathist (*The White
Sheik? I Vitelloni?*) who familiarly remarks to Guido, "It's been
a long time. You've become rich and famous."[2] It's all so beautifully unstressed, but it's there; and, whether or not one can
specifically identify it, it all works.

And all so richly imagined, and with so sharp an eye for a
funny face and comic moment. For I should wish to make it
clear that the masterpiece I believe I saw, in seeing *8½* for the

2. So aptly named, *8½* is not only Fellini's eighth and one-half film but also
a kind of summing up and distillation of his films before to the extent that
I am no longer able with certainty to place details between several films I
saw only months ago, so impressively have I now been brought to see all
Fellini's work as one.

second time, was decidedly a comic masterpiece; and not a comedy of satire despite some finely satirical moments. Satire depends upon distance, upon detachment, and the conclusion of *8½*—with the director announcing, in effect, "I, too, am a fool," and joining in dance with all the others—constitutes an all but explicit rejection of satire; anyway, one would have hoped that *La Dolce Vita* and *Boccaccio '70* had cured anyone of the notion that Fellini is a social satirist; they certainly seem to have cured Fellini. *8½* is a comedy of the fool, but it is a comedy continually underlined by pathos, a pathos diffused throughout the film but most assertively present in the childhood memories and the very end, sequences deeply affecting in ways not easily accounted for. It is the sad comedy of *The White Sheik,* Fellini's first solo film (and, in a sense, also a work about film-making, art, and life); a work which had seemed to me only mildly amusing the first time I saw it but which I found to be an extremely funny, touching, and beautiful film when I saw it again several months ago. Perhaps it is that this is the way, at his best, Fellini works: slowly, gently taking hold on you. Unlike Antonioni, whose work, unmistakably that of a classic prose intelligence, unfolds with a quality like irrefutable proof, the best of Fellini is obliquely metaphorical; elusive and haunting. Despite the enormous deviations of *La Dolce Vita* and *Boccaccio '70,* the genius of Fellini is of a kind that I would wish to call, for all the word's abuse, poetic. And when I think back to such things as the grandmother crooning to the sleeping children in *8½,* as to much else in the film, or recall the deserted seashore scenes and final departure in *I Vitelloni,* or see again that first glimpse of the White Sheik singing to himself and swinging from the treetops high up in the clouds—an image which I think almost definitive of poetry in film—I am convinced that this word is the right one.

And still, although I can hardly hope to exhaust all that is to be found in *8½* in this relatively brief discussion of it, there is so much else that I have scarcely touched upon. For, among all else, *8½* constitutes, from first moment—a nightmare image of suffocation followed by an hallucination of the director flying over Rome (like Christ in *La Dolce Vita*) and abruptly pulled down to "take the cure"—to last, an act of self-criticism and symbolic autobiography so personal as to be almost unparalleled in the history of the film; although, paradoxically, while *La Dolce Vita*, Fellini's "fresco" of modern Roman life, told us more of Fellini's mind than of his society, *8½*, personal as it is, creates for us a large and densely populated external world. I am reminded only of *The Blood of a Poet* (and its companion piece, *The Testament of Orpheus*), another metaphorical self-exegesis, but whereas Cocteau's film is related by means of an heraldic symbolism of highly stylized artificiality, the method of *8½* is, rather, that of the interior monologue; and *8½* is, among other things, the most successfully sustained employment of interior monologue in film of which I know. The achievement of the method, in *8½*, is that of a wholly natural representation of what goes on inside a (wildly humorous and imaginative) mind, much as was the stated intention of the makers of *Last Year at Marienbad;* the mind of a person who also happens to be one of the most convincing artists, nonintellectual species, I have seen depicted in a work of art. But what Fellini has given us with apparent effortlessness, all the labor of Resnais and Robbe-Grillet did not even begin to achieve.

Among those usually considered to be the world's most important film-makers, Fellini must be, with Kurosawa, the most erratic. Roughly half of his films seem to me serious failures, and yet seeing a film such as *8½* makes one realize to what extent Fellini's failures and successes are shaped of common materials: of such things as the evocation of seedy, escapist, and illusion-mongering theatricals, and of the continual reappearance of the sea as representation of both perpetual promise and blank impassivity. I think it is interesting, and revealing of the nature of Fellini's art, that, even in *La Dolce Vita*, in which the sea is associated with very weak ideas of beckoning innocence and salvation, the imagery which conveys them has a force that seems to exist independently of the conceptual weakness. To reduce this to a simple but not, I think, misleading formulation: Fellini is an artist whose intellect is often inferior to his imagination, but whose imagination is capable of a genuinely poetic richness and resonance. *8½* doesn't run deep, but it runs torrentially, and, along the way, it makes an impressive case for the virtues of a luxuriantly imagined, superficial art.

(1963)

VIOLENCE, AMERICAN STYLE

Point Blank is an old-fashioned double-cross and revenge thriller, but made as if by men who had seen some Resnais (or, more likely, films by others who had seen Resnais, like *Two for the Road* and *The Pawnbroker*), and who then, just before shooting their film's conclusion, had had a big experience seeing *Blow-Up*. The result of all this art-in-the-head is a stew of some of the most indigenous ingredients in the American film inappositely dipped into a fancy continental sauce before serving. The ingredients themselves have a distinctively pungent flavor; it's the sauce that keeps it all from going down.

The ingredients of *Point Blank* make up, in fact, the staple diet of the American film: violence; and the film's hero is the American movie hero par excellence: the loner. His name is Walker, and, singlehandedly, he manages to shake up an omnipresent and outwardly respectable criminal organization as he strives to reclaim $93,000 that was stolen from him. It all sounds like and is like lots of other movies before; *Underworld U.S.A.* in particular; but in its very familiarity lies what there is about it that's appealing. Its head may be on the Grand Tour, but its heart is really with the moody, casually violent thrillers of the forties: those films whose impact resided not in any explicable meaning but rather in an image of American life as seen from the bottom, an image that was all the meaning that was needed. There is even a kind of innocence in so ingenuously willed a return to the world of the forties melodramas; the ambitions of *Point Blank* are positively ingratiating compared with those of a *Harper,* simultaneously exploiting nostalgia and straining to appear superior to the materials it feeds on.

And, for stretches, *Point Blank* almost succeeds; the film is so saturated with a random violence as to make one come to accept it virtually as life's condition, life in America anyway, and the director, John Boorman (an Englishman), is gifted with a genuine flair for visual dynamism even if his aesthetic judgment can't be trusted. But it seems you really can't go home again, and, in the end, *Point Blank,* for all its noisome innocence, isn't innocent of intended meaning. So we have a final sequence freighted with ambiguity as Walker (he's given no first name), relentless in pursuit of his stolen booty, declines suddenly to accept it when it is offered to him by the head of the criminal organization, who, it transpires, has been covertly exploiting Walker's lust for vengeance to further his own career. The ambiguity of Walker's withdrawal may be meaningful, and one could argue one's support for this from the film in any number of ways, just as one might, and with as much justification, argue it to be meaningless. All one can say with certainty is that the significance of the ending does not emerge organically from the body of the picture. That, and the fact that, if you're going to flaunt your admiration for things like *Blow-Up,* you had better like them for the right reasons.

II|FAMILY STYLE

If I hadn't known *Bonnie and Clyde* had caused some commotion when it opened in New York, I doubt I would have thought it the kind of film to inspire such commotion. With that humbling thought in mind, I note the fact that *Bonnie and Clyde* provided the occasion not only for another of Bosley Crowther's Sunday ruminations on the menace of violence on the American screen but also a lively defense of the film by Pauline Kael in *The New Yorker* at a length I can't recall that magazine having devoted to any single film before, and a cover story in *Time* with cover by Rauschenberg. *Bonnie and Clyde,* it would seem, is clearly about something; it's only just what it's about that's less than clear.

Like the melodramas of the forties, their meaning merged invisibly into their narrative, *Bonnie and Clyde* frustrates attempts at explication, a coherent explication at any rate, but, unlike them, it fails to leave one with a coherent image that suffices.[1] By far the most interesting suggestion as to what the film is about is to be found in the conclusion of Pauline Kael's piece on it, though not developed there to the point that I can be sure I correctly understand it. As I follow her argument, it is that the strategy of *Bonnie and Clyde* is to make use of attitudes currently available in pop culture—a campy view of the recent past, the ubiquitousness of murder spoofs, etc.—so as to deprive these things of the anesthetic quality they have acquired and make us feel the reality of such things as suffering and death once again. This idea of the film is one I find immensely attractive, and yet I cannot feel that the actuality of *Bonnie and Clyde,* whose life is so indecently dependent on such things as campiness and spoof even as it mocks them, will sustain it.

What *Bonnie and Clyde is* about, definitely if still not clearly, is violence, and, more particularly, the character of violence in American life—the way it arises naturally from the rootlessness of that life and remains consonant with the values which that life sanctions in its milder and more hypocritical forms. Yet one cannot honestly say even this about *Bonnie and Clyde* without adding in the same instant that, in its aspirations toward this theme, the film is continually undercut by compromise; for each cliché it affects to reject, positing another; for every antistereotype, a stereotype of its own. Thus we are meant to see that the Barrow gang is just another family except that it's one which kills people, yet the imagination of what it is to be just folks which fleshes out this conception seems compounded half of liberal pieties about "little people" (as in the glimpses of depression victims and the Wyeth-like homecoming scene) and half of a

1. In James Price's phrase, it has content but no subject.

city person's amused condescension toward hayseeds. And, in the end, all the purported originality of this conception yields only another pair of doomed young lovers, hounded by the world they never made though it made them; for whatever ends the film may attempt to foil conventional feelings, it eventually settles for manipulating our feelings about its principals by means as conventional as anything it disowns. Ultimately, even the very number of scenes that are brilliant seems to reach an equilibrium with those that are banal, the entire film in deadlock—which is the very essence of what is meant by a "good American" movie, in some views.

Some of the ideas in the film *are* brilliant, like the principals' theatrical sense of their own legendary roles ("Good afternoon, this is the Clyde Barrow gang," Clyde announces M.C.-like as they stride into a victim bank), the way in which family bickering takes precedence over even frantic criminal activity, and the suggestion, in the sequence in which the gang temporarily kidnaps two squares, of how criminal and/or journalistic celebrity may confer a godlike freedom to act expansively. Too many others are not so much brilliant as Bright Ideas in the sense that Eric Bentley has defined these ("an invalid idea which has more appeal to the semi-literate mind than a valid one") and, what is worse, seem infatuated with their own Brightness. I think the folksiness of the Barrow gang falls mainly into this category of contrivance, an idea that glitters as it speeds by but gives less illumination the closer one comes to apprehending it; and so does the violence, an unqualified admiration for which I cannot share with·Pauline Kael. As in Arthur Penn's earlier films, the scenes of violence have the air of production numbers, each with its own special message to be extracted, conceived by men with ideas (mainly Bright) about violence but no more than secondhand experience of it. The sequence which Pauline Kael recalls approvingly from *The Left Handed Gun,* another film by Penn in which a legendary outlaw figure is portrayed in thematic modern dress, seems to me a particularly stilted instance of this, but even the stunning scene of the death of Bonnie and Clyde strikes me as lending itself all too easily to diminishing paraphrase. It's not so much that I fail to share Pauline Kael's final estimate of *Bonnie and Clyde* as "an entertaining movie that has some feeling in it" as that I cannot value that accomplishment as much as she. Or, to put it another way, I value it much less, for example, than I do a film such as *Torn Curtain,* a much weaker work which nevertheless contains one passage of violence which, more than all of *Bonnie and Clyde,* puts, in Pauline Kael's phrase, "the sting back into death." And, unlike *Bonnie and Clyde,* it does this without any false sentimentality about the victim.

III | AMERICAN STYLE

Just as we are made to see, in that moment when Walker, the supreme individualist, steps back, if only momentarily, from the values he previously had so assiduously pursued, that *Point Blank,* too, has something to say about America and violence, so does *Bonnie and Clyde,* for its part, share *Point Blank's* willed return to a particularly American genre. Both films suffer from European influences that remain inapposite to their material and from varieties of pretentiousness; stylistic pretentiousness in the case of *Point Blank;* what might better be called cultural pretentiousness in the case of *Bonnie and Clyde.* But what is finally most authentically American about both of them is their sheer energy; this, especially, is the strength of *Bonnie and Clyde;* a kinetic thrust that survives the aesthetic lapses.

Still, for what it fancies itself to be saying about American life and violence, *Bonnie and Clyde,* especially, deserves to be hit over the head. Pauline Kael makes distinctions about the film's writing being let down by its direction which fail, I think, to account for weaknesses which lie at the film's center: the compromises are not only in the execution, as in Bonnie's visit to her mother, but in the very conception of the film, this scene included. One might mind this less if the film weren't always seeming to be congratulating itself on its cleverness in the manner of the new "black comedy." Well, on the subjects of violence and Americana, Arthur Penn and his writers ought to be roped together to see *Kiss Me Deadly* and a few films of the forties, *The Killers* and *The Brasher Doubloon,* for a start.[2] And, to add mothers and black comedy

2. It appears they have already seen *Gun Crazy,* an earlier (1949) variation on the Bonnie and Clyde story, and one from which Penn's film seems occasionally plagiarized, down even to such things as the bickering in the getaway car.

to the curriculum, I suggest *White Heat,* a ferocious and splendid James Cagney film about a psychopathic gangster driven on by his sluttish wife and magnificently malignant mother as he strives to succeed.

A climb-to-success story in the great American tradition—the carnage piling up at the bottom of the ladder—*White Heat* is also genuine black comedy as are few other films (Buñuel's *El* is another) which lay claim to the title. Black comedy will not come of "irreverent" spoofs on "taboo" subjects (like *The Trouble with Harry* or *The Loved One*), but rather from a vision so outrageously terrible that one has to laugh at its very extremity; one must laugh in order to bear it. *White Heat* commands such a vision and does so with such absolute integrity that (because it's not by Buñuel or someone of similar intellectual repute) one can never be sure that the film's makers even know what they're doing. Unlike *Bonnie and Clyde,* no one nudges you in the ribs.

I don't know where on earth one can get to see *White Heat* now off of Forty-second Street; probably, its violence would proscribe it even from television, where most of what was great in the American film now writhes under the cutter's knife. And yet it is among the best films made in this country, and one with much to tell us about the kind of country—its marriages, family life, and corrupting aspirations—in which it was made. This it does with so utter a lack of pretension that its casual brilliance almost seems accidental—surely, since the film was made in Hollywood and doesn't have subtitles, they couldn't have known what they were doing, could they?

As far as our films go, perhaps one might even call that the American style.

(1967)

ANTI-WESTERN

For a moment, at the frontier, the bonds of custom are broken and unrestraint is triumphant.—FREDERICK JACKSON TURNER

The Wild Bunch is the most exciting American film in years, and not the least of those things I admire about it is how resolutely it declines to court any such estimation. Cast in the culturally disreputable form of the Western, it makes an especially charged use (as did *Bonnie and Clyde* with the gangster film) of its form's capacity for violence, in such a way as inevitably to invite the outrage of the guardians of our public morality; given the kind of work *The Wild Bunch* is meant to be, it would be a mark of its artistic failure if the film were *not* execrated by Judith Crist, Rex Reed, *et al., ad nauseam.* For the violence of *The Wild Bunch* goes far beyond that of *Bonnie and Clyde* in its extent and ferocity, and, unlike that of *Bonnie and Clyde,* it adamantly refuses to be paraphrased as a set of liberal statements on the subject.

Yet it would be vain to pretend that the violence of *The Wild Bunch* didn't constitute a real moral and aesthetic problem, for it is a work which—while the violence is contained by its imaginative vision and can hardly be thought to spill over into incitement—does nevertheless offer a vision in which violence is checked by no countervailing values and even bound up at times with feelings approaching a fierce joy. A group of men dressed in soldiers' uniforms rides into a dusty Texas town, circa 1913, as it does, passing some children playfully torturing a scorpion in a nest of red ants; the men aren't soldiers, it soon transpires, but bandits, and waiting for them at the scene of their attempted robbery is an ambush party made up of human refuse more repellent than the bandits themselves—the ambush laid by representatives of "the law." The clash of the two groups engenders a horrifying massacre of bystanders minutes after the film begins, and before one has had a chance to find one's moral bearings relative to the warring parties; the bloodshed is witnessed as morally indiscriminate, while, at its periphery, casually vicious children gawk, smile, and mimic it. Another massacre far more vast, its moral issues equally undifferentiated, ends the film, and, in between, we follow the bandits in their adventures leading to the climactic devastation. In the end, the leader of the bandits is shot in the back by still another pretty and venomous child; the children throughout, whether torturing a scorpion or delighting in the suffering of a tortured man, becoming, as much as the film's rampant violence, the embodiment and image of its overwhelming nihilism. "We all dream of being a child again," a character remarks early on. . . . "Perhaps the worst most of all."

But it is not simply the violence of the film that inescapably calls to mind *Bonnie and Clyde*, for, in *The Wild Bunch*, its director, Sam Peckinpah, has made a deliberate and extensive use of that earlier film's striking device of photographing the moment of death in slow motion, and the radical difference between the films—and the "problem" of *The Wild Bunch*—is epitomized in the different ends to which, in the two works, this device is put. In *Bonnie and Clyde*, the use of slow motion has the effect of glamorizing, not violence, but the film's eponymous principals as, in death, they attain their clichéd apotheosis as teenage rebels, struck down by that world they never made. In *The Wild Bunch*, the protraction of the moment of death impersonally throughout has the effect of forcing one's attention to the physical fact of death by violence as a sensate experience in all its grotesque variations; yet ambiguously protracted also, and inextricably part of the bloodshed's horror, is a sense—virtually orgasmic in the final massacre—of the savage pleasure taken by the killer in inflicting death. Beyond this, the use of slow motion has the effect of giving us, at least insofar as we are capable of responding to the Western genre and have become involved in the action, a heightened consciousness of our own pleasure in the violence of the film, and in the artistic depiction of violence in general. And it is, above all, this confrontation with our own ambiguous feelings that accounts for the peculiar power of the film's violence to shock and disturb us. We watch excitedly; the film remains morally neutral.

The moral neutrality of the film remains inviolate throughout, and is experienced with a particular tension for being set against the conventions of the Western. If the Western has become the last arena for the ritual re-enactment of a characteristically American myth of moral confrontation—the elements of which were fixed for all time in *Shane,* and, now that their innocence has become an embarrassment to our sense of American actualities, are endlessly (and gutlessly) "spoofed" in current-Westerns —then *The Wild Bunch* is the definitive anti-Western, and its brutally rapacious characters the definitive Western antiheroes. *Ride the High Country,* an earlier film by Peckinpah (and, like *The Wild Bunch,* one of the best American films of the sixties), can also be seen as a deliberate attempt to demythologize the Western, but, in its case, so as to reclaim the genre elegiacally; in *The Wild Bunch,* the genre itself is subjected to a relentless excoriation. Wrenched free as the film is from the conventional Western moral scheme, whatever values exist in its world are those which may be found in the domain of the outlaw "bunch," and consist of such things as the bandits' extremely volatile sense of comradeship and their improvisatory daring; yet nowhere is it suggested that, in the absence of others, these values are to be held in higher regard than they intrinsically merit. And, though the bandits' leader occasionally speaks of their code, there is little evidence that the others subscribe to his sentiments or regard the bunch as much more than an alliance for the sake of survival. Following one of his exhortations to solidarity, the leader slips and falls, only to be derided by the others for his previous words; taunted, he rides ahead in that natural isolation in which each of the characters is at different times revealed.

If the bunch seems any more attractive than its antagonists, it is only in the bandits' total commitment to the nihilistic impulse upon which their world revolves. "Why not?" asks their leader toward the end of the film when, frustrated in the attempt to recover one of the bunch who has been taken prisoner by a banditlike Mexican general, there seems nothing to do but wait and pass the time with whores. "Why not?" echoes another of the bunch when, later, the leader decides to try again to retrieve the prisoner. And when the leader impulsively shoots the general who has killed the captive member as they stand surrounded by the general's army, and it becomes clear that they cannot escape, the question re-echoes through the long moment of sudden quiet which precedes the final massacre. It is a moment as charged with a terrible excitement as any in films that I know: a moment almost giddy with a sense of the bunch's psychotic recklessness. In that moment they are already dead, and the giggle of realization and carefully aimed shot which breaks the silence signals their decision to take as much as they can down with them. And, all the while, we watch, amazed to find ourselves admiring as heroism what is so plainly insanity. "We gotta start thinking beyond our guns. Those days are closing fast," the bandits' leader says toward the film's beginning; but the sense with which one is finally left is not of savagery giving way to civilization but of the impulsive violence of the bunch being superseded by the mechanized violence of a society; cars, planes and World War I wait in the wings. When the frenzied killing on which the film closes eventually subsides, the two remnants of the bunch (who happened to be elsewhere and so survived) realign and ride off ostensibly but ambiguously in the name of a "cause"; the frontier ended, a new frontier to be found in Mexico, or Vietnam; ironically, they are the two most sympathetic from a modern, "liberal" perspective. "It ain't like it used to be," one of them remarks. "But it'll do."

If *The Wild Bunch* is an anti-Western—a criticism of us through a criticism of our myths and an indictment of us as one with our heroes[1]—then it remains to add that, in its dramatic and visual excitement, it is also a Western, and a great one. Not since the best of John Ford has there been a director with Peckin-

1. A criticism and indictment, one should add, from which Peckinpah surely doesn't exempt himself.

pah's gift for composing images of men in landscape, and anyone
still doubting that film is a director's medium should compare
the stylistic concentration and control given Lucien Ballard's
beautiful photography in *The Wild Bunch* (and *Ride the High
Country*) with the same photographer's indifferent patchwork in
the lackluster *True Grit;* or, conversely, the way Peckinpah im-
parts these same qualities to the work of another photographer
in *Major Dundee.*[2] Still it is not Ford of whose work *The Wild
Bunch* most forcibly reminds one but that of a professed admirer
of Ford—the Japanese director, Kurosawa—both in its technical
mastery on an epic scale reminiscent of *The Seven Samurai* and
in its profound misanthropy reminiscent of *Yojimbo. The Wild
Bunch* is not without its faults. One might easily wish away the
familiar stage Mexicans ("In Mexico, *señor*, these are the years
of sadness," etc.) and the musical comedy production number–
type scene of the bunch's departure from a Mexican village
which seems to belong to some other picture, as well as a few
other clichés of the genre that remain insufficiently reimagined.
More important, I don't think the slow-motion device quite succeeds as intended in *The Wild Bunch,* except where, as in the
collapse of a bridge, it is used purely for visual beauty and astonishment. Elsewhere, its intended effect must in some degree be
inferred from one's over-all experience of the film's impact, for,
while directing one's attention, the slow motion inevitably has
the additional effect of softening (by aestheticizing) the specific
instance. Beyond this, it may well be that the device was already
used up by *Bonnie and Clyde* and instantaneously converted there
to cliché; in any event, since Peckinpah is capable—as in the
train robbery sequence and throughout—of staging an action

2. Though anyone denying that it is also an actor's medium might also compare the self-indulged, fashionably spoofy performance of John Wayne in
True Grit with the authority and conviction brought to *The Wild Bunch* by
William Holden, Ernest Borgnine, and Robert Ryan; Holden, in particular,
brilliantly used for his vestigial qualities of a particularly American boyish-
ness. There seems now to be a widespread notion that fat, aging stars are to
be congratulated for playing fat, aging stars, and so Wayne, who for years
has gone unpraised for praiseworthy performances in numerous John Ford
films, is generally acclaimed as giving the performance of his career in *True
Grit.* A similar journalistic sentimentality about aging professionals apparently
contributes to Henry Hathaway, who has directed several good films, being
applauded for *True Grit,* a slack and flabby one.

superlatively well so that no detail is lost to us, the device is both somewhat redundant and, in the extent to which employed, excessive. Yet, like Kurosawa's *Yojimbo* (or Godard's *Weekend*), *The Wild Bunch* is a work which by its very nature is excessive, and whose power is inseparably bound up with its excess. And, for all its faults, *The Wild Bunch* has, finally, an imaginative power and energy which take it far beyond anything we have a right to expect now in American films. It is only in its violence and nihilism that it is, like a mirror image, just what we richly deserve.

(1969)

NOTES ON CANT

When MGM, with early indications of having a loser on its hands in *2001*, shifted the film's advertising campaign to tout it as the big-trip movie, it soon became clear from the crowds of stoned under-thirties flocking to it that, given the right sales pitch, the young audience was as susceptible to consumer fraud as any other. Along with the phenomenal success of *The Graduate*, the example of *2001* signaled something new in films—a new market— and the youth market in films has been bullish ever since. Probably it's now not excessive even to say that, apart from the extremes of exploitation films and those made for television, the boom in films geared for youth has been such that the major division into which commercially made American films increasingly fall is that of being with-it or not; the latter chiefly a vast miasma extending from *The Love Bug* to *Bob & Carol & Ted & Alice* with lots of elephantine musicals in between. And certainly it is true that, with the exception of *The Wild Bunch*, virtually all of the commercially made American films of the past two years which have been found worthy of serious attention in the press are distinguished by the extent to which they make a direct appeal to the high-school- and college-age young.

The outpouring of these films is in itself unremarkable enough.

Anyone who has watched the coming and going of the cycles of prize fight or psychological Western or teen-age horror or spy-spoof films knows how predictably successes breed imitations and how soon variety is converted into formula. What is remarkable, and reprehensible, is the rapidity and extent to which an undiscriminating vocabulary of "critical" praise has evolved to greet these films of youthfulness. This is cant—the disingenuous mouthing of a conformity's catchwords—and, like the political liberal's pious encomia of college students, the cant of those desperately afraid of being left behind. The films, when bad, are only bad films. The cant is a cancerous deformation of discourse, and, to the degree that it overgrows such shriveled possibilities of telling the truth on any subject as still exist, a malignant one.

I

> Best movie I've seen in years . . . best I've ever seen on the subject of youth.—REX REED

In recent months, the growing ranks of with-it cinema have been joined by such films as *If . . .*, *Goodbye Columbus, Last Summer, Easy Rider, Medium Cool,* and *Alice's Restaurant.* As might be expected of any such loose grouping, the quality of individual works varies greatly, both in actual artistic accomplishment and in degree of with-it-ness; but then, as a trip movie, *2001* itself proved more Thorazine than LSD. (It's difficult now to talk about *2001* without reacting to the extremes of adulation or antipathy it has provoked. I rather like it, but, for all its gigantism, mainly for the quiet wit with which Kubrick plays off man's stupendous technology against his incorrigible banality, a wit in which the director's attitudes clearly diverge from the fatuous apocalyptic mysticism of Arthur C. Clarke.) Among the recent films, *Goodbye Columbus* is instantly dismissable as an attempt to cash in on the success of *The Graduate,* a pseudo-youth movie product made by a director who, only the film before last, was plowing Stanley Kramer territory, and whose newly acquired mentholated lyricism makes Mike Nichols look like an Eisensteinian genius by comparison. *Last Summer* is something of a ringer, a film about youth made from a distinctly middle-aged, middle-class, middle-brow point of view compounded of some Richard Hughes–William Golding–derived natural savagery business that has been heavily diluted by the we-adults-are-responsible routine. Basically, the film is extended television drama, with everything neatly in its place and a carefully measured dose of "strong medicine" at the end. It benefits greatly from its atmospheric seashore photography and from some extremely good acting, and suffers less than might be expected from Frank and Eleanor Perry, who earlier gave us *David and Lisa, The Swimmer,* and things like that. To judge from a photograph displayed at the San Francisco Film Festival, Frank Perry now wears long hair. Today's fashions can make anyone look like an artist.

II

If you're young, you'll really dig *If. . . .* If you're not so young, it's more reason than ever to go see what it's all about!—LIZ SMITH, *Cosmopolitan*

Lindsay Anderson's *If . . .* is a ringer of another sort, American in its financing only, a film made by an English director and set in an English public school. And, although concerned with youthful rebellion from an extremely sympathetic point of view, it seems unusual also in its lack of any attempt to court the with-it set. This is to honor the work: it seems genuinely and uncompromisedly to spring from its maker's personal vision; yet that vision itself seems compromised by confusions whose consistent evasion finally suggests something like self-deceit. *If . . .* is about schoolboys in conflict with the repressive authority of the system, and has been generally regarded as a work shifting between levels of fantasy and "reality." Yet the film in its entirety has the alogical power of fantasy, and attempts to distinguish between levels within it seem to me to fail to acknowledge the amount of concrete social observation which fantasy may accommodate. The effect of *If . . .* is not of alternating fantasy and reality but rather of alternations between fantasy that has been freely achieved and blocked fantasy, fantasy cut off from the source of its own imaginative power, its elements somehow wrongly related. One senses this inductively: the final scenes in which violent rebellion breaks out, the rebels machine-gunning the school officials and establishment representatives from a roof, have an oddly frustrating, unconsummated quality; the issues and participants blurred, an absence of casualties for all the shooting. The lines of hostility in *If . . .* are drawn from the schoolboys' perspective of "them" against "us," yet, at the end, the rebels fire on their comrades as on their repressers, simply firing on everything in sight. But it is not the "them"-versus-"us" mentality which seems the weakness; indeed, as in *Zero for Conduct,* by which Anderson's film is quite obviously influenced, this immersion in the simple boyhood vision of enmity is a source of strength (although one might wish that, like Vigo, Anderson were able to draw a richer portrait of the enemy, who, in *If . . .,* is caricatured in mere stick figures of malevolent authority). *Zero for Conduct* ends also in the outbreak of rebellion, but there the effect is exhilarating, liberating. The comparable moment in *If . . .* is not in its muffled conclusion but in a scene in the middle of the film in which the rebels' leader, after having made love to a girl met in the course of an illicit excursion to a local café, rides through the countryside on a stolen motorcycle with another schoolboy and the girl held aloft like the figurehead of some speeding ship. The force of this moment comes from its released charge of sexual energy, as does that of all the best moments in the film, whether violent or tender; and it is no small achievement that Anderson is able to bring such feeling equally to the depiction of both homosexual and heterosexual relationships. The repression and liberation of sexual energy are at the heart of what is most moving and powerful, most freely imagined in *If . . . .* But Anderson is a politically committed artist, and committed to Commitment, and so *If . . .* continually attempts to extend its sexual fantasy to the political sphere, to translate the terms of one fantasy into those of another. Yet, in a sense, the artistic failures of *If . . .* are a confirmation of its deepest commitment—for they serve as demonstration that libido can no more be harnessed to the revolution than it can be made for long to serve any other master.

III

The impact is devastating! It tells it like it is with lyricism, remarkable power and rhythm!—JUDITH CRIST

If . . . is an instance of imagination betrayed by intellect; *Easy Rider* an instance of the artistic advantages and limitations of mindlessness. In some ways, *Easy Rider*'s mindlessness is its most authentically turned-on and winning quality. For a time, *Easy Rider* ambles along with so little urgency about destination and such loving devotion to its two cyclist-hippie main characters that it is hard not to go along with it for the ride. For a time. Dennis Hopper, *Easy Rider*'s director and co-star, has, in fact, boasted of the authenticity of the turning on—real grass smoked during all the (many) scenes of grass smoking—and these do indeed have the slowed down, redundant quality of scenes not only acted while high but directed (perforce) and edited on dope as well. (I speak, unscandalized, as someone of Hopper's age, though only a part-time pot smoker.) And, increasingly, the picture postcard views of countryside[1] give way to languorous essays in the iconography of Peter Fonda, a cipher accorded the reverential treatment of an avatar. This reverence is extended in different degrees to all aspects of the hippie life style. A visit to a commune, while welcome as a relief from the Hollywood gloss usually applied to such material on our screens, is nonetheless so stiff with solemnity as to inspire a furtive appreciation of the occasional virtues of slickness and cynicism. Lest one go too far in this direction, however, *Easy Rider* provides its own antidotal glimpse of the worst of both worlds in an obligatory acid trip assiduously reprising every cliché of the genre.

Yet there is authenticity of a somewhat different sort in what is best in *Easy Rider*. The film is structured around a motorcycle trip made by the two hippie characters through the American West and South, the hostility they meet growing ever more menacing, and one scene, set in a Southern café and making use of local townspeople's improvised reactions to the characters' appearance, rather remarkably captures in epitome the tense encounter of the two cultures which the film is about. The film comes most authentically to intelligent life, however, in the hilarious and poignant performance of Jack Nicholson as an alcoholic, Southern, civil libertarian lawyer whom the two pick up along the way; a much praised performance which, if it seizes opportunities that the role richly offers, must nevertheless be said, considering how it could have gone wrong, to deserve the

1. By which (and in conjunction with the music) the hippies are "sold," as Robert Chappetta has remarked, as deliberately as Nixon in 1968.

praise it has received. Nicholson brings to the film not only intelligence but a face, which, after an hour of dwelling on Peter Fonda's empty good looks, has the force of revelation. When Nicholson leaves it, the rest is mainly that acid trip, some Resnais hand-me-down flash forwards, the portentous line, "We blew it," spoken by Fonda while smoking grass, and the sudden, shocking murder of the two motorcyclists by some representative members of the Southern citizenry. The line, reportedly improvised by Fonda while actually high, has been generally regarded as central to the film's meaning, but (though the circumstance of its improvisation need hardly preclude such significance) there seems to me no way coherently to find support from the rest of the film for the weight that it hints of carrying. The film's meaning, such as it is, lies clearly in its violence, which, directed at its own values, has the power of something truly believed. In this—the sincerity of its paranoia—as well as for its tribal loyalties, it is difficult not to like or at least sympathize with *Easy Rider*. And, though the film *is* paranoid, it is hard—and this is the true source of its impact—to say just where the paranoia leaves off and realistic fears begin. In the well-known phrase of folk wisdom: even paranoids may have real enemies.

IV

Staggering . . . Illuminating . . . Magnificent! It is the stuff of now! Young people . . . should be required to see *Medium Cool!*—REX REED

Medium Cool is with-it but not quite of it; a film, like *If . . .*, made by an older director and soberly concerned with the questions of repression and violence, and one, like *Easy Rider*, whose sentiments make it difficult to dislike. Haskell Wexler, the film's writer and director, has been one of Hollywood's most talented and outspoken cinematographers, who, in the past, has been refreshingly candid on the failings of films he has photographed for other directors. Yet, ludicrously unreal as is the black-white confrontation melodrama of *In the Heat of the Night*, *Medium Cool*, however more hip in its black-white confrontation, is both less well directed than the slick Hollywood entertainment and less excitingly photographed. It is one thing to applaud a film for its sentiments but quite another to claim that one is applauding artistic achievement—for, to the extent that the art of film-making involves both the directing of actors and the giving of form to one's materials, it must be said that *Medium Cool* is both stilted and shapeless. Despite being outfitted with a smart McLuhanite title and the stylish trappings of film-making calling attention to itself, *Medium Cool* remains essentially the forced marriage of some very ordinary fictional narrative with a documentary record of the Chicago convention riots. That a genuine excitement inheres in the actual event itself is undeniable, and the film does take an excitement from it. But the relation of *Medium Cool* to the event is chiefly exploitative: the film takes everything, and brings nothing; the riots functioning in it like the exotic locales used to renovate hackneyed plots in standard Hollywood products. Against this actual backdrop, the film places the merest sketch of narrative and character, if the word "character" can even be used to contain divergencies so irreconcilable as the protagonist's shift from callous brutality in the precredit sequence to liberal enlightenment in the scene of his speech while watching a television documentary on Martin Luther King. "Look out, Haskell, it's real!" a crew member is heard to shout on the sound track at one point during the riots as a tear gas bomb explodes nearby. Given the flimsiness of the fiction which *Medium Cool* attempts to impose on this reality and the finality with which that cyclonic reality blows it away, the warning might be taken in more than one way.

V

One of the best films about young people ever made!—*Time*

A while ago, Arlo Guthrie had a hit record, "The Alice's Restaurant Massacree." Shortly afterward, Arthur Penn made a film based on it. Now, in time for the 1969 Christmas season, Random House has published *The Alice's Restaurant Cookbook*. Soon, a chain of "Alice's Restaurants" is to begin opening around the country under franchises sold by Alice Brock, the "real" proprietress of the "real" Alice's Restaurant. . . .

Like *Easy Rider* and *Medium Cool, Alice's Restaurant* is a difficult film to dislike, but by the time I saw it I was starting to
dislike films that were difficult to dislike. The most salient feature
of *Alice's Restaurant*, however, is how little there is in it either
to like, dislike, or otherwise hold onto. If there is anything interesting about the film, it is that somewhere in its meandering
progress from start to finish it changes course, and what starts
looking like another celebration of the new tribal rites finishes
as an elegy to "aging children" and the poignancy of parenthood.
Yet the most interesting thing about this is just how little interest it sustains. Somewhere along the way (or so it would seem
from the film's seesawing uncertainties of tone), Arthur Penn
appears to have sensed that all this is not really heaven, and that
flower children, too, can be up-tight, have problems, destroy
themselves, or reach thirty. This is the news that *Alice's Restaurant* brings, to which at least one possible response might be:
so what?

Yet, to judge from some of the film's sympathizers, another
possible response is paternalistically to indulge its fitful attempts
to "feel its way," as though the film, too, were a fragile flower
child in need of protection, and its groping the badge of its sincerity. *Alice's Restaurant* is sincere all right, in what seems to me
a thoroughly sickening way; disarming resistance by playing on
our knowledge that the real Woody Guthrie lay for years dying
much like the actor who impersonates him in the film and that
his son may be latently afflicted with the same incurable and
fatal disease. (Whether the portrayal of Alice and Ray Brock has
a similar basis in actuality I don't know, though that question
intrigues me far less than does their possible rationales in selling
the rights to the use of their names in connection with events
so intimate as the film chronicles, whether real or fictitious.) As
for the film's fragility, let me offer one possible (if, admittedly,
less charitable) alternative view. Somewhere along the assembly
line on which a catchy tune is converted into Kentucky Fried
Chicken for the now generation, Arthur Penn has made a film, a
kind of updated *Jolson Story* refurbished with lots of the new
candor ("candor": our currently favored form of dishonesty). In it,
Arlo Guthrie, a modestly talented young man with a voice the
sure-fire blend of Dylan's sourness and Donovan's sweetness, a

cherubic simpleton's face sometimes startlingly reminiscent of Harry Langdon's, and a screen presence registration of zero, gets to repeat his big success while Arthur Penn, a director whose films have yet to betray evidence that an original thought has ever crossed his mind, feels his way toward some groping realization that there is trouble in paradise. Our tenderness toward this enterprise is solicited; it is a personal film; it is hard to dislike. I believe, however, that it may be worth making the effort. For, as I write, far from being one of the hundred neediest cases, *Alice's Restaurant* happens to be the next to top grossing film in the country, second only to *I Am Curious (Yellow)*. Again, it seems, somebody is getting rich, and again, it seems, it isn't I. And since somebody is getting rich, in part, on my $2.50, I think I don't have to like it. In fact, I don't think I'd much like *Alice's Restaurant* if it were going broke and I saw it free.

VI

Francis Ford Coppola is, at thirty, a genuinely young director, and already his brief career offers a classical model of Hollywood-style disaffection. A graduate of the motion picture division of UCLA, he quickly acquired such prestigious credits as that of coauthor (with Gore Vidal) of the screenplay of the Franco-American debacle, *Is Paris Burning?* Following a low-budget horror movie, his second feature film as a director was *You're a Big Boy Now*, perhaps the American prototype of coattail with-it cinema, a frantic mélange of Richard Lesterisms joined to music by the Lovin' Spoonful. His next film was a big musical, *Finian's Rainbow*, whether elephantine or not I can't say, not having seen it. Then, with some acidulous comments on working within the studio system, he went on location with a relatively little-known cast to direct an original screenplay of his own, the film now released as *The Rain People*. Given the previous Lester influence, one might reasonably expect something like *Petulia*, jazzed-up soap opera laced with modish anti-Americanism; in other words, a "serious" work, signaling its director's new-found "maturity."

And, following a beautiful, very quiet scene of early-morning rising played under the credits, it appears one's worst expectations will have their confirmation. A young wife is leaving her

affluent home and husband, and stops on her way at the home
of her parents, who only bicker with each other as she tries to
talk to them; you see (for you can't miss), they are too wrapped up
in themselves to listen to her. Yet, almost immediately after, when
the woman stops to telephone her husband, something quite different begins happening. For gradually one becomes aware, in the
course of their conversation (filmed, in a sudden shift from the
fluidly dissolving style of the opening, with the intense concentration of a long single take), that the situation is more ambiguous
than it first appeared; that the husband is not unsympathetic,
and the wife not merely the aspiring spirit fleeing from suburbia.
One becomes aware, in particular, of her tendency to refer to
herself in the third person, speaking of "the married lady" and
telling her husband that "she's pregnant"; and, if at first this
seems no more than a kind of self-conscious criticism of her
domestic role, it soon begins to take on hints of something more
serious and problematical. And when, shortly after embarking on
a drive across the country, she picks up a young male hitchhiker
and later makes herself up in a garishly sexual mask in order to
seduce (and humiliate) him, one's growing sense of witnessing
something approaching a schizophrenic dissociation is reinforced
disturbingly. Yet the effect is not clinical.

The seduction fails, though not the humiliation; the young
man, it is revealed, is a brain-damaged ex-college football hero,
and is, as much as the woman, in flight. And their shared flight
makes up the substance of *The Rain People* as it progresses with
the dramatically unstressed, leisurely pace of the vagrant drive
itself, punctuated by the wife's telephone calls home, and ending
as shockingly as *Easy Rider* in the young man's violent death.
There is much that is erratic along the way—one may wince, in
particular, at the young man's "sensitive" speech from which the
film's title derives, and wish that the episode in which he goes to
see an ex-girl friend and her family were less rigged for easy response—but what emerges from *The Rain People* as a whole is
an extraordinary evocation of the characters' desperation and of
the American road which provides its setting. If there is an influence at work in *The Rain People,* it seems surprisingly to be
that of (middle period) Antonioni, especially in Coppola's eye
for the disorienting strangeness and pathos of familiar things and

places—of a "Welcome Home Mike" banner strung across a small town's main street, a drive-in movie theater entered by day, a passing parade—and even Coppola's penchant for the unusual, proximate camera position, which may strike one as irritatingly mannered at first, seems finally to serve this sense of disorientation and estrangement. It is, of course, the characters' own, yet is most fully realized in their surroundings; and indeed, in its visual beauty and resonant detail, *The Rain People* seems to me, among other things, to create an image of the American landscape with whose vivid intensity the blurred prettiness of *Easy Rider* cannot compare.

With each telephone call home, our sense of the woman's distress deepens. The hitchhiker has become alternately someone about whom she cares and an unwanted burden, someone with whom she shifts unpredictably from tenderness to abuse. At one point, she attacks him as an "idiot" and "freak" whom she only picked up because she "wanted to make it with someone"; then adds, "Don't you see, I can hardly take care of myself!" She tries to leave him, attempting unsuccessfully to find him a job (at a Midwestern "Snake Ranch," another real location with unsettling reverberations), and eventually she does; "You hurt me!" he shouts, as she drives away. Earlier, on the telephone, she has told her husband that she doesn't want responsibility, and he tells her that she *is* responsible—for herself, for the baby she's carrying. . . . She withdraws again behind her mask for an encounter with a cop she meets but whom she only discovers to be as much a damaged person as the hitchhiker and herself. The hitchhiker breaks in on her while she's with the cop, and, thinking she needs his help, attempts to defend her. A fight breaks out; he is shot; and the film ends with the woman hysterically weeping, mothering the hitchhiker's dead body with the consoling promise that she and her husband will take him in and look after him.

The Rain People is hardly a wholly successful work; both somewhat lacking in definition and, despite the closing burst of violent action (in itself, something of a betrayal of the film's character), unfulfilled. Like the Beatles' "She's Leaving Home," it continually skirts bathos, and may (as may the song) occasionally overstep the line. It is also beautifully acted and directed, and a work which rather admirably declines to bend with fashion or seek easily accessible applause. Its vision of the flight from responsibility ending only in discovery of the inescapability of responsibility isn't an ingratiating one, nor is the sympathetic portrayal of a character who happens to be a cop likely to find favor with the young. Indeed, to judge from the speed of its disappearance in San Francisco, *The Rain People* is likely to find favor with almost no one. Yet, for all the current rage of youthfulness in films, the occasional appearance of a young film-maker's work so little with-it and so clearly a personal creation as *The Rain People* (or Noel Black's *Pretty Poison* of the year before) is an encouraging sign that there are still those who, faced with the rewards of joining the new conformity, choose instead to drop out.

(1969)

THREE | **FILM-MAKERS**

THE CLOSED MIND OF

SERGEI EISENSTEIN

The great success of the 1925 Moscow film season was not *Potemkin*, but some undistinguished Hollywood colossus; some thirty-five years later, Eisenstein had his season in New York. His huge presence looms even larger now than then; somehow, the twilight casts a more enhancing shadow than the dawn. The Museum of Modern Art Film Library is perforce becoming a mausoleum. Where will one today find a work so vast, so ambitious, as to challenge the pre-eminence of the early classics? Is it only twilight that descends, or some more permanent darkness?

Which is, perhaps, a somewhat elaborate way of saying that things are not so good, and, perhaps, suggesting that they were not ever so good as it may now seem. The Museum of Modern Art's retrospective Eisenstein exhibition struck me as being as much significant of our past excesses as our present dearth. We still do not really know what has been genuinely important in the brief, tragical history of the film; at least, we seem incapable of discriminating it from the flamboyance of mere specious success. It is not the forest that the trees obscure; rather, other trees,

111

those closer to the center. The presence looms large; with the Soviet Union's release of *Ivan the Terrible*, Part II, for cultural export, the recent rediscovery of *Strike*, his first and previously almost forgotten film, and the present availability of his writings, Eisenstein stands before us whole. The figure imposes upon our imagination, demanding judgment. There once was a man named Sergei Eisenstein, and, somehow, we must attempt to come to terms with him.

Eisenstein once called *All Quiet on the Western Front* a good Ph.D. thesis, and Dwight Macdonald has described *The Film Sense* as a bad Ph.D. thesis. Events have now, I suppose, come full circle; Eisenstein is dead, Macdonald a reviewer for *Esquire*, and Milestone is still making movies. Even those for whom Eisenstein was a modern Shakespeare (always excepting the Jay Leydas, for whom, presumably, Shakespeare was a premature Eisenstein) have tended to dissociate Eisenstein the film-maker from Eisenstein the theoretician. And even Eisenstein himself, whose sympathies are rather more with the Jay Leydas, remarks, with his customary heavy-handed wit, upon his deficiency as a literary stylist. And, certainly, what could be further from the stunning virtuosity of *Potemkin* than the gnomic phraseology and leaden pedantry of *The Film Sense*, or, for that matter, *Film Form*[1] as well. Eisenstein on *pars pro toto* is a hilarity too good to be missed. One is tempted to say, as Eric Bentley has remarked of another artist become theoretician, that Eisenstein begins a new paragraph every time he does not have a new idea, which is usually a good many times per page. Yet this kind of writing is what George Bluestone has found to be related to Susanne Langer's analysis of symbolic thinking, and to Merleau-Ponty's application of phenomenological psychology to cinema. I am reminded of the famous, if, perhaps, apocryphal, doctoral dissertation on The Function of Cleaning the American Living Room, in which it was discovered that there was a Definite Correlation between the Spatial Relationships Factor of the area in question and the Furniture Quantity Factor in determining the Cleaning Time Figure.

Perhaps the most likable quality which Eisenstein displays in

1. *Film Form and The Film Sense*, New York, Meridian Books, 1957.

his writings is an honest admiration for his own films. With some justice, he treats *Potemkin* as a classic; it is nothing if not that. *Alexander Nevsky* receives similar reverence, perhaps as deservedly. Less honest is the vein of disingenuous self-congratulation that runs through his writings, usually expressed in rallying cries in praise of the Soviet cinema in general. More disturbing still is the impersonal way in which he speaks of his "mistakes." Thus of *Strike:*

> . . . our enthusiasm produced a one-sided representation of the masses and the collective; one-sided because collectivism means the maximum development of the individual within the collective, a conception irreconcilably opposed to bourgeois individualism. Our first mass films missed this deeper meaning.

Thus a sequence in *October* was an "error." Is this a man, not to say an artist, or a committee speaking?

And Eisenstein is not above urging that the cinema is the greatest of arts, an extravagance scarcely inclined to diminish his own reputation.

> Here we shall consider the general problem of art in the specific example of its highest form—film. . . .
>
> The cinema would seem to be the highest stage of embodiment for the potentialities and aspirations of each of the arts. . . .
>
> The inexhaustible potential of all art, having achieved its highest level of development in the form of cinema . . .

He quotes Lenin's famous remark that "the cinema is the most important of all the arts to us," leaving off the "to us." He devotes one article to a condescending consideration of the limits of all other arts, explaining how the older arts are subsumed and augmented by cinema.

> Moreover, the cinema is that genuine and ultimate synthesis of all artistic manifestations that fell to pieces after the peak of Greek culture, which Diderot sought vainly in opera, Wagner in music-drama, Scriabin in his color-concerti, and so on and on. . . .
>
> Here is a unity of man and space. How many inventive minds have striven unsuccessfully to solve this problem on the stage! Gordon Craig, Adolphe Appia, and how many others! And how easily this problem is solved in cinema. . . .
>
> How narrow is the diapason of sculpture. . . . How frustrated have

been those efforts by composers. . . . How bound is literature. . . . How imperfect and limited, too, is the theater in this respect! . . .

The full embrace of the whole inner world of man, of a whole reproduction of the outer world, cannot be achieved by any one of them. . . .

As for their expressive means, escape here lies in a transition to a more perfected stage of all their potentialities—to cinema.

He will speak patronizingly of Joyce in order to establish a point in favor of cinema.

When Joyce and I met in Paris, he was intensely interested in my plans for the inner film-monologue, with a far broader scope than is afforded by literature.

Despite his almost total blindness, Joyce wished to see those parts of *Potemkin* and *October* that, with the expressive means of film culture, move along kindred lines. . . .

The most heroic attempt to achieve this in literature was made by James Joyce in *Ulysses* and in *Finnegans Wake*.

Here was reached the limit in reconstructing the reflection and refraction of reality in the consciousness and feelings of man.

. . . None of the "previous" arts has been able to achieve this purpose to the full.

He carefully explains that the film-maker must necessarily be a supreme master of all the arts.

No one, without learning all the secrets of *mise-en-scène* completely, can learn montage.

An actor who has not mastered the entire arsenal of theater craft can never fully develop his screen potentialities.

Only after mastering the whole culture of the graphic arts can a cameraman realize the compositional basis of the shot.

And only on a foundation of the entire experience of dramaturgy, epos, and lyricism, can a writer create a finished work in that unprecedented literary phenomenon—film-writing, which includes in itself just such a synthesis of literary forms as the cinema as a whole comprises a synthesis of all forms of art.

The least one might hope for in reading Eisenstein on film theory is a clear exposition and definition of montage. For those who share Eisenstein's belief that there are such things as knowable "fundamental laws of art," there may be some accomplishment in his positing five categories of montage—metric, rhythmic, tonal, overtonal, and intellectual—but certainly this is only the prelude to a definition. And when that definition comes it is either absurdly self-evident:

> Example 3 (from *Potemkin*): . . . In the thunder of the *Potemkin's* guns, a marble lion leaps up, in protest against the bloodshed on the Odessa steps. Composed of three shots of three stationary marble lions at the Alupka Palace in the Crimea: a sleeping lion, an awakening lion, a rising lion. The effect is achieved by a correct calculation of the length of the second shot. Its superimposition on the first shot produces the first action. This establishes time to impress the second position on the mind. Superimposition of the third position on the second produces the second action: the lion finally rises.

or densely metaphysical:

> An example: the "fog sequence" in *Potemkin* (preceding the mass mourning over the body of Vakulinchuk). Here the montage was based exclusively on the emotional "sound" of the pieces—on rhythmic vibrations that do not affect spatial alterations. In this example it is interesting that, alongside the basic tonal dominant, a secondary, accessory *rhythmic* dominant is also operating. This links the tonal construction of the scene with the tradition of rhythmic montage, the furthest development of which is tonal montage. And, like rhythmic montage, this is also a special variation of metric montage.

You have to admit that's a lot of . . . montage. The fog sequence remains one of the most beautiful passages in Eisenstein—significantly, one without people—reminiscent of a Ryder mystical seascape, and, perhaps, reminder of how much the best in Eisenstein owes to Tisse, his photographer. What Eisenstein claims for it, however, is quite simply beyond human ken. Probably, no statement is so frankly revealing on the subject of the mystique of montage as Eisenstein's casual reference, in another context, to "Fira Tobak, my wonderful, long time montage assistant"—like Shakespeare and his wonderful, long-time dialogue assistant! With characteristic bureaucratic bluntness, Hollywood has reduced the meaning of "montage" to a special-effects sequence. In France and Italy, it just means editing.

There is, of course, behind all of Eisenstein's theoretical writing, a dazzling display of erudition. But what is one finally to say when he cites Flaubert, Kabuki, Haiku, the whole of Japanese culture, Plato, Dante, Spinoza, Newman, Michelangelo, Rembrandt, Delacroix, Debussy, *King Lear,* the fundamental principles of thought and speech, Polynesian birth customs, Milton, da Vinci, El Greco, and Walt Whitman in order to establish precedent for . . . montage! All extant culture becomes fair game when a point must be proved. At this point, however, one must distinguish between the intellectual, the mind which is open, free, inquiring, and skeptical, and the ideologue, the mind which is closed, committed, and intent on marshaling all knowledge only toward the end of ratifying its own preconceptions.

As Robert Warshow has observed, the real hero of the classic Russian movies was neither the individual nor the masses, but, as every good Hegelian knows, history. (Always, of course, excepting Peter, Nevsky, Ivan, and Stalin, Riders of the Purple *Zeitgeist.*) When history is the hero, the best the individual can hope for is to recognize the forces at work, and, if he is lucky, sacrifice himself to them when the right opportunity arises. Vakulinchuk, the martyr of *Potemkin,* simply senses the tremor of revolutionary excitement in the air, seizes it, and sets inevitable events into motion. His individual destiny is simply to die at a good time, and in a good cause. More important, he makes a good symbol, and lies in state with the legend, "For a spoonful of soup," pinned to his chest. His death has meaning only as it serves higher purposes: provoking a mass demonstration, and providing Eisenstein with a good montage sequence. It is occasionally difficult to tell which of these consequences is the more important; it is, perhaps, not inapposite to note that the People's State came to suspect it was the latter. Reading Eisenstein on the sequence of the Odessa steps is, in this respect, particularly illuminating. For him, the famous moment in which the woman with a pince-nez is wounded in her eye is a good instance of Example 2: an illustration of instantaneous action (under) Capital Letter A. Logical (under) Roman Numeral II. *An artificially produced image of motion* (under) Heading: *a tentative film-syntax.* Photographs of the trampled child and the mother carrying the dead child advancing to meet the soldiers are reproduced above the captions "Graphic Conflict" and "Conflict of Planes," respectively. His detailed analysis of the "pathos" and "organic-ness" of the entire sequence concludes:

> Then the *chaos* of movement changes to a design: the *rhythmic* descending feet of the soldiers. . . .
>
> Suddenly the tempo of the *running crowd* leaps over into the next category of speed—into a *rolling baby-carriage*. It propels the idea of rushing downward into the next dimension—*from rolling, as understood "figuratively," into the physical fact of rolling*. This is not merely a change in levels of *tempo*. This is furthermore as well a *leap in display method* from the figurative to the physical, taking place within the representation of rolling. . . .
>
> *Chaotic* movement (of a mass)—into *rhythmic* movement (of the soldiers). . . .
>
> Stride by stride—a leap from dimension to dimension. A leap from quality to quality. So that in the final accounting, rather than in a separate episode (the baby-carriage), *the whole method of exposing* the entire event likewise accomplishes its leap: a *narrative* type of exposition is replaced (in the montage rousing of the stone lion) and transferred to the concentrated structure of *imagery*. Visually rhythmic prose leaps over into visually poetic speech.

Need one be a socialist realist to cry "Formalism!" Eisenstein's approach to his material is supremely that of a *metteur en scene*. Masses enter on left ("then the *chaos of* movement changes to a design") and arrange themselves in stunning patterns; soldiers come on and perform an exquisite massacre ("*chaotic* movement [of a mass]—into *rhythmic* movement [of the soldiers]"). And so another montage is born. What is this if not the conception of a *decorator?* Now a healthy art has a place for its decorators; sometimes, as in the case of a René Clair, the decorator may combine taste, wit, sensitivity, and elegance to a point at which he may, occasionally, become indistinguishable from a complete artist. But it is one thing to decorate with Labiche, even Goethe, and quite another to arrange human beings and catastrophic events into merely pleasing or exciting pictorial patterns. To reduce *Faust* to pretty pictures may be merely frivolous, but to make a beautiful arrangement of terror-stricken, dead and dying people is, in addition, aesthetically and morally reprehensible. Robert Warshow has called the films of Eisenstein and Pudovkin "a triumph of art over humanity." Perhaps it should be added that the remark was not intended as praise.

Montage: it has so long been the shibboleth of intellectual enthusiasts of the cinema, for whom the experience of the silent Russian film was virtually sacramental, that one who similarly considers himself a partisan of the medium cannot but utter the word without some sensation of pride. *Here,* certainly, is the art of the film. And so we behold a massacre of peasants intercut with the butchering of a bull in *Strike.* ("As a matter of fact, homogeneity of gesture plays an important part in this case in achieving the effect—both the movement of the dynamic gesture within the frame, and the static gesture dividing the frame graphically.") And so the famous sequence intercutting shots of stock exchange and battlefield in Pudovkin's *The End of St. Petersburg.* A bridge is raised in *October,* and a dead woman's hair hangs over the edge, while a dead horse dangles limply from its harness over the river below. To what extent do such sequences enlarge and illuminate the human experience? Rather, to what extent do they simplify and diminish its meaning? Don't ask—it's montage! Perhaps as significant a comment as one can make on such episodes is merely to note that, in lieu of "movie magic," a real bull and horse were slaughtered for their occasions. One need not respond sentimentally to this fact, but one might reasonably wonder if, given the opportunity, Eisenstein wouldn't mind similarly slaughtering a few extras, providing they might "die" better.

"Down to feed the maggots," flashes the title, while the image is of a pince-nez belonging to the *Potemkin*'s doctor dangling from a rope along the ship's side. The title is adequate to the image; another bourgeois has been disposed of, and by an ingenious display of *pars pro toto* (which Eisenstein enthusiastically submits to protracted analysis) we don't even see the body. Another life has been adequately converted into a slogan. In a sense, it is no different from Vakulinchuk's motto, "For a spoonful of soup." All grist for the same revolutionary mill, in which all experience is relieved of its individual dignity and meaning outside of its value to a cause. History is our hero, and for history one individual is pretty much like another, only the slogans change. It really *is* the triumph of art over humanity. Faced with the Art of the Film, it is always impolitic to talk politics. But pinning a slogan to a corpse would have been equally an act of moral crudity, emptiness, and barbarism in democratic Athens. Only it wasn't done in democratic Athens. Even Socrates was allowed to possess his own death. For human beings, individuals change, but one slogan is pretty much like another.

And so, in the West, where the notion of the individual is given some currency, however debased, it was possible to regard Eisenstein's political circumstances as a "tragedy," albeit in the modern mode of "unheroic tragedy." In Russia, it must have seemed more nearly just another comedy, bureaucratic comedy. Eisenstein was no Meyerhold, and no one had the right to ask him to be. And so the melancholy chronology of public declarations.

> The intellectual cinema . . . is too vulgar to consider. *The General Line* was an intellectual film. (1935)

> There was a period in Soviet cinema when montage was proclaimed "everything." Now we are at the close of a period during which montage has been regarded as "nothing." Regarding montage neither as nothing nor everything, I . . . (1938)

> The formalist temptations left me. The Gordian knots untied themselves. (1939)

> There [in cinema] montage . . . was a mere *sequence* . . . (1946)

> We artists forgot . . . those great ideas our art is summoned to serve. . . . We forgot that the main thing in art is its ideological content. . . . In the second part of *Ivan the Terrible* we committed a misrepresentation of historical facts which made the film worthless and vicious in an ideological sense. . . . We must fully subordinate our creations to the interest of education of the Soviet people. From this aim we must take not one step aside nor deviate a single iota. We must master the Lenin-Stalin method of perceiving reality and history so completely and profoundly that we shall be able to overcome all remnants and survivals of former ideas which, though long ago banished from consciousness, strive stubbornly and cunningly to steal into our works whenever our creative vigilance relaxes for a single moment. This is a guarantee that our cinematography will be able to surmount all the ideological and artistic failures . . . and will again begin to create pictures of high quality, worthy of the Stalinist epoch. (1946)

As Robert Warshow has observed, "If there is one thing we should have learned from history—and from the history of the Russian Revolution above all—it is that history ought to be nobody's hero."

And so in the year 1958, a dismal body described as "117 film historians" (everyone knows there just *aren't* 117 film historians) solemnly, and to the surprise of no one, put its collective head together, reaffirmed the opinion of 33 years' abdication of intellect, and cast its ballots for *Potemkin* as The Best Film of All Time. And so it goes with an audience that still cannot distinguish what is merely brilliant and clever from what is great; that mistakes its innovators for its creators, its artisans for its artists, its hacks for its geniuses. So it goes with an audience for whom historical and artistic importance are synonymous, committed irrevocably to the notion of a cultural hit parade. Such an audience always gets its Eisensteins. It always gets what it deserves.

(1960)

POSTSCRIPT, 1969

Nine years ago, when I wrote the preceding piece, polemics seemed called for. Eisenstein was firmly installed high in the cinema's hagiography, with only Robert Warshow, to my knowledge, saying different; and my piece was heavily indebted to him, not so much in its particulars as for the general example of truth-telling he provided. But now the pendulum has swung the other way, thanks, in great measure, to the indirect influence of André Bazin and the critical climate he created for understanding the genius of Jean Renoir, and dismissing Eisenstein has become something of a commonplace. At times such as these, I might even feel tempted to defend Eisenstein. Yet I think I can resist this temptation still.

There are things one can say in Eisenstein's behalf though, and they are not the usual ones. Despite its textbook-pleasing repellencies, *Strike* remains a work of great theatrical verve in a mode for which he had perhaps his most congenial flair: political cartooning; Eisenstein encountering history may not have yielded the achievement of a Michelet, but it did reveal the gifts of a Thomas Nast. And then there is the pseudo-operatic pageantry of *Alexander Nevsky* and *Ivan the Terrible;* work which, if essentially pictures to accompany music, shows at least the good judgment to choose music by Prokofiev to accompany. In between these divergent works which came at the beginning and end of his career, lies the bulk of what we mean by "Eisenstein": it was this that was the subject of my earlier essay.

But, for a number of readers, it was this—my subject and its boundaries—which posed the greatest problem of that essay. Despite its stated intention to attempt to judge Eisenstein whole, there was a tendency still for people to read that essay as an attack on Eisenstein's theoretical writings, and an unwillingness to extend its judgments to the films. My point, of course, was not that the latter are bad because the former are so, but rather that the same distinguishing traits which account for the particular badness of the former inevitably enter into and drastically mar the latter. Everything in Eisenstein that is dogmatic, deadening, and dehumanizing is *in the films.*

Still, there is one further observation I would wish to make specifically about the films. Most film theory has emphasized the visual aspect of moving pictures, but there have been few sustained considerations of them as movement, that is, as visual images in motion. The most profound difference between the visual character of a film by Eisenstein and one, say, by Renoir is not so much in the nature of their visual composition seen in isolation, different as these would be, as in the quality of their movement. For Eisenstein, every movement is a relevant part of the Grand Design, all smacking of some rigid, overriding choreography and painted footprints on the floor. Eisenstein yields striking stills, but a still is at best a fragmentary and at worst, in that it *arrests* motion, a distorted representation of a film; emphasis on the visual elements *within* the single shot is where textbook-fostered "film appreciation" has so often gone wrong. You can't look at the composition of a movie shot as though it were a still, or framed painting; the shot, seen "purely" (that is, abstracted from content), is part of a line of continuous movement that is perhaps closer by analogy to the dance than to any of the other arts.

In Renoir's films, people come and go as the frame opens up and deepens; the movement is flexible, fluid; above all, free. It is human, dramatic movement as opposed to abstract, decorative movement, and in this difference it reveals, I believe, the essential polarity of the two directors' attitudes toward the human figure in art; subject versus object. Even Eisenstein's justly celebrated editing techniques may be seen as the results of a furious attempt to *impose* movement on material that is, in its rigidity of conception, essentially static, however swiftly it is marched through the preconceived paces. And even Eisenstein's editing, grounded always in half-baked scientific laws and formulas, pulse counts, heartbeats, and other paraphernalia of the closed mind, seems to me less satisfying artistically *and* aesthetically (a distinction with a difference for, though Eisenstein may well have been the greatest aesthete the cinema has ever known, the aesthetic preoccupation virtually murdered his art) than the effortless, "invisible" flow of a film by Renoir. And one is left, with Eisenstein, to ponder the implacable dictum that no truly living art ever sprang from impulse that was purely aesthetic.

AMERICAN MADNESS

I suppose that merely to bring oneself to see a film with a name like *Pocketful of Miracles,* no less like it, it is necessary simply to like the movies, and, at least in part, in a strictly noncerebral way. I saw it, and I liked it, and I can't say that the experience of it much involved the faculty of mind. Nor, even on the level of mindless diversion, can Frank Capra's new movie, his second following a retirement of eight years, be said to be impeccable. It is an expensive job, and gives occasionally onto those big, dull, vacant spaces which money seems infallibly to buy; it suffers from the Hollywood disease—elephantiasis ("A ninety-minute picture, Jules? You must be talking about the coming attractions!"). At its best—a bravura performance by Bette Davis as "Apple Annie," some wonderfully funny bits and pieces, a knockdown brawl which assails and exhilarates by its sheer kinetic energy—the insubstantiality of the whole is almost justified. At its bad moments —particularly those featuring an incredible ingenue and her Valentino-like Latin fiancé, in whom even Capra does not seem to believe—one has the sense not so much of talent lacking as of talent not engaged. Yet Capra is his own producer, wholly independent; he hops to no mogul's barked command. Among important Hollywood directors, only George Stevens has recently

123

had this kind of independence, and, with the financial collapse of his last film, he now has probably lost it. Indeed, with the exceptions of John Ford and De Mille,[1] Capra is perhaps the most conventionally successful director Hollywood has ever known: consistent maker of profit; winner of several Academy Awards.

And, despite these credentials, Capra *is* a director of considerable importance. Among Hollywood directors, perhaps only Preston Sturges has so consistently concerned himself with a comedy of the contemporary scene; yet, for all Sturges' cosmopolitan wit, he was essentially a *farceur,* and Capra, for all his occasional air of being merely topical and his apparent sentimentality, works in a much more Aristophanic tradition. Billy Wilder also comes to mind. But his films seem to me almost the inverse of Capra's; hard cynicism on the surface, soft sentimentality underneath; and, in a film like *The Apartment,* the surface becomes scarcely distinguishable from the core. What is sentimentality if not a deficiency of feeling expressed as an excess of response; and what is cynicism if not the reciprocal of this?

Capra has called his latest film a fairy tale, and this it is, a fable of innocence out of Damon Runyon. There are a number of things wrong with it, but never does it become sentimental; if anything, one is rather conscious of a sharp edge of cruelty running through the work, an edge which cuts. Capra has populated his film—and this is one of its pleasures—with the greatest array of character actors assembled since the thirties, but the familiarity of their faces serves a purpose beyond nostalgia. The faces, like the rest of the movie's artifice, seem there constantly to remind us we are in a theater, and, indeed, Capra seems always to be saying of his fairy tale, you'd better enjoy it while you can because it only happens in the movies.

But the faces—epitomized by the marvelous mask of cosmic incompetence which is the face of Edward Everett Horton— serve still another function: inescapably, they date the work. One of the film's shrewdest strokes was in Capra's decision not to modernize his material, as, for instance, Billy Wilder refurbishes Molnar. *Pocketful of Miracles* is a fable of the twenties set in the twenties; its innocence remains inviolate. In the per-

---

1. In this, as with the question of independence, I exclude Hitchcock as a special case.

vasive ambience of the fairy tale, even a joke on implied homo-
sexuality is redeemed for innocence. The audience with whom
I saw it laughed at the comedy and cried at the pathos as at
no other film of my recent experience; in fact, my impression
was of seeing, in the audience as well, faces that had not been
inside a movie theater since the thirties. How one aches for
the simple innocence of the world on the screen; I found myself
nostalgic for a time in which I had not yet been born: clue,
perhaps, that it was a time which never existed. Never, that
is, but in our movies; and who would deny the reality of our
experience of them? It is the movies themselves for which the
film evokes nostalgia. But the pastness of *Pocketful of Miracles*
exceeds mere nostalgia, both more profound and more complex; the film, in its totality, has the aura of some earlier
experience. And, in fact, the film is a remake of one of Capra's
earliest successes, a remake in the sixties of a film made in the
thirties and set in the twenties. The final effect left by Frank
Capra's latest film is that of having seen a revival.

In an enterprise as vast and impersonal as the making of a film,
it is rare enough that a director creates his own style; if, then,
he also creates his own genre, it is indeed a signal accomplishment. That Frank Capra did both, and then abruptly climaxed
his spectacularly successful career by a self-imposed premature
retirement, would serve to make him an absolute conundrum.
For Hollywood directors are notoriously like old soldiers in the
way in which they just fade out and away.

The unique Capra genre has been defined by Richard Griffith, the film historian, as the "fantasy of goodwill," and he has
also described its archetypical pattern. "In each film, a mes-
sianic innocent, not unlike the classic simpletons of literature
. . . pits himself against the forces of entrenched greed. His
inexperience defeats him strategically, but his gallant integrity
in the face of temptation calls forth the goodwill of the 'little
people,' and through their combined protest, he triumphs."
This ritual of innocence triumphant did little to ingratiate
Capra to an intellectual audience to whom he represented only
the triumph of the *Saturday Evening Post*. But though the
apparent vein of cheery optimism which informs this ritual's

re-enactment *is,* of course, precisely that quality which both endears Capra to his popular audience and alienates an intellectual one, yet, in seeing the films again, this quality seems strangely elusive, forever asserting itself on set occasions, but always dissipating itself finally in a kind of shrill excitement. There are even intimations of something like melancholy constantly lurking beneath the surface glare of happy affirmation.

The sense of this becomes particularly emphatic if one views the films—and I restrict myself to his most famous and characteristic comedies—in chronological sequence. From this perspective, although the pattern is already set in such early work as *The Strong Man,* a 1926 Harry Langdon seven-reeler, *Mr. Deeds Goes to Town* is its first major exposition, at once the prototype and the exception. Compared to Capra's subsequent films, it is the most unreservedly "positive" in tone. Longfellow Deeds does, indeed, win out, and innocence triumphs. The rustic poet *cum* tuba confronts the powerful presence of metropolitan venality, and not only effects a personal victory, but manages to impress the cynical—a reminder of their own lost innocence —with his exemplary goodness as well. The memory of innocence lost is a crucially disturbing one in Capra's films, and central to any understanding of them. While the progress from small-town purity to big-city corruption may not, in fact, be part of the audience's personal history, it remains a fact of its acquired cultural legacy. That is, it is part of the inherited myth of an American past—of quiet, shady, tree-lined streets of white wood homes—which is so concretely a part of an American childhood that it persists into adulthood as a psychological fact, with the force of memory. And while the audience is asked to, and indeed must, identify with the innocent hero, it cannot fail to recognize itself, if not quite consciously, more nearly depicted in the images of his antagonists—the cynics, smart guys, hustlers, chiselers, opportunists, exploiters, hypocrites: all the corrupt; all our failed selves; what we have become. We respond finally to the classic Capra hero, whether Mr. Smith or John Doe, the uniquely American Everyman, with a kind of reluctant longing. He is our conscience *manqué,* the image of our childhood selves, reminding us, as we do not wish to be

reminded, of the ways and degrees to which we have failed
this image; all reaching some comic apotheosis in the figure of
Jimmy Stewart, as Mr. Smith, in Washington, quite literally,
a big Boy Scout.

What moderates the merely Sunday school piety of the Capra
hero, what keeps his meaning just short of the moralizing
"essay" on the page before the murder case in our Sunday sup-
plements, is always some specifically foolish, specifically human
trait which becomes the comic correlative of virtue: Mr. Deeds
plays his tuba, John Doe plays his baseball, and Mr. Smith is
not simply a patriot, but an absurdly fanatical one, who cannot
pass the Washington Monument, however casually, without
adopting some posture of ridiculously extravagant reverence.
The virtue of the characters seems inseparable from their absurdity, and, bound up as it is with this absurdity, passes from
the ideality of the Sunday moral to the reality of a concrete
human embodiment. It becomes a human possibility; that is
to say, the peculiar impact of the Capra hero is as an assertion that it is possible to be that good . . . and human, too.

It is the formularized happy ending which has always seemed
the fatal weakness of Capra's films; the apparent belief that
everything will turn out all right in the end serves, finally,
only to nullify any serious moral concern. Yet this convention
of the happy ending seems, on closer look, to be curiously
quarantined in Capra's films, and the observance of it has often
been strangely perfunctory. Only *Mr. Deeds Goes to Town*
appears comfortably to adopt a happy ending, and, while this
film remains the prototype of the others, much of their interest
derives from the variations they work on the original pattern.
In *Mr. Smith Goes to Washington,* the dramatic climax is
brought off with such astonishing abruptness as to be over
before we can consciously comprehend it. The filibuster has
dragged on interminably. Mr. Smith seems defeated, and with
the arrival of the hostile letters he suddenly becomes aware of
his defeat. More suddenly still, the corrupt Senator leaps to
the railing—admits the truth of Smith's accusation—Smith
collapses in exhaustion and disbelief—wild commotion—Jean
Arthur smiles—The End. The entire dramatic reversal takes
place in less than a minute. The finale of *Meet John Doe* is

almost the reverse in quality. With John Doe's suicide an apparent inevitability, the film closes on an episode of almost dreamlike tranquillity. It is Christmas Eve; there is an all but unendurably slow elevator ride to the top of a deserted skyscraper; the snow is falling, thick and silent; John Doe appears and moves to the edge of the roof; Edward Arnold appears with his henchmen; the Girl appears with specimen types of little folk who have regained faith in the idea of John Doe, and Doe allows himself to be persuaded to return to life. Distant church bells. In both cases, the tone and tenor of the final sequence are seriously at odds with the rest of the work: in *Meet John Doe,* it seems to take place in a vacuum; in *Mr. Smith Goes to Washington,* on a roller coaster. I am not at all sure that Capra rejects the validity of the happy ending, but what one detects, in the abrupt changes of style, is some knowledge, if less than conscious, of the discrepancy between the complex nature of his film's recurring antitheses and the evasive facility of their reconciliation.

To understand this is to come to a film such as *It's a Wonderful Life* with a fresh eye. For it is in this film that Capra effects the perfect equipoise between the antitheses he poses and the apparatus by which he reconciles them; there being, in fact, no recourse in "real life," the end is served by the intervention of a literal *deus ex machina*. And, as George Bailey, the film's hero, jumps into the river to commit suicide as the culmination of his progress of disastrous failures, he is saved . . . by an angel! This is, of course, the perfect, and, in fact, only, alternative for Capra; and the *deus ex machina* serves its classic purpose, from *Iphigenia in Tauris* to *The Threepenny Opera;* namely, to satisfy an understanding of the work on every level. It creates, for those who wish it, the happy ending par excellence, since it had already become apparent, in the previous Capra movies, that the climaxes, by the very extremity of the situations which gave rise to them, were derived *de force majeure.* Yet, for those who can accept the realities of George Bailey's situation—the continual frustration of his ambitions, his envy of those who have done what he has only wanted to do, the collapse of his business, a sense of utter isolation, final despair —and do not believe in angels (and Capra no more says *we* must believe in slightly absurd angels, although *he* possibly does, than Euripides says we may not believe in slightly absurd gods, although he surely doesn't), the film ends, in effect, with the hero's suicide.[2]

It's a Wonderful Life is the kind of work which defies criticism; almost, one might say, defies art. It is one of the funniest and one of the bleakest, as well as being one of the most technically adroit, films ever made; it is a masterpiece, yet rather of that kind peculiar to the film: unconscious masterpieces. Consciously, except in the matter of his certainly conscious concern with the mastery of his medium's technique, I don't imagine Capra conceives of himself as much different from Clarence Budington Kelland, from whose story *Mr. Deeds Goes to Town* was adapted. *It's a Wonderful Life* is a truly subversive work, the *Huckleberry Finn* which gives the lie to the *Tom Sawyers*; yet I am certain Capra would not think of it in this way, nor boast of pacts made with the devil. I mention Twain and allude to Melville not haphazardly; Capra's films seem to me related in a direct way to the mainstream of our literature; and the kind of case Leslie Fiedler makes with regard to the American novel, leaving aside questions of its truth or falsity, might equally have been derived from the American film. Just as *Pull My Daisy* is clearly out of *Huckleberry Finn,* so *A Place in the Sun* (once one forgets Dreiser, as the film itself was quite ready to do) is pure *Gatsby;* and Capra seems to me, in many ways, the analogue of Twain, always, but once, flawing his genius. I would not wish to press this analogy, for, as artists, Twain and Capra are vastly dissimilar; yet they seem to me comparable in their situation with respect to art and consciousness. And, like Twain also, Capra is a "natural"; a folk artist in the sense of drawing imaginatively for his substance on some of the most characteristic matter of our national folklore.

Capra (whose life, in actuality, was in imitation of that most classic American cliché: poor Italian immigrant makes good) has made our clichés the stuff of his art; compounding his most

2. I don't mean to give the impression here that Capra employs his *deus ex machina* with any Euripidean irony (all the film's irony is contained in its title). The agonizing pathos of the film's climax derives precisely from the tension one senses between Capra's deeply felt desire to save his protagonist and his terrible knowledge that he cannot.

significant films of the ritual elements of the peculiarly American mythos of innocence. The image of metropolitan corruption, the hatred of the city slicker, the suspicion of sophistication, the distrust of politics and the fear of government, the virtue of the rural: what is this if not a compendium of the beliefs of Populism and of Progressivism, which, in turn, are Jeffersonianism, grown ossified and anachronistic. Even the agrarian quality of Jeffersonianism has been curiously preserved; Mr. Deeds wants to use his twenty-million-dollar inheritance to aid homeless farmers with free land and seed, and Mr. Smith wants the disputed tract of land to be used as an outdoor camp for boys. And there is, in addition, in Capra's work, a preoccupation with still another aspect of our national subconscious. All of his heroes are made to undergo some extraordinarily harrowing ordeal before their final triumph: Mr. Deeds is placed on trial; Mr. Smith is forced to filibuster; John Doe is hissed, jeered, and ridiculed before an assemblage of his followers; George Bailey is humiliatingly bankrupt. There is, as Dwight Macdonald has observed, something very American in the idea of an uncrucified Christ.

But Capra's genius is a comic one, and there remains that quality of irreducible foolishness in the Capra heroes, a foolishness that is the emblem of their humanity: Mr. Deeds' tuba and awful poetry, Mr. Smith's patriotic mania, John Doe's hobo language and legends, George Bailey's consummate awkwardness. And their innocence, their virtue, their beauty is inextricable from this. In a world of cleverness and corruption, they have allowed themselves to be "fools for Christ's sake"; and it hardly seems a flaw in this scheme that George Bailey's antagonist in *It's a Wonderful Life* is made a Dickensian caricature of villainy, embodying his single trait; rather, he becomes an abstracted converse of the George Baileys, the incarnation of pure, natural malignity. He exists not so much as a human being as an operative force in this world; and, by the suicide of George Bailey, the triumphant one; in the end, the cross will not be cheated of its suffering.

I have mentioned the breaches of Capra's style, but it remains to mention the style as such. It is a style—although one might never guess it from the most part of his recent work—of almost classic purity; and it seems somehow appropriate to the American ethos of casual abundance that the director of quite probably the greatest technical genius in the Hollywood film, post-Griffith, pre-Hitchcock—a genius, as Richard Griffith has suggested, on the order of those of the silent Russian cinema at its zenith—should have placed his great gifts at the service of an apparently frivolous kind of comedy. It is a style, one is tempted to say, based solely on editing, since it depends for its effect on a sustained sequence of rhythmic motion. There is very little about Capra's style which may be ascertained from a still, as, say, each still from Eisenstein has the carefully composed quality of an Old Master. A Capra still is unbeautiful; if anything, a characteristic still from Capra will strike one as a little too busy, even chaotic. But whereas Eisenstein's complex and intricate editing seems, finally, the attempt to impose movement on material which is essentially static, Capra's has the effect of imposing order on images constantly in motion, imposing order on chaos. The end of all this is indeed a kind of beauty, a beauty of controlled motion, more like dancing than like painting, but more like the movies than like anything else.

A comic genius is fundamentally a realistic one, and, in his films, his various conclusions notwithstanding, Capra has created for us an anthology of indelible images of predatory greed, political corruption, the cynical manipulation of public opinion, the murderous nature of private enterprise, and the frustration and aridity of small-town American life. There is always a gulf between what Capra wishes to say and what he actually succeeds in saying. He seems obsessed with certain American social myths, but he observes that society itself as a realist. The most succinct statement of this discrepancy between intention and accomplishment is put by Richard Griffith, in his monograph on Capra, simply by juxtaposing a commonplace phrase of Capra criticism—"engrossing affection for small American types" —against a still of the witnesses at the trial of Mr. Deeds. Their faces remain more expressive than any comment one could make upon them: mean, stupid, vain, petty, ridiculous; they form an imposing catalogue of human viciousness.

And Capra seems always to realize this. His films move at a

breath-taking clip: dynamic, driving, taut, at their extreme even hysterical; the unrelenting, frantic acceleration of pace seems to spring from the release of some tremendous accumulation of pressure. The sheer speed and energy seem, finally, less calculated than desperate, as though Capra were aware, on some level, of the tension established between his material and what he attempts to make of it. Desperation—in this quality of Capra's films one sees again the fundamental nature of style as moral action: Capra's desperation is his final honesty. It ruthlessly exposes his own affirmation as pretense, and reveals, recklessly and without defense, dilemma.

Perhaps mention should be made, in passing, of what was, in effect—the rest being only a few remakes, a few frank time-killers, and eight years of silence—Capra's last film, *State of the Union;* despite its prodigal talent and virtuoso style, an acknowledgment of defeat. With *It's a Wonderful Life,* the ideal form for the Capra comedy had been established, but it was a form which could be employed only once. Despite the fact that, in *State of the Union,* such actual names as Vandenberg and Stassen (*O tempora! O mores!*) are mentioned with considerable irreverence, these ostensible signs of daring only serve to emphasize a more fundamental lack of it. Unlike any of Capra's other films, *State of the Union* seems anxious to retreat into its subplot, one of romantic misalliance. And all the hoopla of its finale, as frenetic and noisy as anything Capra has put on the screen, cannot disguise the fact that the hero resigns from politics with the implication being that he is, in fact, *too good* to be involved. In one sense, this is Capra at his most realistic, but also at his least engaged. For the artist, withdrawal from the world—the world as he perceives it—is never achieved without some radical diminution of his art.

Perhaps, having made *It's a Wonderful Life,* there was nothing more Capra had to say. His only fruitful alternative, having achieved a kind of perfection within his own terms, had to be to question the very nature of those terms themselves. Without a realization that the dilemma existed inherently in the terms in which he articulated it, he could, in effect, go no further. It remains only to note that he went no further.

(1962)

THE LIGHT IS DARK ENOUGH

Ingmar Bear-ih-mahn[1]—not quite seven syllables, and somewhat less musically mellifluous on the tongue than Federico Fellini —but then whose memory is so faithful as to recall the enthusiasms of four years past? Which is not to suggest that Ingmar Bergman is *merely* the Federico Fellini of 1960 (and even less that Fellini was merely the Bergman of 1956);[2] only to reaffirm a few platitudinous sentiments on the transience of our earthly affections: my old flame, I can't remember her name; yesterday's kisses are just memories; it's a long, long time from May to December; etc., etc. Bergman seems durable enough to survive what James Baldwin has called his "precarious vogue," but are we?

And then, much of what may fairly be attributed to Ingmar Bergman does seem to be genuinely extraordinary. At forty-one, he has managed to create a body of work without parallel in the theatrical film for continuity and consistence; for, whereas with most directors the touchstone of their work is style, with Bergman it is theme and meaning, an achievement which looms

1. Erudition courtesy *Time* magazine.
2. At the time of writing, the American Fellini boom still centered mainly on *La Strada*.

even larger as one reflects upon it. It is as though a film director were at last to create a succession of films as shot through with the mark of his unmistakable, personal identity as the plays of a Strindberg or Ibsen. And few film directors' work has been less erratic; by which I don't mean that Bergman's films have been uniformly good, but that even his failures may be seen and understood in the light of his central preoccupations and most serious concerns. And, certainly, no contemporary director has served as more of a focal and rallying point for the young intellectual enthusiasts of the motion picture, nor has so fully articulated, not as victim but as master, the central anxieties of our age. All of which is to pay high compliment, and still to have avoided the most crucial questions; indeed, not even to have asked questions at all.

Perhaps the best work of which to ask these questions is Bergman's latest, *Ansiktet,* translated as *The Magician* or *The Face* for the Swedish word may mean both,[3] the ambiguity which informs the title proliferating richly throughout the entire film. It is the film in which Bergman has been able to expose all of his dominant themes, and the multiplicity of their presence gives the film its complex, yet curiously uncomplicated texture, its finished, definitive character. In *Ansiktet,* the dialectical clangor of faith and reason, which rings through such a film as *The Seventh Seal* and echoes resonantly throughout his other work, combines harmoniously with Bergman's preoccupation with the artist and his audience. Vogler, the mesmerist, looks like both a charlatan and a Christ, and this resemblance seems to be at the heart of what Bergman is saying: that the most salient cause of the artist's inevitable failing of his audience is the latter's impossible demand that the artist be also savior, both magician and messiah, ingenious impostor and immutable face. It is not a role which the artist exactly desires, but one to which he nevertheless seems inescapably to pretend; and though Vogler may suffer some awful, mute agony at his stigmata, he seems ineluctably to adopt the postures—vainly attempting to be healer instead of entertainer, dumbly mothering the dying actor—of redeemer. He is doomed

3. Erudition courtesy the author, who shall employ, in this case only, the Swedish title, in order to retain the nice ambiguity of its meaning.

to fail in this imposture, and fail, furthermore, as artist in the attempt; in attempting to transcend the natural limits of art. The power of art is not curative but diagnostic, and while the magician's attempt to play at divinity and weave inexplicable wonders is mercilessly exposed as pathetic sham, he is stunningly successful at exposing the sham illusions of his audience. The audience does not love him for this—for revealing the hypocritical foundation of a respectable marriage, for disclosing the invisible chains that bind a physical brute—but then the artist's passion to be loved is always at odds with the nature of his art. "People pay anything for love," says the magician's old witch as she prepares to desert his company: "You must know your limitations."

Yet the artist cannot relinquish his desire to be loved: thus the eternal appeal of the Christlike mask. But such a disguise is only able to excite responses accidental and irrelevant to art: the religious *cum* sexual attraction of the housewife; the fear and anger of the coachman: "There's something special about charlatans: their faces drive you mad. A face like Vogler's drives you mad." It is not until Vogler is stripped of his disguises, lost to his defenses and wholly abased in his person, that he is able to achieve the successes proper to his art. But first he must confront his audience without pride or pretension and reveal to it his naked face, as when Vogler finally appears before his audience without his makeup:

"I've never seen you!"
"I was made up then; what's the difference?"
". . . Put on your makeup again so that I can recognize you!"

Constantly allied to this theme is that larger one of faith and reason, the ultimate duality wherein Bergman conceives his universe. For the doctor and his associates, Vogler's performance has become the test of nonrational phenomena, and Vogler's performance fails miserably. In the test of faith and rationality, reason wins the public performance, and even later, when Vogler "performs" privately for the doctor alone, he proves, despite his impressive array of tricks, incapable of any real, substantial creation, producing only "a strong sensation of the fear of death." The doctor and his fellows actually hope for the magician's tri-

umph over their own rational skepticism; they are eager, even
hungry, for his promised sensations; and, at one point, the
doctor confesses to fighting a liking for the performers' faces. But
what the audience is seeking cannot, finally, be publicly demonstrated, only perceived in a dangerous leap of faith. The audience proves inadequate to such audacity, as do most of the
artist's company, deserting him, in the end, for the comforts
of the serene, domestic life and its attendant pieties. Only the
artist is finally capable of so hazardous, so presumptuous an
act, and, somehow, out of his abysmal despair, failure, and
frustration, his metaphysical courage is accorded some ultimate
bestowal of grace: a royal command performance.

Much of what is resolved in *Ansiktet* has already been adumbrated in such earlier films of Bergman as *The Naked Night* and,
especially, *The Seventh Seal;* or suggested indirectly by such
lighter works as *Smiles of a Summer Night;* in all these films,
a dialectic of reason and faith, often a peculiarly unreligious
kind of faith manifesting itself as pure feeling, moves toward
some transcendence by a final leap of faith. Yet to observe all
of this is still to have said nothing, still to have deferred the
most serious kind of question: for to discover a theme's continuity is not necessarily to honor its profundity; to have seen
evidence of thought not necessarily to have established its value.
    According to a definition of Harold Rosenberg's, an intel-
lectual is someone who turns answers into questions, and, as
Vernon Young has noted, Bergman's is essentially a comic intelligence in that he tends always to *reconcile* contradictions.
Even a film as rife with conflict and crisis as *The Seventh Seal*
attempts finally to settle itself, and arrive at something like an
affirmation. Thus the enigma of the juggler's ball standing
motionless in the air, and the serene endurance of the juggler,
Jof, his infant child, and his wife, Mia; neither a ball dropped
nor a symbol. But the thrilling discovery of divinity in innocence is something even less than novel; it is null. To turn
from some glimpse of life's terror, of its terrible complexity,
to a serene innocence, is no viable alternative, no real choice.
This grasping for panacea has its counterpart in the ambiguity
of its final image: the motionless ball. Is it meant to suggest

a confutation and transcendence of nature; is it to represent an artistic creation of unprecedented, incredible beauty? The ambiguity of the image here serves not to enrich but to confuse the meaning. Bergman's flair for epigram and paradox seems, here as occasionally elsewhere, a bit too brilliant, too facile and merely clever for his own good; too often one feels it to be the substitute for some deeper confrontation. And one comes, finally, even to suspect the strategy of representing the artist as nomadic clown and entertainer as essentially too easy and tractable an evasive simplification: is the synecdoche really adequate to the complex charge he wishes it to bear?

All Bergman's answers seem similarly inadequate to the implications of his questions, soft where the latter are hard, and all his questions call forth answers. Much has been made of Bergman's famous feminism. I would say his preoccupation with women is less a theme than an attitude, not so much philosophy as philosophic stance. What it amounts to is Bergman's submission to the female principle, to a celebration of natural force as it triumphs over mind, and to an image of woman as indomitable life-giver; what begins as biological half-truth becomes grounds for intellectual abdication. Strindberg, too, imagined his women as creatures of an amoral, natural power, but saw in the superiority of their power a fact to enrage him; Bergman depicts this disparity only eagerly to surrender to it. A recurrent cliché in Bergman's films is that of an intellectual discussion aborted to the precedence of some natural fact, as in the Squire's rejoinders in *The Seventh Seal*, the students' theological debate in *Wild Strawberries*, and Tubal's interruptions of the dying actor in *Ansiktet*. All ideas are dissolved in some *homme moyen sensuel* "reality," and one cannot but suspect that, although Bergman is willing to exploit ideas and abstractions, he finally distrusts and wishes to disengage himself from them. He can imagine terror, but seems finally unprepared to face it; all his final reconciliations amount to a flight from ideas into a suffusion of feeling. And thus the familiar pieties of Bergman's climactic affirmations: "I'm tired of people, which doesn't prevent my loving them"; "Hell together is better than hell alone."

But the particular genius of the truly charismatic artist—and

Bergman certainly is this—is not only to give the right answers
but to ask the right questions, and the remarkable thing about
Bergman is his ability to sound the temper of his age, to embody
and express the spiritual unrest and distress of what he has
called "the current dilemma." The extraordinary element in
Bergman's uncannily barometrical readings of the *Zeitgeist,* what
makes him a truly representative, symptomatic artist, assimi-
lable even to the sanctimony of *Time* magazine, is his ability to
transform the prevalent malaise into an article of faith; and
the degree to which, at the highest level, Bergman tells his
audience what it wants to know. The characteristic trait of our
contemporary messiahs is the extent to which they resemble us;
we want them in our image, rather than vice versa; telling us
what we want to hear, and bringing us an apocalyptic revelation of what we already know. With Bergman, an existential
position, characteristically a gesture of despair and negation,
and traditionally an opening blow in philosophic inquiry, has
become a quasi-religious affirmation, and a final resting place;
what is properly a beginning has become an end. The kind
of relentless excoriation which informs a film like *The Naked
Night,* Bergman's most pitiless film (and also one of his most
ponderous stylistically), remains largely intact in *Ansiktet,* but
has been fundamentally redirected to become a simulacrum of
faith.

> "Is your husband of the same opinion?"
> "Well—he doesn't speak."
> "Is that true?"
> "Nothing is true!"

Again:

> "Step by step you go into the darkness. . . . The movement itself
> is the only truth. . . . "

Such passages, properly an expression of the agony of such
fundamental existential confrontation, have instead the effect
of justifying an embrace of irrationality; and what should be
a *cri de coeur* becomes a credo.

It is this strangely complacent quality of Bergman's celebrated
restlessness that enables such as *Time* magazine to honor his

quest, indulging him in his experimentation and excess so long as he continues to come out of it, as he does, on the right side. *Time* quite accurately exposes the philosophical drift of Bergman's later films: that man's essence is God's existence; and what an astonishingly orthodox and inadequate proposition this turns out to be, especially when one considers the extent to which Bergman's films are finally brought up short, swerving off course from its more daring converse. But that man's existence may be God's essence seems always to be beyond the point Bergman wishes to go; his vision of the world seems to rush headlong, irreversibly toward this conclusion, but always, as in *Ansiktet,* Victoria's messenger riding comes, and the threatening confrontation is averted. The conclusion of *Ansiktet,* wrenched bodily from *The Beggar's* and *Threepenny Opera,* is a brilliantly impudent tour de force, but its triumph is that of Bergman's zeal for reconciliation, his drive toward the final reconciliation of conflicts and contradictions which, in his earlier films, resulted in the evasive affirmations and obfuscations on which they closed. The ending of *Ansiktet* constitutes the stunning adoption of an artistic device for strategic purposes; as art, however, it is mere sham. What the unmitigated irony of the Gay-Brecht invention forces one to see is the absurdity, wishfulness, and self-deception behind all our happy endings; by their manufacture of such a delusion, we are made to see its perfect impossibility. But, in *Ansiktet,* the final note is somehow triumphant; the irony dissipates itself in mere audacity, and the terrible, irreconcilable spirit of the work has been successfully exorcised.

The borrowed conclusion of *Ansiktet* reminds one also how much else in Bergman's work seems to wear a face that is slightly familiar. Large portions of Bergman's films seem now to be an exercise in Carl Dreyer, now Buñuel-Dali, Cocteau, Renoir, Germanic expressionism, or still another studied derivation. This eclecticism is not synthesized in Bergman's work as is the stylistic eclecticism of a Picasso or Stravinsky; rather it is only in aggregate and by virtue of the characteristic preoccupations to which such borrowings are turned that this pastiche becomes recognizably the work of Bergman. The chameleonlike styles of Bergman's films seem finally to serve much the same purpose as do the changing colorations of chameleons, and to be as much manufactured to meet the exigencies of the moment. The stylistic versatility is impressive, and one wouldn't wish to demand that Bergman restrict himself invariably to any single stylistic identity. Still, in great art, style is something more than method and strategy: it is identical to and indivisible from the artist's vision. In great art, style and meaning become as one, the object perceived inseparable from the mode of perception. And, conversely, as long as Bergman's style remains something manufactured on demand, one cannot avoid questions about the manufactured nature of the vision. Unlike a Strindberg (to cite another of his sources), Bergman seems a deliberate rather than a demonic creator; compulsive rather than possessed; and the style of each finally reflects the differences between an art of furious passion and one of careful intellection.

It is particularly in the darker side of the world of his films that Bergman seems most willfully to be working against the natural bent of his temperament; in the special sense which Vernon Young has noted, a comic temperament; and to be most in need of buttressing. This is why a film such as *The Seventh Seal* fails stylistically, forced and derivative; and why *Ansiktet* seems finally, despite its audacity and self-assurance, no more than brilliant sleight of hand, a magic lantern show. Its deepest level is irony, but irony freed from commitment is merely frivolous. Bergman has likened himself to a conjurer, with the camera his marvelous apparatus of magic and deception; and perhaps, in his ability to mesmerize us with mere shadows, he is closer to Vogler than we have cared to imagine. "Your tricks are old-fashioned; they can't be explained," says a character in *Ansiktet* to the old witch. Bergman's tricks are anything but old-fashioned, as a generation of college professors and *Time* magazine have borne witness.

If the dark side of his films seems alien to him, it is in the brightly lit world, the glitter of his comedies, that Bergman seems to be temperamentally at home; it is only in the comedies that his style loses the ponderous, deliberate character of his dark films and takes on the qualities of lightness and grace. Paradoxically, as his darker, more self-consciously serious films tend to suggest frivolity—as in the typical "serious" conversation abandoned to some natural fact, or earthy, physiological joke—so do his light, comic films imply something very like philosophical seriousness. Perhaps because Bergman's vision is temperamentally so unalterably contemporary (as Dreyer's is so irrevocably wedded to the past), it is *Wild Strawberries,* alone among his serious films, that, despite obvious stylistic derivations, leaves one with the satisfactions of art rather than of brilliant legerdemain; in it, form and theme—the unlived life—have become one; and it is unique among Bergman's serious films in its relative relaxation; in its establishing something like a perfect ratio between capability and intention. And, alone among his serious films, its visual texture is predominantly light, even blindingly white. It would be pointless to compare the pastoral imagery of a film such as *Wild Strawberries* to that of a Ford or Renoir; but *Wild Strawberries* succeeds in establishing its own order of visual beauty, an astringently severe, intellectual beauty. It is not a tragic film; James Baldwin has rightly observed that Bergman's intelligence is, even despite itself, too consciously rational and Protestant to submit to the terrible, catastrophic vision of tragedy. Bergman's vision is pre-eminently ironic, but it may subsume, as in *Wild Strawberries,* if not the terror of tragedy, certain profound images of flux, irreversibility, anguish, and compassion. The penultimate image of the film, that of the old man's confrontation of his parents after having made the merciless, heartbreaking trek back to the innocence of his origins, exquisitely achieves a perfected distillation of Bergman's vision that, at the end, is only the beginning: only the shatteringly fragile arc of the fishing rod; the image of eternal quest.

If a film like *The Seventh Seal* seems born of confusion, and *Wild Strawberries* of a vision, *Ansiktet* presents Bergman in an act of exposition, riding on top of his material, and in absolute control of it. This poise shows itself most plainly in the joke of the film's rain to sunshine ending; implied in such audacity is almost a confident calculation of how good you must be to get away with it. Yet the film's easy outdistancing of risk explains also why it finally rings hollow, while a film such as *Wild Strawberries,* even, in its somewhat less resonant way, *Smiles of a Summer Night,* reverberates with the kind of infinite suggestiveness of a work which serves vision. These are films which, if not great, are nevertheless permanently a part of what has been most serious and intelligent in the modern cinema, and which makes Bergman's presence in that cinema, however much claims for his accomplishment have been inflated, a salutary one. He has been a director of intelligence, and he has opened the eyes of an audience to the fact that the film is a medium responsive to the uses of an artist of intelligence; that it is responsive to ideas and their dialectic drama. And he has offered the proof, if we ever really needed it, that intelligence, in itself, is not enough.

(1960)

POSTSCRIPT, 1960

In a sense, it hardly matters what one says about *The Virgin Spring*, or about Bergman. No matter; the latest Bergman is upon us, and, predictably, the college kids will once again be queuing up, along with all those other species of intellectual, academic and nonacademic, full- and part-time, that surface at the art theaters for the ritual Saturday night. The time is now; Bergmania rules the waves; even the French New Wave is somewhat overwhelmed by its momentum. Not to know the work of Ingmar Bergman is to be ignorant of much that is most impressive in the contemporary film; yet to know only Bergman is to be, in another way, equally ignorant. And too many people who watch other and better films still see only Bergman's.

Nevertheless, *The Virgin Spring* should be seen. It, and, indeed, all of Bergman's work, has earned for itself a place in the history of all that is serious and ambitious, seriously ambitious, in the cinema. Compared to Bergman, men far more talented—Renoir, for example—are made to look merely frivolous: a man talking of God and a man staging a cancan. And stamped upon this seriousness is always the mark of Bergman's own, unmistakable preoccupations. A young girl, riding through the medieval forest on her way to Mass with a gift for the Holy Virgin, is brutally assaulted and slain by three vicious herdsmen; the girl's father avenges her by taking the murderers' lives, then prays to God for forgiveness of his act, and vows to build a church; and, on the spot where the girl was slain, a spring gushes forth from the earth: a miracle. From whom else but Bergman could such a film derive? Dreyer, perhaps; but the difference is in the details, such as Bergman's ubiquitous, earthy servant types, in this case a beggar, with their characteristic philosophical reflections: ". . . human beings. They tremble and worry like a leaf in the storm—because they know, and because they don't know." All is mystery, all is depth.

The Virgin Spring opens abruptly on a startling image. A dark, slatternly girl is blowing on a smoldering hearth; suddenly, the smoking embers burst into flame. No premonitory swooping gulls, creaking coaches, or slanting coffins; we open *in medias res,* starkly, mundanely in the thick of things. Gone is the complex visual texture that has marked Bergman's recent work; instead, all is now deliberate simplicity. The family figures move with apparent artlessness about their plain, rough rooms; they sit at table in a row, resembling, in their lack of perspective and adornment, some primitive Last Supper. As Vernon Young has noted, it is camera placement rather than camera movement which characterizes Bergman's style. It is this fact which enables Arthur Knight to write with awe of one of Bergman's films that "these are long dialogue sequences daringly played from a single camera position." It is only in the uncompromising context of a Bergman film that such deliberate stasis could be described as "daring." In *The Virgin Spring,* it is only by a difficult effort that one realizes there is a camera there at all.

All this is to the good, for simplicity is prerequisite to the success of such a film. The source of *The Virgin Spring* is a folk ballad of seventy-two brief lines of concentrated power and beauty. In a preface to her published screenplay for the film, Ulla Isaksson has described some of the difficulties in translating the ballad into a film:

> Insofar as possible, the film tries to retain the original story of the song, its simultaneously cruel and beautiful visual nature, the relentless insight into human life, and the Christian message. But in print the song takes only three pages and leaves out every kind of personal characterization and psychological motivation. The film must, in quite another way, make this story of young Karin and her

parents realistic, comprehensible, coherent, convincing in psychology and milieu. However, it did not seem possible to reproduce with entire realism the norms and attitudes of such a distant time, and expect modern men to understand them. The crucial task was to find as much common ground as possible and to build the film on that, so that the song might be both preserved and communicated. Certain additions to the story were therefore essential.

Some of what has been added to the original ballad, particularly in the way of nuance and emphasis, is extraordinarily fine: as the mournful cry of the cuckoo when the herdsmen first catch sight of the girl in the forest, and the mother's slight, involuntary move backward when one of the murderers, having shown her the dead girl's garment in an effort to sell it, moves forward to touch it; the mother's senseless attempt to prevent from being touched what has already been defiled provides what is perhaps the truest dramatic movement in the film. One can also admire the sophistication with which Bergman treats the clash of paganism and Christianity, a theme which he has introduced into the film. In the terms of the film, both beliefs are granted equal reality, and their conflict is made not one between truth and superstition but rather between an equally potent good and evil, in which Odin's curses have all the efficacy of God's miracles.

And yet all the film's intelligence and sophistication seem finally less shatteringly profound than the irreducible simplicity of the ballad. In the film, the miracle occurs only after the father, having revenged himself, begs God's forgiveness and vows to build a church; in the ballad, the spring appears immediately upon the girl's death; all else is subsequent. Contained in this rearrangement of the event is all the difference between a world conceived in terms of total faith and one of subtle meanings and symbolic justices; in short, all the difference in the world. In expanding his source, Bergman has lost the crystalline simplicity of the ballad, and not gained anything to equal it. In Bergman's film, the miracle comes as a poetic apotheosis, an emblem of goodness; in the ballad, it is simply *there,* God working full time, without glosses for his audience, his inscrutable works to perform.

But, for Bergman, a world without explanations is finally un-

endurable, however much he may flagellate his rationalism with
the lash of faith. Bergman has written: "To me, religious problems are continuously alive. I never cease to concern myself
with them; it goes on every hour of every day. Yet this does not
take place on the emotional level, but on an intellectual one.
Religious emotion, religious sentimentality is something I got
rid of long ago." In *The Virgin Spring*, against every natural inclination of his temperament, Bergman has attempted to give
us a miracle play, pushing himself deliberately onward into
an alien religiosity. But it is really no less credible that a real
spring should miraculously burst forth from the real ground
than that such should happen in a film of Bergman's. If there is
a lesson in *The Virgin Spring*, it is that the one thing which
sophistication cannot will is true simplicity.

POSTSCRIPT, 1968

Soon after *The Virgin Spring*, I stopped attending Bergman
films regularly. In part, this was because, as Robert Warshow
has said, "a man watches a movie, and the critic must acknowledge that he is that man," and though the critic in me felt
some sense of obligation to keep up with what Bergman was
doing, I was, for the rest, more interested in other things. But,
in part also, because the critic in me took seriously the implications of my previous criticism: that Bergman, for all his skill
and artistry, was essentially the middlebrow's highbrow, in
whose work his audience could find intellectual pieties without
content, metaphysical journeys without commitment to destina-
tions, tragic gravity without tragic anguish. Seen in 1956, *The
Seventh Seal* could seem for many the birth of a new seriousness
in cinema; seen today (and I certainly don't mean to say seen
in its difference from today's fashions), it is difficult not to see
it as something of a last stand of the well-made film, the cinema
of Jacques Feyder and Marcel Carné, refurbished by an infusion
of serious ideas. But the ideas, too, seem, chiefly, well made,
divested of resonance, each nailed neatly into place within the
cabinet of a master carpenter. Recently, on television, I watched
Bergman being interviewed on what was then his just completed

film, *Hour of the Wolf,* and heard him say of it things like "The demons possessed me."[4] It was a portrait of the artist as prefabricator of phrases for admiring quotation in *Time* magazine.

It is probably of no critical consequence whether one personally prefers the groaning emptiness of *The Silence,* the muffled mystification of *Persona,* or the message-laden thud of *Shame.* Bergman's celebrated attempt to create a "chamber music" in cinema by the radical paring down of his films' elements has resulted only in the loss of their surface variety and complication without gain in profundity; or, rather, has revealed, in the absence of profundity, how much his best work has depended on variety and complication of surface all along; if you're going to write a suite for unaccompanied cello, you had better be a Bach and not a Rossini. It was Shaw, I believe, who described someone or something as a sphinx without a riddle. A film such as *Persona* seems to me a riddle without a sphinx, an infinitely portentous mystery, lying inert, without the intellect, or art, to make it reverberate. It is impressive, in the manner of extinct volcanoes. It looks like a volcano. But it is extinct.

4. A compendium of such remarks appears in two speeches, collectively entitled "Each Film Is My Last," which are reprinted in the *Tulane Drama Review* of Fall 1966.

PARTS OF SOME TIME SPENT
WITH ABRAHAM POLONSKY

In 1948, a writer, whose experience, with the exception of two previous screenplays and two unmemorable novels, had been primarily in radio, made an adaptation of another writer's undistinguished, journalistic novel to the screen, and directed a film of it. The event would not seem to be a particularly auspicious one nor much of a novelty for Hollywood, where every other day finds one hack adapting the work of another hack into a piece of adapted hack work. Nor would it have been much more promising to know that the film made use of several elements that were sufficiently familiar—the good-bad guy involved in the rackets who finally goes straight, the ingenue who tries to reform him, etc. Yet, apparently, to have known all this was not to know enough. How else to account for the fact that out of it all was created an original, moving, and even beautiful work, whose only tangency with clichés was at the point at which it transformed and transcended them? I think it is accounted for by that phenomenon which never ceases somehow to be inexplicable and unpredictable: by the presence of an artist.

But the event was, perhaps, not quite so unpredictable as I may, somewhat Hollywoodishly, have made it sound. The artist's name was Abraham Polonsky, and his film was *Force of Evil;* previously, he had written the original scenario for the film *Body and Soul. Body and Soul* did not lack acclaim; although independently produced, it won an Academy Award, and was financially successful. *Force of Evil* went largely without acclaim or appreciation; noticed chiefly by the British film periodicals, it was allowed to die an inconspicuous death, a gangster film with only muted violence, a love story without romantic apotheosis, a Hollywood film without a happy ending. Both *Sight and Sound* and *Sequence* cited it as among the best films of its year, and it still occasionally crops up in catalogues of neglected works. Lindsay Anderson, in his analysis of the last sequence of *On the Waterfront* which appeared in *Sight and Sound,* invoked *Force of Evil* as foil to that film's inflation and dishonesty. The habitual British reader may have caught the aptness of the comparison; for the American one, it must have been merely a little baffling.

In theme and meaning, *Body and Soul* and *Force of Evil* form an extraordinary unity. In each, the protagonist, played in both films by John Garfield with his most characteristic combination of tough cynicism and a dreamy sense of the city's promise of exaltation, allows himself knowingly to become involved in some kind of corruption only, finally, to experience an intense self-revulsion, and to attempt to wrest himself free. In both films, the protagonist is not moved to this final breach without first having caused some irrevocable violence to those most close to him, and both films end not with any cheap and easy redemption, but deep in anguish and ambiguity. "What can you do? Kill me? Everybody dies," are the final words of *Body and Soul,* as the fighter says them to the gambler whose fight he has refused to throw, and, heroic as the words may be, they do not undercut the essential bleakness of the film's concluding prospect, or transform it into any conventional concession to an audience's expectations. What the audience was given, however, was the physical excitement of the prizefight scenes, dynamically photographed by James Wong Howe on roller skates, and the comfortable familiarity of the basic plot: ambitious young man from slums climbs ruthlessly to success. Probably, it is these elements in *Body and*

Soul that account for its commercial success and Academy Award, but the film's true distinction is rather to be found in its lyrically rich language, its evocative sense of an urban poetry, and the sensitively observed drawing of characters and their relationships which flesh out the success story's skeleton and give it life.

Force of Evil is not so accessible a film, one without *Body and Soul's* more immediate compensations for its serious demands. Joe Morse, the protagonist of *Force of Evil,* is not so simply and understandably the product of social determinations as is the fighter in *Body and Soul.* We first see him as a successful lawyer, propelled not by lack of advantages but by the drive to acquire more. Nor is he unaware of the nature of his corruption, or without moral insight. One is never certain to what extent the protagonist of *Body and Soul* is capable of self-knowledge, but Joe Morse acknowledges responsibility for his acts, and without pleading weakness. In his own words, he is "strong enough to get a part of the corruption, but not strong enough to resist it." But this is not so much weakness as a perversion of strength, a defect not in quantity but in kind. The progress of *Force of Evil* is that of the painful burgeoning of a moral imagination. This is not miraculously attained through romantic love, but achieved only after the death of Joe's older brother, whom he had tried both to advance and protect within the racket into which he tempted him. There is a romantic love story in the film, but the relationship which lies at its heart is that of the two brothers, a relationship exacerbated mutually by guilts and thwarted love, and ending agonizingly in the death of one brother and the other's acceptance of his responsibility for this. In its unfolding, the film moves with great charm and vivacity, but also with an underlying tragic momentum toward its painful conclusion, and the painfulness remains largely unmitigated. There is no final, solipsistic kiss; "I decided to help" are Joe's last words as the film concludes on his decision to confess after he has found his dead brother's discarded body. It is a moment entirely free from the pieties which customarily attend Hollywood-style reformations, nor has it any of that sense of straining to engage some good, gray abstraction like Society, which hangs so heavily over the last sequence of *On the Waterfront. Force of Evil* ends in moral awakening, but it reaches not so much outward toward society as inward toward communion: toward a shared responsibility; toward a sense of the oneness of human involvement without any diminution of that involvement's complex difficulty and ineluctable pain.

Were this all, one might still have simply a film of the delicacy, compassion, and, I believe, somewhat vitiating softness of, say, *They Live by Night*. Even *Sight and Sound* tended to relegate *Force of Evil* to the status of a sensitive but "minor" work; I think this is other than the case. The film was said to be too essentially literary, and there can be no doubt that it is a work which relies indispensably on its language; we have still to free ourselves entirely from the constrictive dogma that language is not properly an element of film. Simply to observe that the language of *Force of Evil* is beautiful is probably not to the point. The impression of that language is of really hearing for the first time in films the extraordinary sound of New York City speech, with its distinctive repetitions and elisions, cadences and inflections, inarticulateness and cryptopoetry; much as Odets had brought it to the stage. As in Odets, the effect is naturalistic, and, as in Odets, it is achieved by an extreme degree of stylization. But the radical accomplishment of *Force of Evil*, perhaps more obvious now in the light of such conspicuous rhetorical experimentation as that of *Hiroshima, Mon Amour*, is in the way the word works with the image. Nothing is redundant, or unnecessary. Joe Morse finds his brother's battered body where he has been told he will, flung upon some rocks, and says in narration what has already become known both through dialogue and image: "He was dead"; yet the effect of this is never superfluous. The narration is the image refracted through an individual consciousness, and thus, however subtly, reimagined. Throughout the film, the protagonist is constantly commenting upon the action, telling us not only what he and the others are thinking but describing events even as we see them; creating, through the free flow of language, a context of perception and volition which constantly urges on us the sense of his moral responsibility. But, beyond this, the aesthetic effect of all the film's oblique repetition, with its language overlapping image and language overlapping language, is to impart an almost musical resonance to the agon of the brothers which is at its core.

The more one sees *Force of Evil*, the more one becomes aware of the intricate synthesis of formal means by which it is unfolded. The language becomes a kind of insistent presence, and the images move both congruently and dissonantly with an extraordinary autonomy and freedom. A brief conversation is composed from a remote angle above a gracefully curving stairway; the moment exists both in and independent of the action; and, independently, in its abstraction of light and space, it is startlingly beautiful. Such astonishment is to be found in profusion throughout the film, from so relatively simple an instance to others as complexly moving as the image of Joe Morse running senselessly down a deserted Wall Street at night, knowing that he will never again be returning to his "fine office up in the clouds." The film's critics are right. *Force of Evil is* a literary film, but only insofar as the film *is* a literary medium, and perhaps no other work until Godard's has pressed forward with such exploratory imagination to test the boundaries of the literary capacity of films. But beyond its exploratory thrust, the achievement of *Force of Evil* remains in what it is in itself: an original, moving, and even beautiful work. Its beauty directly engages the paradox of art: that it can both be deeply painful and provide pleasure; the pleasure, ultimately, of having one's vision extended. Perhaps nowhere in *Force of Evil* does this fusion of the harrowing and beautiful command more power than in the film's concluding passage. In the breaking light of early morning, Joe Morse descends a seeming infinity of stairs to discover his brother's body where it has been discarded "like an old rag" upon the rocks at the base of a bridge. It is a descent to "the bottom of the world," to a kind of hell; the symbolic death that must be suffered before regeneration. "Because if a man can live so long, and have his whole life come out like rubbish, then something was horribly wrong . . . and I decided to help."

(1961)

Abraham Polonsky wrote *Body and Soul* in 1947, directed *Force of Evil* in 1948, and was politically blacklisted in America until

1968. A little simple arithmetic will reveal that one of the richest talents and arguably the richest literary talent to have appeared in the American film was, for twenty years, unable to work in the medium. One need not respond emotionally to that fact. One need not respond emotionally to any fact.

In 1962, I contacted Polonsky, and soon after published an "interview" with him done solely through correspondence. I met Polonsky a short while later, and have seen him on those several occasions when we have been in the same place at the same time in the years since; a time during which our relationship progressed, I think it fair to say, from that of critic and film-maker to one between friends. And it was, I think, in the latter relationship that Polonsky telephoned to tell me the news that he was going to direct a film again and to invite me to visit him once shooting had begun, though it was more in reversion to the former that I brought along a tape recorder which ran intermittently throughout much of a long day that I spent with him soon after.

I visited the set of *Willie Boy*[1] several weeks after filming had begun; I had hoped to observe filming at one of the desert locations, but was frustrated in this by some last-minute changes in the shooting schedule. I arrived at the studio some twenty minutes after the beginning of the working day at 9 A.M., and reached the set to find it had been cleared of the crew, while, as I learned subsequently, some disagreement was taking place between the director and Conrad Hall, his director of photography. Later, Polonsky spoke of it; he was going through a stage with Hall that was not uncommon, he thought, to the working relationships between directors and their directors of photography: he was trying to get Hall to loosen up. "I need more freedom for the actors because they're complaining bitterly. He's holding them to too many marks." But Polonsky wasn't complaining. "He's interesting, temperamental, and a gambler with light. The actors are both obedient and creative. What more can you ask?"

It had been some time since I'd been on a working set, and, generally harmonious as this one was, the feel of it—the numbers of people performing small tasks or just hanging about, and the numbers of temperaments requiring solicitous orchestration—

1. The film was subsequently retitled *Tell Them Willie Boy Is Here.*

reminded me how unappealing I had always, by my own temperament, found that side of film-making. Yet Polonsky seemed not
only good at it but genuinely to enjoy it, and I asked if he did.

"I enjoy it, yes. It's almost as good as writing because it is a
form of writing. I like it and I feel it as we do it. It's excellent;
I feel this whole thing, and I feel it all coming together and
coming apart all the time, and that's part of the pleasure and
part of the operation and part of the contest you have with
yourself, if you have any contest at all. That's the wrong word;
it's . . . it's the living sense of the set. The set is a live thing—
a more complex writing experience."

I asked if, in seeing someone else's films, he could see from
what was on film where, if there's some failure, it may be that
kind of failure—a failure in working with people.

"I don't think I could. . . . I mean, I wouldn't know."

Though I had read a copy of the script, the scenes being taken
that day weren't in it, and one thing in particular, the start of a
tracking movement, was giving the camera crew some difficulty. I
asked if it might be possible to achieve the desired effect with a
particular cut, a jump cut, though I'd failed to visualize it as
that.

"Jump cut? . . . Why not, if you intend it. It's all right; there's
nothing wrong with it if you mean it. . . . You feel that at once
in a picture where that isn't the style. If it's not a general style,
then it's a particular emphasis. But, if it's an emphasis, what do
you mean? Well, I don't mean that sort of emphasis here."

Someone suggested what a jump cut there *might* mean.

"That's true. But that would be an explanation after the event,
not an intention now. That's what you can do, rationalize a meaning. When you shoot, that's a prediction; not an explanation . . .
after something happens."

The shot was finally made as Polonsky wanted it, and, while the
next one was being lit, the director secluded himself with his
actors in rehearsal. Afterward, Polonsky spoke of this and ampli-
fied on the issue over which he had confronted his director of
photography.

"The reason for the rehearsal was to find out where they would
go naturally in the scene. I don't want to tell them to go there
and go there and go there—just to help out with the lighting.

Not today, anyway. It turned out they were going to go exactly to the places I had asked them to originally. That happens very often. Excluding documentaries where you take the camera and expose yourself to the scene, whichever way it works . . . in this kind of a film, what you do is construct a *cage* of light around these actors—and they are not really free in this cage because, if they are really free, neither the sound nor the light works in it. One of the ways to eliminate the sound problem is to loop it. But you can't eliminate the light problem. You can't eliminate the cage of light, and this is true outdoors too. Depending where the sun is in the sky, and how your scene is going, you can't see the expression on a face even if you're two feet away. So what you do with the kind of film we're used to seeing—clearly full of expression in every detail—is construct this geometrical thing . . . and live with it.

"If you ask the cameraman to loosen up, and if he just falls back and lights it generally, you're not going to see anything. I'm shuffling around from heads to bodies in the same shot and moving them. There are very grave difficulties for the actor and all the technical crew. . . .

"Now the problem is that professional actors, in this cage, give you *their* performance, which enables them to survive the cage. And if you want anything else, they're fighting with the cage. So there's a dynamic set up between how much you're going to go for and how much the technical crew can give you without hobbling the actor."

Later, at lunch, some comments on a few of the stars whose giant photos decorate the walls of the studio commissary led back to the subject of actors.

"Well, some have a performance that they own. Let's say they have nothing but this one performance. It's often more than enough for a film, where personality is rampant and effective."

Someone remarked that most actors don't even have one performance.

"Not really . . . Most of them have many. But most of them come to *rely* on one performance for other reasons. When it's a successful one, for instance."

Thinking of *Madigan,* I said, "Now Henry Fonda's been doing that bit—"

"That's right!"

"But Henry Fonda can do a lot of other things."

"Oh, yes! . . .

"When I cast these characters for the posse, I was very careful not to pick Western actors simply on the grounds that they wouldn't have a stock set of performances as a posse to give. Otherwise, you have to fight that battle too. I'm not sure what I'll get from them, but I won't have that."

The conversation turned to the direction of actors.

"Very often what you do is substitute energy for expressiveness. You drive the actors and get a lot of energy going on the set, and it feels like life, but it's not necessarily life; it's mechanical life. The way we live."

"Of course," I said, "if you're not as concerned with your actors as you are, you can get expressiveness in other ways, and use the actors more as props."

"But then you can't use my actors; you'd have to cast others."

"Well, you can't use you as a director on that film either," I said.

We discussed the morning's takes, and I mentioned my interest in seeing how some things looked in the rushes.

"Dailies can fool you. They're full of momentary energy. You have no way of knowing till they're cut together in the whole film if anything is going there. . . . Accidental energy cancels out, and things just lie there."

With us through the day was Robert Gilman, one of the most talented and technically proficient young Americans now making short films outside the industry. He asked Polonsky: "How do you work with your editor? His idea of rhythm is going to be different from your idea of rhythm."

"Well, when we first met, I picked the takes I thought were best and gave him a general idea of how I wanted to go, and he went and edited and assembled. And he showed it to me, and the rhythm was different from what I wanted. So I went back with him to the Movieola, and edited it piece by piece, and he saw what I wanted.

"Now, as we go along, I select the takes I prefer and give him a general idea of how I want it to go. Then he edits the film. Where the rhythm is different from what I want, we work together until it has my feeling, where that's possible. Then my rhythm runs."

"He's quite willing to do what you want?"

"Yes. He's good. There are editors who won't do that; you can't work with them. He's only done two films, I think, before this one. The last one was *Finian's Rainbow*; he worked with Coppola, who works the same way I do: he edits his own films."

One difference between them, I remarked, judging from the one film of Coppola's I'd seen, was that Coppola didn't seem to care about his actors.[2]

"No. He's interested in technology," Polonsky said.

The afternoon's shooting moved slowly, a few brief takes surrounded by long intervals for lighting. During one of these, I commented to Polonsky that it seemed a peculiar predicament for an artist to have such periods of tedium inescapably interwoven with periods of working creation.

"That's why experienced directors learn to live their lives between shots—writing letters, calling on the phone, making dates with girl friends, investing in the stock market. . . ."

Later, during one particularly long pause for lighting, we left the set, where, the actors having been rehearsed, the director was as dispensable as I was. In a small trailer, the director's equivalent of a dressing room, we were able to talk without interruption.

"Now to maintain full expression throughout the course of the film, and freedom, is the problem."

"By full expression you mean the expressiveness of the actor?"

"And my own. But the liberation of the actor in the scene, the liberation of the content of the script, and the excellence of the technical apparatus to make it visible . . . and audible; to make this all come together in sound and talk and light and clear expression. What you tend to do is *settle* . . . for technical excellence. What you do is find yourself settling for a passing grade. It tells the story, it's pretty good, there are no big mistakes; thank God, let's go on. Disaster."

"Settle for technical excellence?"

"And performance; competent, excellent performance. That's

2. Obviously, at the time of this conversation, Coppola hadn't yet made *The Rain People*, on the basis of which I gladly retract my earlier comment on his direction of actors, justifiable as it may once have been.

not the same thing as a real performance by anyone, including the camera. By the end of the day, you're willing to settle too. This is where you have to stop. Your greatest problem is not to settle for what's good enough; to try to go a little further. You have pressing on you schedule, cost, all those things which are forcing you to settle."

"I suppose the advanced stage is when you don't know that you're settling."

"Well, then, as in all things, you've succeeded in your profession. You are now successful."

A bit later, while we were still alone, Polonsky said, "I'm kind of amused by all this."

"What do you mean, it amuses you? You love it."

"I love it, but this is, in a way, too late."

"Too late to be struck by the glamour of it, you mean?"

"Well, it's not glamour. . . . Marcel Proust said—or was it Marcel Proust who said someplace that—don't wish too intensely for anything because you'll get it . . . but too late. . . . Or something like that . . . some witty remark of that nature . . .

"I don't know, it isn't really too late, but there's a lot of— something of that in what I feel . . . like I don't really care any more, but I do. Twenty years is too long. . . . In a strange kind of way I'm doing this and I'm saying, well, I'll do it, but I don't really think it's worthwhile bothering with all this stuff any more. Now that may just be—"

"What do you mean by all this stuff? Films?"

"No . . . perhaps just weariness as you work . . . I mean so many people are such a drag. . . . I'm surrounded by hundreds of people. . . . I ought to retire to my mountain and meditate, that's what I mean. . . . "

"Maybe you should be making films in a different setup?"

"Maybe I shouldn't make anything is what I mean. . . . I don't know what I'm saying really. . . . I mean—I don't know what I'm talking about. . . . I'm talking about something . . . I don't know what it is . . . I mean something."

"I've often had that feeling."

". . . There's something wrong with what I'm doing. On the set, everything's fine. I'm having all the freedom anyone gets. . . . The management doesn't even look at the rushes. . . ."

"Is it anything to do with the feeling that you could make a good film or a bad film and it wouldn't make any difference to most of the people you're working with—I mean that they wouldn't *see* the difference?"

"No. No, it has nothing to do with that. They'll see the difference; of course they will. They may not like the same things I like, but, in general, they know the difference. All they want is for it to be a good film. If it turned out not to make money, they wouldn't be horrified because they know that happens very often . . . so there's no problem with that. . . . I'm talking about something else, I think . . . but I don't know what it is. . . . I don't know how it even came out. I didn't intend to say it. . . ."

Before returning to the set, we talked a little about the blacklist, which Frank Rosenberg had broken for Polonsky with a co-author's credit for the screenplay of *Madigan,* a project to which Polonsky had come late, following the departure of the first writer, Howard Rodman (who has pseudonymous co-author's credit for the film as "Henri Simoun"). Earlier, I had referred to *Madigan* (a film I had enjoyed despite or, probably, as much because of its forties-melodrama clichés, as well as for its occasional passages of genuine feeling and the performance of Richard Widmark) as "hack work," meaning only that I assumed it had been a job undertaken while waiting for or as a means to the more meaningful work of direction, and Polonsky had been somewhat defensive, thinking I was simply accusing the work of mediocrity. (He agreed with me, of course, that there was a good deal of mediocre work in the film, but hoped I'd realized that his share of it wasn't done with a free hand.) He had thought there would have to be a succession of *Madigan*-level assignments before he'd have a chance to direct again. But then he was given the chance to do *Willie Boy* as a film for television, and, as the project took shape, the studio was persuaded to produce it as a theatrical feature; Polonsky, all the while, buying directorial independence by relinquishing his own financial prerogatives in the film as a business venture. Yesterday, and for twenty years, he was anathema; today he is, with an unusual degree of freedom, directing a film budgeted at three million dollars, and planning three other projects to follow. In America, there is always a happy ending, and all wishes come true. Sometimes, too late.

"And there are still people blacklisted?" I asked him.

"It's about over now. . . . Till there's a new one. . . . It's part of the way the world goes. . . ."

I asked about a few people in particular; John Berry, and Bob Roberts who had produced *Body and Soul* and *Force of Evil*. "They're making films again?"

"Yes . . . Everybody is . . . unless they're dead. Some died . . . some of them left. . . . Everything comes to an end, including you and me. And that's a relief."

After the day's shooting was finished, we went to see the previous days' rushes. In the audience, Katharine Ross and Robert Blake, who hadn't been involved in the present day's shooting, joined Susan Clark and Robert Redford, who had. I saw on film some of the scenes I had read in the script, but there was little I could tell about the finished work other than to get some sense of its visual style and see how those actors whom I hadn't seen working looked in their roles.

Willie Boy is the story, based on an actual incident, of an Indian hunted for killing the father of the girl with whom he has fled; the action takes place in 1909, at a time when President Taft is on a speech-making tour through Southern California, and the single Indian is so incredibly resourceful in eluding his massing pursuers (at one stage, including eleven posses) that rumors reach the press of an Indian uprising and an attempt to assassinate the President. Robert Blake, whom I hadn't seen in films before, plays Willie Boy, the hunted Indian.

Afterward, Polonsky took me to his office; he had something to show me. There, spread over two walls, were photographs of the actual Willie Boy and others involved in the events: Willie Boy in what seemed to be a studio portrait; individual pictures of the participating sheriffs; the full posse, posed for the press, stiff and erect as a graduating class or early baseball team; and, finally, the full posse again, its members proudly smiling, like fishermen with their big catch, as they stood over the corpse of their solitary quarry; all interspersed with pictures of the Banning and Twentynine Palms desert landscapes where the action had taken place. Somehow, it had never occurred to me that the entire episode would be so fully documented. I turned again to the studio portrait, but could not fathom the pathos in that blankly impassive, young yet ancient face; though I had known there was an actual Willie Boy, it was not until the instant of seeing his photograph that he ceased for me to be fictional. Seeing Robert Blake's to me unfamiliar face on the screen while viewing the rushes, I had been impressed by the unactorish verisimilitude he bore as an Indian, but now I felt humbled in this presumption by the eloquent presence of what James Agee used to venerate as "the real thing."

Polonsky, too, seemed slightly awed before the photographs' mute authority. I think Polonsky knew that I had reserved feelings about the script; one of the first things I had asked him that day was whether his commitment to this film was of a kind with that he had given *Force of Evil*, and he seemed surprised and irritated that I had any doubts that it was. Other than that, the day's conversation had tended away from any discussion of the film as a whole to concentrate instead on the meaning of this or that particular shot, a natural course of direction when all one's activity on the set is centered upon the particular shot that is being made. One comes to take it for granted that an actor's performance in a film is pieced together bit by bit from shots made out of dramatic sequence, the sequence of takes in most films being dictated by economic rather than dramatic necessity; but one is less inclined to consider that the director must then perforce work this way too. I had thought that much of the unevenness in even the best of films, especially those made in America, owed to the participation of too many hands, but now it occurred to me that virtually everything in the conventional processes of commercial movie-making operated as a threat to the work's artistic unity. Unless a film-maker's work was episodic of its nature, as, for instance, Godard's, what a feat it must be to keep before you an imaginative vision of the work as a whole through all the fragmentizing stages of its creation. And, given the further enervation in having to bend great numbers of other people around to your vision while yourself striving to sustain it, the sheer labor of making a film suddenly seemed to me almost heroic.

And now, for the first time that day, and in the presence of those photographs, Polonsky began to talk about his vision of the film; of how he imagined it and of its meaning. I had no illusion that the script I had read was any adequate imaginative equivalent to the film that might be made of it, but Polonsky spoke now of possibilities in the material which I simply hadn't seen in the reading; and possibilities not simply for visualization but of realizing the meaning of the action and relationships. It would be untrue to say that what he said utterly dispelled my reservations about the script; whether the film would fulfill those possibilities he saw in it, I couldn't know; but, for the first time, I was brought to see that those possibilities were there. And I recalled what Robert Redford had said to me earlier that day when I had asked him if Polonsky was an easy director to work for. "Yes," he said. "He has passion."

It was almost nine, and dark outside. I didn't run the tape while we spoke thus, or for the short time remaining that we spent together. Exactly what Polonsky said then would mean little without one's having read the script, and, in a sense, it wasn't important; either it will be in the film or it won't. Either it will have its life as art or join the ghosts in that crowded limbo of unrealized intentions. It will be important or it won't. ". . . Like I don't really care any more, but I do."

(1968)

TRIALS

To love things as they are is to make a mockery of them.—GEORGE SANTAYANA

Admittedly, I went to *The Trial* burdened with prejudice. I expected it to be bad, and my expectation seemed to me perfectly reasonable: Welles hasn't given us a film not aggressively bad in over a decade, and, even then, what we were given for years previously was not exactly good. Still, while I expected *The Trial* to be bad, I went to it truly hoping for the best. And, in fact, while I expected it to be bad, bad as a mannerist painting can be bad, bad, for instance, as Welles' *Othello* is bad, I had not been expecting the worst; I had not expected that it might be boring. Orson Welles boring! And boring to stupefaction.

Now let me make it clear at the outset that the least of my reservations about the film, before having seen it, was that *The Trial* by Welles was not likely to be much like *The Trial* by Kafka. Apart from the fact that it might be difficult to imagine two individuals temperamentally and stylistically more dissimilar, I like to think I take a liberal attitude in general toward the free adaptation of literary works for the screen. After all, we don't reject Berg's *Wozzeck* because it is not Buechner's; as soon as we hear the music, we realize we are in the presence of something related to but also enormously different from the play. Similarly, as soon as we *see* a strange man enter Joseph K.'s bedroom "one fine morning" (although, in the film, this isn't the first thing that we see), we are plunged, or should be, into an order of experience quite different from that of a reader of the novel. Furthermore, in the particular case of *The Trial*, Welles has been provided with a rather considerable precedent in the way of free adaptation; I mean *Le Procès*, the version made for the stage by Jean-Louis Barrault in collaboration with André Gide. It is a production I did not see, but, to judge from the account given of it by Eric Bentley in *In Search of Theater*, Welles' film would seem to derive from the prior theatrical adaptation to an even greater extent than from the original novel; indeed, the one photograph of the Barrault production included by Bentley shows the stage, via the designer's distortion of perspective, given the effect of a camera's low angle, exactly the kind of camera setup which Welles made virtually his own in his earliest films. At one point, in the film, we see an aggregation of what appear to be victimized Jews, inmates of a ghetto or concentration camp, standing motionless, in tableau, in front of the tenement to which K. goes for his interrogation; these Jews have their antecedent not in the novel but in the play alone, in which they figured as a kind of chorus. But, whereas their repeated use on the stage played its part in the larger theatrical conception, their single, brief appearance in the film serves only to create an eerie effect, for the instant; they recede into the movie's *mise en scène;* they are picturesque. Much else of what is in the film is not so much a departure from the earlier adaptation as a merely physical extension of it beyond the boundaries of what can be presented on a stage. In Kafka's novel, an office is recognizably an office; what is surreal is what is taking place in it. On Barrault's stage, according to Bentley, the telephone on Joseph K.'s desk was about eighteen inches long. In Welles' film, K.'s office has been given the dimensions of a large aircraft hangar.

In fact, it is not an aircraft hangar but a great unused industrial fairground, complete with fifteen hundred desks, which alternates with the film's primary location, a huge, abandoned railway terminal, scheduled for demolition, the finding of which as a set for *The Trial* Welles is reported to consider his greatest stroke of good fortune in the making of the film. And, indeed, it is this set, with its vast, cavernous expanses of space, redecorated and used for almost all of the interiors, which provides the film with its most impressive feature. Kafka's novel, too, conveys a vivid sense of space, but space, in the novel, is always cramped, confining, oppressive, stifling. In the novel, the interrogation chamber is described as a medium-sized, two-windowed room just below the roof of which is a gallery "where the people were able to stand only in a bent posture with their heads and backs knocking against the ceiling." In the film, the interrogation chamber becomes an arena on the order of Madison Square Garden, packed by the proverbial "cast of thousands." The airless labyrinth which is the law court offices in the novel becomes, in the film, a balconied edifice of files. The painter Titorelli's studio, a room in which "you could scarcely take two strides in any direction," and in which, as at the law court offices, K. nearly faints from the airlessness, becomes an area large enough for Welles to execute some elaborate movements of the camera, and the stairway leading up to Titorelli's place—"extremely narrow, very long, without any turning . . . enclosed on either side by blank walls"—on which K. encounters the "several" monstrous young girls in the novel, now accommodates throngs of them; again, the principle of the cast of thousands. And on, and on. Describing the design of *Le Procès* as theater, Bentley mentions the influence of *The Cabinet of Dr. Caligari;* in Welles' film, what one sees are occasional bits and pieces out of *Caligari* inflated to a scale more nearly reminiscent of *Metropolis*.

But, whereas the design of *Le Procès* strove for an interpretation and theatrical restylization of the novel, the film manages to achieve neither interpretation nor style, unless decor may be called style. The sole impetus of the film appears to be the immensity of the set; it is as though the film were made to display the set; Kafka's *The Trial* just an afterthought, something with which to fill it. Through the space of this set, Welles can practice unrestrictedly what has become his chief contribution to the art of the film in recent years, the conversation held between two people as one walks briskly away from the other. So Fräulein Montag, who limps, heard but unseen, through the halls of K.'s boardinghouse, moving her belongings, in the novel, now drags a steamer

trunk across a vast empty landscape as K. pursues her; and the
advocate's lodgings attain the size of a gymnasium so that the
characters may run laps around it. It all has so little to do with
Kafka's *The Trial,* or any interpretation of it, however free, that
I almost feel it irrelevant on my part to make any comparative
mention of the two. Throughout the film, action and events
taken from the novel have been telescoped and transposed so
meaninglessly that the only purpose of the alterations seems to
be to prove that Welles, as director of the film, has the power to
make them, which, obviously, he has. In Kafka's world, surreal
happenings arise almost imperceptibly out of a setting of everyday
reality, so that it is virtually impossible to tell where what is
ordinary ends and what is mad begins; in Welles' film, one bizarre
event follows another, without connection. Specifically: in the
novel, K. is supposed to conduct a foreign business colleague,
interested in ancient monuments, on a tour of the local cathedral;
when the man fails to arrive at the appointed hour for their meeting inside the almost entirely empty cathedral, K. makes ready
to leave, but a verger directs his attention toward a side aisle, in
which, he becomes aware, preparations are apparently being made
for the preaching of a service. Although there is no congregation
present other than K., a priest begins to mount the pulpit; K. attempts to leave before the beginning of the sermon obliges him
to stay, but, just as he reaches the exit, he is stopped by the voice
of the priest calling after him, calling him by name. As this incident appears in the film, K. simply walks from one part of the
huge expressionistic set to another, and, in just vaguely identifiable surroundings, a vaguely identifiable man addresses him from
a vaguely identifiable balcony. It isn't Kafka. It isn't style. Nor is
it an interpretation.

But, to be sure, minutes before the end, we are given what is,
I believe, intended to be recognized as interpretation. It comes in
the form of some dialogue, or, more precisely, chatter, about the
responsibility of the individual and society which passes between
K. and his advocate, who, in departure from the novel, makes a
reappearance in the cathedral following the business with the
priest. This food for thought having been served, the advocate
relates to K. an abridged version of Kafka's great parable of the
Law by means of a series of slides, "visual aids," as the advocate

calls them. I realize, as I put this down, that these inventions of the film may actually sound audacious, in the way that Welles could once be genuinely and excitingly audacious, but, in the seeing, it all has the stale air of yesterday's audacity.

And then—in one final stab at something like interpretation—there is the Bomb, its blast, in the film's final, prolonged image, hovering significantly over all that has gone before. What has happened immediately before, as I understand it, and I think I do, is that K. dies in an explosion of dynamite, but manages also to kill his executioners; at the end, he laughs, maniacally but also, perhaps, somewhat triumphantly, if anything about the film may be described as triumphant; at any rate, the laughter does stop. Gone is the novel's knife plunged into K.'s heart, and twisted; gone K.'s dying realization: "Like a dog!" Instead, the familiar mushroom cloud, with all its attendant, unearned Significance. It is Significance on the order of the "crucifixion" of Ahab—Ahab, the Antichrist!—in John Huston's film of *Moby Dick*. It is Significance in the abstract; Significance emptied of all significance.

But by now you've got the point. Yes, it's not Kafka. Yes, yes, it's bad. But how to account for the merciless boredom—my trial?

For the moment, let me postpone that question.

More and more, the career of Orson Welles has come to take on distressing parallels to that of his creation, Charles Foster Kane, and as Welles said of Kane, in the previews of his first film, "Ladies and gentlemen, I don't know what you'll think about Mr. Kane. I can't imagine. You see, I play the part myself. Well, Kane is a hero and a scoundrel, a no-account and a swell guy . . . a great lover, a great American citizen, and a dirty guy. That depends upon who's talking about him." One hardly knows whether to laugh or cry.

And thus, depending upon who's talking about him, Welles' later failures are either treated with a doting indulgence or his earlier achievements belittled, both being instances of that form of rewriting history by which the inconveniences of fact are triumphed over by the consistency of criticism; at least one would probably have to be a film critic to be able to believe some good was served by either eulogizing the later failures or gloating over them. Well, they *are* failures, but they *were* achievements. It is possible, perhaps, to dismiss *Citizen Kane* as little more than a bag of tricks, good tricks but tricks nonetheless; yet, although much of that film's excitement derives from the sheer exuberance and audacity—real audacity—of its exploration of the medium's techniques, I think this is considerably to underestimate the work. But one may concede the case of *Citizen Kane*, and still there is *The Magnificent Ambersons*, a less perfect work, perhaps; also, I think, a finer one. Beginning with its apparently random and casual collection of nostalgic images of bygone styles in clothes and motorcars, like so many snapshots from a family album, the film quietly deepens and extends itself into an almost achingly sorrowful picture of a vanished style of life, and of irrecoverable loss; and, in so doing, manages to achieve what *Citizen Kane*, in all its brilliant eclecticism, never does: a unified style of its own. And it is style as practiced by a film-maker capable of raising style to the level at which it becomes indistinguishable from genius.

But it is style—as, in Welles' work, it was never again to be—pressed wholly into the service of meaning. Nothing is gratuitous; from the sleigh ride through an impossibly soft and radiant snowscape—the snow as surreal as that which floats through Kane's crystal globe, the sleigh itself thereafter to give way to fuming, sputtering automobiles—to the "last of the great, long-remembered dances" at the Amberson mansion, all of the film's imagery is darkened and complicated by a sense, an almost tragic sense, of the impermanence of all that appears solid and substantial, and of the evanescence of all that is beautiful. *The Magnificent Ambersons* is, like *Citizen Kane*, about a man's fall, but also about the fall of a house, and of a society. The film's narrative remains faithful to that of the novel by Booth Tarkington from which it was adapted, but what Welles brings to that narrative, not in the novel, above all, is mystery. It is a quality which arises, in part, from the difference between the grayish naturalism of the novel's language and the rich chiaroscuro of the imagery of the film. But the film's imagery itself seems, finally, to arise from the apprehension of some deeper kind of mystery: that mystery inherent in the way men come to be as they are, and in the way all power declines and dies.

And, when all the tricks are emptied from *Citizen Kane*'s bag of tricks, it is that sense of mystery which still remains. Although an audience conditioned to psychological explanation may suddenly grow acutely attentive when one character says that Kane wanted to be loved, and nod in perfect understanding at the closing confrontation with "Rosebud," the psychological explanation is, finally, just one of several explanations offered by the characters in the film, and this in a film everywhere filled with the implication that any single explanation, indeed, any explanation, must remain inadequate to the mystery which a person may contain. As the reporter and his staff prepare to leave the Kane mansion, a photographer asks him if he ever did find out what Rosebud means. "No," he replies, "I never did. Maybe Rosebud was something he couldn't get, or something he lost, but I don't think it would have explained anything, anyway. I don't think any word can explain a man's life. I guess Rosebud is just a piece in a jigsaw puzzle. A missing piece."[1] It is the film's final irony: we *do* discover what Rosebud is, and still do not know what it means. A burning sled . . . a sled, outside the Kanes' old cabin, gradually becoming buried in the ceaselessly falling snow . . . a line: "I was on the way to the warehouse in search of my youth"; what is it all but an evocation of the past, of irretrievable loss, retaining all its mystery, explaining nothing? And so the film ends: the sled in flames; the fire obliterating the painted word; the great castle, its lights extinguished, its chimneys billowing forth the smoke of Kane's possessions as they burn; antique statuary, mysterious wharves, silent pools; and the camera moving down a wire fence, gliding past a posted warning, ending the film with the words with which it began, now deepened in meaning, now implicating us: "No Trespassing."

If I appear to dwell on Welles' two earliest films, it is because, for all the attention that has been paid to them as works of

---

1. Although the usual objection to *Citizen Kane* is that the character of Kane is, finally, too simple-minded in its conception, I would argue, rather, that Kane does not even exist as a character in the sense in which we conventionally construe the meaning of this. Kane is a force which we know only through its impact on various bodies; our sole "objective" glimpse of him is at the moment of his death, at which the force that he contains escapes him. Or he is an image, a fragmented image, which, unlike that of a jigsaw puzzle, cannot be put back together; for what we see of Kane, in the various evocations of him, is contradictory, and incomplete; we can never possess all the pieces, and those we have can never exactly be made to fit.

technical brilliance, they yet remain insufficiently appreciated as works of art; that, and the fact that, among Welles' subsequent films, there is little else to dwell upon. *Citizen Kane* is not a profound work, but, aside from that, it is almost everything else one might wish a first work to be: unmistakably individual, exploratory, exuberant, charged with an excitement undiminished after twenty years; and *The Magnificent Ambersons* is, I think, one of the most mysteriously beautiful films ever made. Probably, the course of Welles' work since cannot be wholly understood without taking into account the conditions under which he has had to struggle for that work's existence. Given carte blanche to make *Citizen Kane,* he had virtually to enjoin R.K.O. to release it. *Citizen Kane* was preceded by two projects, one of them an experimental treatment for the filming of Conrad's *Heart of Darkness,* both of which the studio chose finally to reject; *The Magnificent Ambersons* followed only after two more aborted projects. By the time *Journey into Fear,* Welles' third Mercury production, was to be filmed, Welles was replaced as director by the studio with some safe nonentity. Several hundred thousand feet—footage of sufficient length to complete a feature—of a fourth film were shot in South America before Welles was recalled, and his relations with R.K.O. terminated. Footage for the unfinished film was entombed in the studio's vaults, where it resides to this day (if, with the demise of R.K.O., these vaults themselves still exist), and both *The Magnificent Ambersons* and *Journey into Fear* were released in mutilated versions; the former shorn of some forty-five minutes, and concluding with a sequence Welles neither wrote nor directed. In fact, what one sees in *The Magnificent Ambersons* now is only a version of Welles' conception of the film, one onto which has been tacked the proverbial Hollywood happy ending. In the twenty-two years which elapsed between his making *Citizen Kane* and *The Trial,* Welles has directed only eight other finished films (including *Journey into Fear*), his own film-making usually financed by his acceptance of acting roles in the hack work of others, and, of those made since *Citizen Kane,* it was not until *The Trial* that another of his films was released in exactly the form in which he wished it. But life is not so prodigal as Hollywood with happy endings.

Yet *Journey into Fear,* despite the fact that the credit for its direction is not given to Welles, is everywhere stamped with the mark of his individuality, as are the two other melodramas which sporadically succeeded it, *The Stranger* and *The Lady from Shanghai*. All are witty, exciting, above all, enormously entertaining; and, if their brilliance seems to reside largely on their surface, well, where else should brilliance be? They are melodramas; only their enthusiasts have pretended they are more; although, at least in the case of the last, one alarming, three-dimensional character is quite indelibly created: Glenn Anders as the monstrous Mr. Grisby. Then, in 1948, Welles made his first film of Shakespeare, *Macbeth*, with himself in the leading role. It is a film easily dismissed as a production of the play, with its drastic textual rearrangement and, but for Welles and Dan O'Herlihy, generally impoverished acting; it is also by far the most interesting film made of Shakespeare to pursue the idea that an adaptation of a play into film requires as radical and complete a transformation of the original materials as does the adaptation of a play into opera. Welles made his *Macbeth* on a slender budget in little more than three weeks—he has called it, "for better or worse . . . a kind of violently sketched charcoal drawing of a great play"— and, if he allowed most of the performances to go flagrantly awry, it was not because of any inability on his part to direct actors; it would be difficult to match the ensemble playing of Welles' Mercury Theater company in his first two films with that in many others. Welles' preoccupation in *Macbeth* is clearly with inventing a line of visual imagery raised to the level of the language, even if, in the accomplishment, what more often resulted was a reduction of the language to the level of the visual imagery; one would really have to be, at the least, a Verdi wholly to succeed in what Welles was attempting, and Welles is not this. Still, while the achievement of Welles' film is decidedly not that of Shakespeare's *Macbeth*, the film does manage to achieve a striking, genuinely barbaric splendor of its own. And, despite the film's many failures, if one considers the respectfully dull ways that *Macbeth* has been done badly on our stages, one might be less inclined to undervalue that achievement.

What happened to Welles' great gifts as a film-maker during the four years that elapsed between *Macbeth* and the completion of his *Othello*, I cannot pretend to be able to say. It is not that it is difficult to speculate upon the causes of so spectacular a decline; it is all too easy. But the facts are these: *Macbeth* was made in approximately three weeks, at the end of a period during which Welles may be said to have worked with some regularity as a film-maker; *Othello* was made over a period of four years, one of only three films Welles directed between *Macbeth* in 1948 and *The Trial* in 1962. What happened, I cannot pretend to say, but I can guess, and I would guess that Welles has always been the kind of artist whose genius lies in his intuition, who is, time and again, betrayed by his premeditation; and four years is a long time to premeditate. But more important, I think, is that, unlike a Bresson, Welles is a film-maker whose talent is necessarily impaired by disuse, being bound, as it is, less to some commanding imaginative vision than to an ardent exploration of his medium, and needing the constant renewal of a continuing contact with that medium to keep it from stagnation; for the apparent consequence of Welles' inability to work in his medium has been a virtual obsession with the medium per se. In any case, the special badness of Welles' *Othello*,[2] with all its fussy inflation of eye-catching details, is of a kind to make the free-wheeling carelessness of his *Macbeth* seem positively invigorating by comparison. It is the details, in fact, which take over this *Othello*, crowding out character, crowding out action, almost, but not quite, crowding out everything that is the play. All is sacrificed to the *mise en scène*, but it is a *mise en scène* now become an orgy of tilted camera angles, intricate composition, and florid chiaroscuro. Concern is now exclusively for effects, and not effects directed toward the end of any total meaning but rather isolated effects, singular flashes of brilliance (and some, admittedly, brilliant), indulged in only for themselves. Each scene is invested with an impact out of all proportion to its meaning or its relevance to context; each scene played and shot as though it were climactic. Gone is the marvelous rhythmic continuity of *Citizen Kane*; given way to a monotonous fluidity (almost every transition is a quick dissolve) as discrete, supercharged images flow one into the other. There is a word for Welles' film of *Othello*. It suffers

2. For a thoroughgoing autopsy of Welles' *Othello*, and one that is eminently fair, I refer the reader to Eric Bentley, "Orson Welles and Two Othellos," in *What Is Theatre?*, New York. Atheneum, 1968.

not from lack of talent; rather, from a conspicuous waste of it. All has grown overripe; the individual cells have developed at the expense of the organism as a whole. The word is decadent.

And it is that word which best characterizes all of Welles' films since. There is little to choose from between *Mr. Arkadin* (known also by the title, *Confidential Report*) and *Touch of Evil;* of the two, I tend to prefer the former, which seems to me more willing to accept itself at its own level of preposterousness, rather than go rummaging about among half-baked profundities. But, whatever one's preference, such distinctions as may be drawn between the two are fine, and *Touch of Evil* is, I think, profoundly bad, its badness only somewhat obscured by such things as the long-take crane shot on which it opens, a virtuoso exercise which exhibits more skill in three minutes than is to be found in the life's work of most other directors. The film is melodrama again, as was *Mr. Arkadin,* but, whereas Welles was once able to use his camera ingeniously to enhance such material, here the camera, with few exceptions, just gets in the way, intruding on the action, complicating it unnecessarily, further cluttering a film already, in its narrative, prodigally cluttered, and generally providing graphic evidence of what kind of artistic disaster may occur when a medium whose propensity is to reveal is taken in the hands of a director whose proclivity is to obscure. *Touch of Evil* probably contains more irrelevant movement per frame than anything else yet committed to film, movement finally signifying nothing so much as Welles' radical failure as a director; yet what remains glaringly apparent, despite all the camera's agitation, is Welles' corresponding failure as an actor. In *Touch of Evil,* he manages wholly to accomplish what one saw only intermittently realized in his playing of Othello: the reduction of himself to the status of a prop, a fabrication of the makeup room, a triumph of paste and putty. Even his fatness fails to exist as a human quality; it is simply another grotesque; fatness in the abstract. Among more zealous lovers of cinema, *Touch of Evil* has attained something of the status of Welles' masterpiece; and for those, not necessarily cinema enthusiasts, who just relish the spectacle of a prodigious talent recklessly exploring all possible ways to squander and parody itself, *Touch of Evil* is, indeed, highly recommended. I found it deeply depressing.

Still, bad as *Othello* and *Mr. Arkadin* and *Touch of Evil* are, they manage to remain enjoyable on some level, however disturbing in their implications; *Othello* as an exercise in the rococo; *Mr. Arkadin* as nonsense; *Touch of Evil* as camp, with Marlene Dietrich and Zsa Zsa Gabor running through their bits as special "guest stars," unbilled appearances by Joseph Cotten in spectacles and white mustache and Mercedes McCambridge in black leather jacket, and a prominently displayed player piano presumably left over from *Beat the Devil*. Bad as they are, they aren't boring. Which brings me back to *The Trial*, and my postponed question. For, if the essential difference between Welles' *Macbeth* and his *Othello* is that of using the medium to serve the play and using the play to serve the medium, what we have in *The Trial* is a case of there being no play, only medium. Even *Touch of Evil*, largely, I would guess, thanks to what is left of the thriller from which it was derived, has its characters and plot, threadbare and tattered as they may respectively be. To some extent, simply because *Othello* is a play, because it exists in its language and its action (not to mention, that is, its greatness), there is enough inherent strength in what remains from the play, in Welles' *Othello*, to survive even so bad a production of it as his—and it would be difficult to imagine one worse. But take away Kafka's style, and his tone, and what have you? Take away the logic and order of Joseph K.'s nightmare, and what is there left? What Welles gives us is a succession of disjointed grotesqueries, each exploited for its own grotesqueness to the end of being picturesque. Again, what is paramount is the *mise en scène*, but it is *mise en scène* finally freed from the dictates imposed by some narrative or dramatic necessity. For a subject makes certain demands of an artist; in an absolute sense, it limits his freedom of choices; but Welles, in surrendering subject, has attained a kind of absolute freedom. The *mise en scène* no longer has a reason, no longer is governed by some controlling center. As if by centrifugal force, things fly apart; everything moves out toward the marvelous periphery. The vacuum created, Shakespeare can fill, Kafka cannot. All the activity on the surface of Welles' latest film will not disguise the lack of substance, the gaping void, at its center. And, elaborate as is the superstructure, it cannot but collapse.

So *The Trial*, boredom and all, is, finally, not without meaning, though not so much one it contains as one which contains it. In an idiom which appears to be narrative or dramatic, Welles has actually given us an instance of pure *mise en scène, mise en scène* freed of all necessity, concerned solely with independent visual effects. Perhaps a director of greater genius than Welles could do this and make it continuously interesting; but I doubt it. For I think that, with something like the regularity of a law, any attempt to make pure cinema, or, for that matter, pure poetry, out of the materials of narrative or drama, materials whose natural end is in the discovery of meaning, results in something neither meaningful nor good cinema nor good poetry. Were *The Trial* visually beautiful to see, there would be no boredom, but the fact is that, for all the attention lavished on the refinement of the film's surface, that surface is one of an almost unrelieved ugliness; to John Grierson's famous dictum—when a director dies, he becomes a photographer—one feels compelled, on such evidence as *The Trial*, to add the corollary that, when the photographer is a dead director, he will be a bad photographer. How to begin to do justice to what is projected on the screen: that incoherent litter of bric-a-brac which passes for its composition; the crude contrastiness of its lighting; those graceless movements of actors and camera; that spastic cutting; those static setups, and takes which seem to last forever? For anyone familiar with Orson Welles' talents at their peak, even more shocking than how bad *The Trial* is, is how bad it looks: it looks like the dregs of Cinema 16. And, like every message from the avant-garde, species Cinema 16, from three minutes in length on up, it closes with the Bomb, that all-purpose, photogenic emblem of deep meaning and universal significance. Only never before has that well-known mushroom cloud been so unphotogenic; never so meaningless.

(1963)

THE DIRECTOR VANISHES

> Whenever the characters of a story suffer, they do so at the behest of their author—the author is responsible for their suffering and must justify his cruelty by the seriousness of his moral intention.—LIONEL TRILLING, *A Gathering of Fugitives*

Sometime in 1959, I experienced a particularly disturbing instance of the not unusual occurrence of seeing a film generally regarded as a triumph and finding in it something of a disaster. Actually, I wasn't entirely alone in sensing that something was wrong, however light others chose to make of it. Reviewing *North by Northwest* (favorably) in *The New Yorker,* Whitney Balliett diagnosed it as a case of self-parody of a kind he suggested to be prevalent in the recent work of a number of contemporary artists: Hemingway, Picasso, Louis Armstrong, and Orson Welles among them. Arguably, Hitchcock did laughably exceed himself in strafing his harassed hero over a Midwestern cornfield from a low-flying airplane and executing a climactic chase atop the monuments of Mount Rushmore; yet this kind of excess seems to me in many ways the best thing in the film. Such extravagant contrivances legitimately provoke laughter; they are nothing if not the manifestation of wit, which, as much in intelligent melodrama as in comedy, depends on the artist's imaginative capacity to take

175

his audience by surprise; in this, a gasp and laughter may register much the same sort of delighted astonishment. Alfred Hitchcock may not be an Oscar Wilde, but the difference has often been rather more of degree than of kind, and Hitchcock may be a Shakespeare when it is the Shakespeare of *Titus Andronicus.* Melodramatic invention may misfire, but not in the direction of prodigality. To send the heroine scampering across the face of Mount Rushmore in high heels is quintessentially of the Hitchcock art, and, for the rare excitement of this kind of palpable nightmare, our disbelief is willingly suspended.

But such excitement is rare indeed in *North by Northwest*; for every five minutes of it were fifty-five of being nudged in the ribs with facetious "self-parody." Yet for self-parody you need a self to parody and in those fifty-five minutes there was none to be found; only the blank spaces left by the film's vanishing director. In fact, Hitchcock had been a long time in vanishing; almost as long as he'd been in America. Vanished the shopkeepers' world of his British films, and, in its place, the drawing room: blank spaces. The world of *The Thirty-Nine Steps* is a sharply observed, substantial reality, from the pitiless confinement of a farmwife's rough cottage to the music hall; that of *To Catch a Thief* and *North by Northwest,* a flimsy paste-up of the fashion magazines. It is not on the cliffs or in the cornfields that *North by Northwest* goes awry; rather at the point at which some sort of solidity should anchor the weightless improbability of the melodramatic invention. Instead of this, we have Cary Grant at his most relentlessly blasé and the director's vanishing act of ersatz Noel Coward. What these later films lack is equilibrium, a center of gravity, and, in its absence, even the most ingenious inventions merely levitate aimlessly.

If these later films surrender a tangible world for pallid repartee, this loss of a material reality equally vitiates the period's one direct attempt at comedy. Earlier in his American period, Hitchcock had directed (as a favor to Carole Lombard) another straight comedy in *Mr. and Mrs. Smith,* and, if his contribution to it was chiefly that of his professional skill in handling actors (insufficiently appreciated) and keeping things moving (justly renowned), the film was at least deftly paced and beautifully played, as well as funny. In contrast, *The Trouble with Harry* is easily the nadir of Hitchcock's career, an arch whimsey that, alone among his films, seems to have been directed by his persona as a television host, and equally confirms the fact that his humor is virtually nonexistent as divorced from his wit, which is to say his invention, which is to say his imagination. The comedy in Hitchcock derives properly from the tension between a palpable world and improbable events. In *The Trouble with Harry,* one slack joke is stretched into invisibility.

But Hitchcock's American years embrace another loss: the loss of contact with his audience; and I think it is revealing of the peculiar nature of his art that it seems in many ways a larger one. What is truly ruinous to the bulk of *North by Northwest,* as to much of what preceded it, is its eagerness to please, and to please everybody. I don't mean to imply in this any cynical calculation of audience response; if anything, the film seems desperately unsure of its audience and how to relate to it; nor do I even mean audience-consciousness. In any case, Hitchcock's audience has always been a central concern of even his best work; even, in some sense, the work's theme. But never, at his best, was this preoccupation with his audience based on any flattery or accommodation; rather, on something very much like antagonism; his object to frustrate expectations, harass, and unnerve. Over the years, Hitchcock has punched, kicked, thrown knives and fired guns at his audience; he has, in effect, loosed a virtual war of aggression through the inventions of his films, subjecting his audience as his protagonists to the terrors of paralysis, agoraphobia, confinement, vertiginous heights, impotence, and, above all, the unknown.

To do this, and make an audience pay for it, requires, at the least, a certain equanimity and poise, the kind of poise one finds splendidly evident in Hitchcock's earliest American films, *Rebecca* and *Foreign Correspondent,* which remain largely British in character, and still essentially intact as late as *Shadow of a Doubt,* his first distinctively American one. Yet increasingly the confidence crumbles, and the films veer schizophrenically toward empty entertainments on the one hand, and something like art on the other (with the self-conscious experiments of *Lifeboat* and *Rope* two casualties of this latter front); for Hollywood is a place where one learns perforce to have a highly specialized pre-occupation with an audience, and you're only as good as the box-office receipts of your last picture. I wouldn't want to distort particulars to convenience generalities; there are brilliantly successful things in a number of Hitchcock's films from the mid-forties through the fifties, and two of them, *Notorious* and *Strangers on a Train*, achieve a fair proximity to his best work; but, increasingly, the period is one of trying to recover lost composure. And, increasingly, the attempts grow more self-effacing: *I Confess* and *The Wrong Man*, aborted attempts to resuscitate the familiar materials in a more serious form;[1] *Dial M for Murder* and *The Man Who Knew Too Much*, the cautious reproduction of a proven theatrical hit and remaking of an earlier success of Hitchcock's own; *The Trouble with Harry*, vacuous reflection of the television personality public image; *To Catch a Thief* and *North by Northwest*, lobotomized commodity entertainments.

There *is* something much like self-parody in *North by Northwest*, but it is not in the audacity of the invention, which is fine; rather, in the relentless tendency to mock that invention. Already this tendency is adumbrated in a film such as *Rear Window*, in which the brilliant central contrivance is continually cheapened and coarsened by the excrescence of easy clichés with which it is padded. The contempt for his audience which such things evidence is relatively new to Hitchcock; by contrast, his earlier antagonism was a mark of respect. The penultimate

1. Both films attempt to engender a kind of moral suspense, and both dissolve this in final alibis, a melodramatic alibi for the religious issue in the former, a religious alibi for the melodrama of the latter. In *I Confess*, a priest is accused of a murder, the responsibility for which has been confessed to him by the true murderer in the inviolable secrecy of the confessional; this seemingly insoluble dilemma "solved" by having the murderer gratuitously reveal himself in a closing burst of conventionally melodramatic action. In *The Wrong Man*, another person falsely accused of a crime finds himself in an apparently hopeless situation, and kneels to pray; at that moment, the real criminal is "miraculously" apprehended in as extraordinarily cynical a contrivance as Hitchcock has ever manufactured, since, despite his admirers' occasional claims for his films' Catholicism, there is clearly not a trace of actual religious feeling in them. Much has been made of the fact that the culprit in Hitchcock's films is usually given some opportunity to confess his crime, and it would probably make no difference to people who want to make much of such things to point out that surely the confession is as much a ritual of the thriller as of the church.

moment of *North by Northwest* finds hero and heroine dangling precariously from the peaks of Mount Rushmore, where they engage in some dialogue to the effect of:

SHE: Incidentally, why did you say your first wife divorced you?
HE: She thought I led too dull a life.

This is something very like self-parody, but it is much closer to self-loathing; Hitchcock's contempt for his audience being only another aspect of that self-contempt, so inextricably are this artist and his audience allied.

Thus far generalities, less one outstanding particular: *Vertigo,* the least apparently characteristic, most extraordinary creation of the American Hitchcock through the fifties. It is, visually, an extravagantly beautiful work, perhaps the most sustained essay in a sensuously romantic iconography in the American film since Ophuls' *Letter from an Unknown Woman* a decade before; but it is also something else, and something far more difficult to comprehend. For the film's beauty unfolds to disclose a narrative of unremitting cruelty, as its protagonist and we who are identified with him are subjected to an ordeal of callous manipulation, expectations established only to be frustrated, hopes offered only to be shattered, and a final, pervasive impotence as the film concludes with a reversal of its apparent direction so stunningly sudden and shockingly antithetical as, to be virtually unassimilable for protagonist and audience alike. The experience of all this is enervating to exhaustion, a profoundly harrowing one; and yet the film actually *means* nothing, is *about* nothing beyond the exposition of its narrative. Or, rather it is *about* suffering, the experience of suffering which the narrative engenders is its meaning. But we suffer, in effect, for the sake of entertainment; certainly not to the end of any greater understanding; at best, to the end of beauty. This we are given, in an unfolding succession of dreamily transfixing, breathtakingly sensuous imagery: in the streets—the mesmeric movement of gliding cars on San Francisco's hills and labyrinthine byways; in the graveyard of the Mission Dolores—a mist of luminous, filmy white light all but forming an enveloping halation; in an old bookshop, where we are drawn more closely into the narrative's net—an almost imperceptibly deepening, tragic darkness, descending like a mourning veil; in Muir Woods—a splash of filigreed light spilling through the highest leaves to the floor of the forest below. It is, perhaps, to the end of this kind of pleasure that we consent to endure the pain.

Yet it is not enough, nor will it disguise the fact that much of the latter part of the film, in which the preternatural events that have gone before are fitted with their naturalistic explanations, is shockingly miscalculated in its dissipation of the film's previous hypnotic power. Dealing with similar materials by the same authors in *Les Diaboliques,* Clouzot, at least, did not delude us; sordid machinations were accorded sordid treatment; but *Vertigo* attempts to engage us on a level more profound, and, at its best, through its beauty and narrative engrossment, it succeeds; we are affected. But we are deceived. In the name of beauty and feeling, we are tricked into responding deeply to mere contrivance; we have, indeed, suffered for nothing. Yet the experience, the fact of this suffering remains, nightmarishly persistent. If *North by Northwest* remains the apotheosis of Hitchcock in his role of clown and pander, *Vertigo* represents the culmination of two decades' inclination toward something like a serious art. Yet the attempt finally aborts, neither fully realized art nor successful entertainment. Instead, it remains, both anomalously and characteristically, the most deeply schizoid creation of the American Hitchcock.

Thus Hitchcock in 1959, at the end of a succession of eight failures and one deeply flawed but enthralling anomaly. Who could have known it was not in those failures, but in the best of *Vertigo,* most emphatically in its final moments, that the real Hitchcock was to be found; who could have predicted *Psycho?* For I was mistaken, in 1959, in thinking I was attending a wake; the coffin was empty; the vanished director elsewhere. That missing person lives in every frame of *Psycho;* and *Psycho* is, without a doubt, one of the most profoundly frightening films ever to reach the screen.[2] All that one has now come to know as

2. And, in its dark way, one of the funniest, although, seeing it for the first time, one is so busy being frightened as perhaps not to notice this. Who, anyway, could get, the first time around, a joke like Anthony Perkins' apology to Janet Leigh upon returning to the motel from his house, from which a noisy quarrel has just been overheard: "My mother isn't quite herself today"?

being of the essential Hitchcock is delivered by the film, and
with force. Perhaps, most prominently this is the movie's audience, those persons who queued up to *see it from the beginning!*
and were enjoined *not to reveal the end!* The story has it that,
prior to its release, *Psycho* was expected to be a box-office failure,
and the unusual publicity campaign was an attempt to drum
up interest in a movie thought to be badly in need of it; that
the film, one of Hitchcock's most personal and least compromised
creations, was, in fact, an extraordinary popular success may
offer some partial explanation of the regained freedom of his
subsequent work. But, whatever the origin of *Psycho*'s publicity,
the fact remains that in its aggressive intimidation of the spectator, even before he is in the theater, it is wholly in keeping
with what distinguishes the personality of the film's director.
The injunctions of the advertisements had the effect also of a
warning; and the atmosphere surrounding *Psycho* was deeply
charged with apprehension: something awful is always just
about to happen. One could sense that the audience was constantly aware of this; indeed, it had the solidarity of a convention assembled on the common understanding of some unspoken
entente terrible; it was, in the fullest sense, an audience; not
merely the random gathering of discrete individuals attendant at
most plays and movies. And this fact of an audience was one of
Psycho's most important accomplishments; for, in a certain
sense, Hitchcock has always been more the director of audiences
than of films; his films being only the means through which
that other end might be achieved.

Having created his audience, there is, once again, the director's frontal assault on its nerves and sensibilities: a particularly
gruesome murder which manages somehow to be both joltingly
graphic and exasperatingly indirect; some excruciatingly meticulous details of the fastidious mopping up of blood; a climactic
nightmare of American Gothic, replete with late-afternoon sunlight, Victorian cornices, ponderous bedposts, marble-topped
washbasins, and decaying cadaver. For almost half of the film,
the audience allows itself to be misled—engrossed in the rational
while the director relentlessly pursues the terrible; so a cache
of stolen money which Hitchcock allows to be misleading is
prominently exploited until such time as he sees fit casually to

dispose of it; in effect, it is only a prop with which to harass his audience, and the audience is ruthlessly punished for its credulity. They *would* be thinking about the money, Hitchcock seems to be saying, while something far more terrible is at play.

In effect, *Psycho* represents something like a complete triumph of the director *over* his audience; with Hitchcock always at his most detached exactly at that point his audience is most excited and disturbed, most intensely and fearfully involved. So, while the audience is writhing at the clinical details of the blood, Hitchcock is off matching shots of the shower nozzle, drain, and victim's eye; amusing himself with the conceits of purely physical analogies while his audience suffers and squirms. And so, during what is, perhaps, the single most frightening moment in an intensely frightening film, Hitchcock shifts abruptly to the remote impersonality of an overhead angle; the very ultimate in aplomb; managing, thereby, not only to analyze and anatomize the action with an almost scientific, cool precision, but, almost inexplicably, succeeding in making it incalculably more terrifying as well. For, in classic nightmare fashion, the overhead perspective has the effect of showing you everything and yet revealing nothing; the essential secret is left more unknowable than ever. The shot recalls, most of all, the terror of the final moment of *Vertigo,* in which the heroine falls in fear, for the second time, from the mission tower, in a nightmarishly recurrent image: the spectral appearance of the nun; the girl's look of fear and her fatal plunge; the man's stance of cosmic impotence; his legs apart; his clothes softly flapping, hair blowing, in the sinistrous breeze; his arms at his sides, hands cupped outward in a gesture of bewildered helplessness; all taken from a portentous low angle, with the camera's final, slight, appalled movement back—the withdrawal an epiphany. Like that camera movement, the overhead angle in *Psycho* bespeaks a knowledge of the medium that can be neither taught nor learned; an intimate, almost instinctive, deeply intuitive sense of how things work in film.

Psycho is, in fact, so good a film—marred only by the useless and redundant psychoanalytical aria delivered at its end—that it is all too easy now to be generous to the films which immediately preceded it; it is one thing to see *North by Northwest* in its context, climaxing Hitchcock's failures of the fifties, and quite another to see it knowing *Psycho* was in store. And now there is *The Birds*, a film every bit as terrifying as *Psycho,* but a different kind of film, and terrifying in a different kind of way. What frightens us in *Psycho* is what we do not know; in *The Birds,* it is what we do. The terror of *Psycho* lies hidden in concealment. In *The Birds,* it is presented to us in a sweepingly overt revelation. Everything in *Psycho* is reticent and ambiguous, but *The Birds* has the explicit clarity of a demonstration. What is happening is always unmistakably in evidence. The sole mystery is: why?

And, just as the secretive character of *Psycho* extended to its publicity, so also with the directness of *The Birds.* The spectator would virtually have to be a Martian who was so estranged from the mass media, newspapers and magazines, as to be able to go to see *The Birds* unaware of what it was about—good God, I even heard Hitchcock being interviewed and discussing the technical problems of staging the birds' attack as an intermission guest during the broadcast of a New York Philharmonic concert! But it is only once one is inside the theater, and the film has begun, that one is struck by the realization of, for all the fore-warning of an attack by birds, how little one actually knows.

Why is it that a film by which we are prepared to be frightened should open with a scene so manifestly light and play-ful? The credits appear to the accompaniment of the beating of wings and the shrieking of birds, from diminuendo to a crescendo which reaches, if it does not cross, the threshold of pain; then, abruptly, we are into the kind of scene which has opened countless Hollywood romantic comedies, the lovers-to-be, at first meeting, reacting to each other with an antagonism we immediately know is destined to be short-lived. It is a conventional beginning, which, in a conventional movie, would be re-laxing, confirming us in our expectations of what is to follow; in *The Birds,* jarring as it is to expectations of a very different nature, it is slightly unnerving; the scene communicates an undercurrent of tension it does not seem inherently to contain. Or does it? Isn't it merely a case of our expecting the terrible, and so being oversensitive to any possible portent of it; despite the presence of birds, there is really nothing even remotely sinister in the film's first sequence. A *Vogue* model–type blonde enters a San Francisco pet shop; while the saleslady is temporarily off the floor, she pretends to be a saleslady herself to a man who enters subsequently, and who addresses her as such; she is revealed in her pretense by the man, who has, in fact, recognized her from some previous occasion, he having encouraged her in her deception only so as to be able to expose it. Leaving the girl irritated, the man exits. It is a prank which might have been agreeably amusing in another film, in another world; in this film, this world, something is not as it should be. Where the participants should be bright and playful, they seem, instead, just slightly smug; the whole business has a vaguely unpleasant edge. This is, perhaps, as good a place as any to remark that, while the characters and their conversation tend at times through the film toward a kind of vapidity, it would be as beside the point to defend the banality of some of their lines with the fallacy that Hitchcock is portraying the characters' banality by imitation of it, as it is to commit another fallacy in identifying him with the things his characters say. Even when the characters in the film appear most vapid, there is always something happening on another level in the scene, something larger and more meaningful than whatever the characters may be saying. Part of our difficulty with the film's opening sequence, seeing it for the first time, is in our not being able to distinguish Hitchcock's concerns from those of his characters. Yet is the chief source of what disturbs us, in the opening scene, in the action or ourselves? Isn't it the very lightness of the scene which unnerves us? For, surely, we know that this film will not long remain a comedy. And, if we allow ourselves the frivolity of laughter now, how much will we later have to pay?

For payment is exacted, although neither at the time nor in the manner we expect it. The first prank is followed by a second, more calculated one. As a means of getting even, the girl obtains a pair of lovebirds, for the purpose of buying which, as a birthday present for his young sister, the man had originally entered the pet shop. As she is about to leave them anonymously outside his apartment, she is informed by a neighbor that the man has gone for the weekend to his family home in the country, some sixty miles away; already involved in her scheme beyond abandoning it, she proceeds to follow him. In fact, the film is well under way and the locale shifted to the small fishing community of Bodega Bay before the birds make their first massed attack, and, by this time, we have been introduced to the people who become the attackers' prey: the self-absorbed young lady whose practical joking initiates the action, the smug young man who is the object of the prank, his excessively attentive mother, and an ex-girl friend who has moved from the city to where the man spends each weekend with his family—mother and sister—because she wishes merely to remain near him; by this time, too, the light and playful atmosphere of the film's opening has given way to one darkened by a vague but pervasive menace. We begin to scrutinize everyone—a casual passenger on an elevator, the proprietor of a gloomy general store, the mother, the ex-girl friend—and everywhere—the family's barn, and house, and hallway within, which we see in eerily moving shots constructed from a subjective point of view—for signs of peril without yet knowing what the nature of that peril might be; the one thing which seems certain, however ill defined, is our growing sense that something is unnatural, something not as it should be. That a pretty girl should go to such lengths to perpetrate a trifling, slightly malicious prank, that a handsome, well-to-do, marriageable young man should be so devotedly attached to his mother, or that his mother should gaze at him with such intense absorption, that another attractive girl should alter her life to the design of merely living in proximity to a man who no longer loves her—surely, all this is not natural; surely, these people must be hiding something. Even after the first, singly attacking bird has swooped from the sky and drawn blood, we still succumb to a stray suspicion that someone—the strangely aloof mother, perhaps—is somehow responsible for the deed. Yet, unlike *Psycho,* there is not a single way in which Hitchcock has misled us. It is by our own expectations alone that we are deceived.

Once the birds attack, the film is full of violence—much more so than *Psycho*—yet the film's violence remains entirely unrelated to what may be said to be its sadism, which is directed not at its characters but at its audience, and consists, as it always has

in Hitchcock, of such things as the exacerbation of the spectators' sensibilities by such devices as the sound behind the credits
and by sheer terror, and, above all, of the constant thwarting of
the audience's expectations. The violence in the film is integral
to its vision of nature, and wholly appropriate to it. No doubt,
were *Hamlet* to appear for the first time as a film today, *The
New Republic* would have something edifying to say on the
subject of gratuitous bloodshed; but you'll have to check your
New Republic notions at the door if you wish even to begin to
understand *The Birds* (not to say *Hamlet*), to begin to find an
answer to the: why? Why do the birds attack? Who is responsible? The connection between the people to whom we are introduced in the early part of the film and the attack of the
birds is the film's sole enigma: all else is demonstrably evident.
Perhaps, it is enough to say that the relationship of the characters to the birds is simply that of victim. "There's no reason,"
says someone to the "hero" after the birds have attacked in
force, and the man replies, "Well, it's happening; isn't that a
reason!" It is; and yet, while no causal relation is ever
established between the people and the attack of the birds, the
film is filled with implications that what is incontrovertibly
happening is not without a kind of reason of its own.

The Birds: the name seems deliberately to sound a classical
echo: but there is a resemblance which extends, I think, beyond
the character of a name. The people, in *The Birds,* no more
cause the birds' attack than Orestes can be said to cause the
vengeance of the Eumenides, or, for that matter, the affliction
by the flies; persons are not the *cause* of the punishment of the
gods, they are only its provocation. There are no gods in the
world of *The Birds,* but there is nature; nature outraged, and
nature revenged. It is a revenge the people in the film somehow
provoke, although the precise grounds of the provocation we
never know; it is enough to know that something is unnatural,
an affront to what is naturally fitting, and that, as traditionally,
the disturbance and provocation seem to reside in an unnatural
household. At one point, the ex-girl friend offers the "heroine"
a possible psychological explanation of the mother's attachment
to her son, and then more or less dismisses it. It is not what is
wrong that counts, but the very fact that something is wrong.

In a sense, we see enough reason for the birds' attack, even before we are acquainted with the members of the household, when the heroine, driving with the lovebirds up from San Francisco to Bodega Bay, makes a sharp turn, and the birds, their cage on the automobile's floor, are forced comically to tilt on their perch by the car's sudden movement. The birds are there only as an object in the girl's scheme, creatures appropriated to the end of a trivial joke, and their ridiculous tilt is only a trivial indignity; yet, embodied figuratively in the image of that indignity is an offense to nature already reason enough to provoke the subsequent catastrophe. Nature, natural function, has been interfered with, without respect, and that is an outrage.[3] The offense, the outrage, is largely figurative; its scale is so small; but what is everything in *The Birds* if not this? *The Birds* depicts for us an event which we recognize to be impossible, yet the quality of the film is neither that of fantasy nor of allegory. Rather, the action has the effect of containing completely, in a figurative image, a certain vision of nature and of natural order. Hitchcock is not a poetic filmmaker as we usually mean the word "poetic," despite the great visual beauty of a film such as *Vertigo,* but *The Birds* has, as a totality, the integrity of poetry, of a dramatic poem, wherein all the meaning is contained within an action rather than in any individual's particular role in or understanding of it. Nature outraged, nature revenged: it is classical in its boldness and simplicity. I tremble to pronounce the name of the dead, yet it's almost like tragedy.

But it isn't. In the birds, we have, indeed, a modern image of the furies with something much like their traditional tragic force, but *The Birds* is not tragedy, and if I have spoken of sev-

3. Much later, in the final minutes of the film, as the people are abandoning their house, the young sister asks if she may bring the lovebirds—"they haven't harmed anybody"—and, ironically, the pair of birds is once again placed in an automobile. Although they are the only birds that have remained tranquil throughout the film, faithful to their natural function, the audience is manifestly unnerved by the decision of the characters to take them: in the course of the film, the lovebirds have been transformed from an object in a joke to an object of fear. And, indeed, it is not altogether certain that the fear is unmerited; the lovebirds accompany the people when they finally drive away, but the sister's plea remains, nevertheless, the most ambiguous line in the film.

eral of its similarities, I should mention its differences as well. In *The Birds,* action is tragic, character is not. The characters of *The Birds* figuratively initiate the film's main action, but, once having set the machinery of that action into motion, it proceeds with an inexorable logic and momentum of its own, and they cannot exert the slightest effect on it. What they suffer, they provoke, and yet what they suffer is not actually punishment, at least, not just punishment; the suffering is incommensurable with the provocation. Only once in the film does there appear to be something like a direct and proportionate relation between the provocation of the characters and what befalls them, when, after having smuggled the lovebirds successfully into the house, the girl rows back across the bay and is met by the man, who has discovered the birds, spied her boat, and raced by automobile around to the opposite shore. Aware of his attention and pleased by her success, she fusses with her hair, and smiles in perfect self-satisfaction; the moment is that of the apex of her smugness; then, suddenly, a single gull dives at her head from the sky, slashing her scalp; it is the first attacking bird. The wound is a minor one, but it momentarily spoils her appearance, and the prank, and she cannot subsequently quite regain her lost composure. What remains of her smugness disappears soon after, disappears decisively in the scene on the hilltop above the sister's outdoor birthday party; but it is too late, and the party becomes the target of the birds' first concerted attack. So, too, the man's smugness, and his mother's distant coldness, and the apparent hostility of the ex-girl friend crumble not long after, but it is too late for all of them. There will be no respite from the furies until the heroine has been systematically reduced from the fashion model we meet in the opening scene to the shocked, bruised, haggard, virtually insensate creature she is left at the end; first her hairdo and makeup go, the outermost mask, but none other will be allowed her either, and, by the end of the film, she remains little more than a tattered sack. Certainly, this exceeds anything which might be understood as punishment, both by the birds and by Hitchcock, who seems, in a sense, as much as his characters, to be the servant of the independent, self-propelling logic of the action. Once having provoked the birds' attack, nothing the characters may do can avert it. And, once having decided to make a work like *The Birds,* there is almost no way in which Hitchcock might have made it differently.

Once the birds attack, all else recedes into the background; the scope of the film properly becomes the macrocosmic one. The people in the film have played their part, but there is no longer any effective part in the action they may play. And, although the characters do change in the course of that action, even, one might say, become better people, it is hardly through any understanding of what is happening to them. In the face of the birds' attack, their masks and poses become luxuries they can no longer afford; they change simply because they have no choice. Not one of the characters we see in the world of the film seems capable of moral awareness, not to say moral understanding; capable of the kind of confrontation of and coming to terms with their situation which one sees in a truly tragic character; they are people in a world which inspires us to terror, but not pity. The vision of *The Birds* is not a moral but an aesthetic one; that of a world ordered not by justice, but by fitness, balance, and design. In one of the most amazing images of the film, we suddenly see the town, now burning in destruction, in a view from great aerial elevation; from this perspective, one sees everything as part of a vast design, and the scene of chaos appears almost peaceful, even beautiful; then, gradually, the silence gives way to the flapping of wings and the birds' awful shrieking, and the image, without losing its beauty, is filled with terror as well. The incommensurability between human provocation and cosmic retribution is suggestive, in a way, of the world of Job, a world of reasons surpassing human understanding; but, while the vision of Job seems, finally, beyond morality, that of *The Birds* is, one might say, a premoral one. There are no gods, only nature; not right and wrong, but natural and unnatural; the sense of nature antecedes morality. In this world, the greatest offense is an aesthetic one: above all, one must not violate the design.

Yet, if this is, finally, not the world of tragedy, it must be said that *The Birds* closes on an image which is authentically cathartic, an image truly worthy of tragedy. I must confess that, beneath all my tremendous excitement on first seeing *The*

Birds, was an undercurrent of extraneous apprehension: the film was so good, I thought, but would he, as he did to some degree in the psychoanalyst's speech in *Psycho,* throw it away? Would the militia really come in, as a radio commentator is briefly heard to conjecture with absurd and pathetic inadequacy? Would he again bow to the audience in a conciliatory act of explanation, explaining away what was, in fact, its own explanation? ". . . It's happening; isn't that a reason!" It is; and it is allowed to be. For, in *The Birds,* we are met with first causes; there is no cause of the birds' attack; the attack is, in itself, the assertion of the primacy of nature; it happens. From the large audience in which I first saw *The Birds* came audible cries of protest at the film's closing image; and that Hitchcock has given his audience this ending, which it does not want and which is the only proper ending for the work, is both the gesture and the measure of his present independence. In a shot held so long as to make the audience gradually come to realize that it must be final even before it ends, is an image of the landscape, now blanketed by birds, as the characters are, in effect, permitted by the attackers to abandon their besieged house, and drive away: in the sun-streaked light of early morning, the foreground is revealed to be occupied everywhere by the birds, most of them at rest; in the background, the car drives off, remaining visible for a while, but dwindling in size until it disappears completely somewhere beyond the range of vision; and, as it disappears and the sound of its engine fades from audibility, there are only the birds, sole inhabitants; the only sounds those of subdued chirping, the rustling of feathers, and an occasional flutter of wings. It is an image of great serenity and beauty, and an image which overwhelms one with awe; an image of order restored, of nature triumphant and man reduced to his place in the whole design of it. It is, as I've said, cathartic; an image worthy, in the profundity of its terror, of tragedy; and who would have thought Hitchcock capable of it? Which is by way of apologizing, because, until I saw it, I had not.

Let me be perfectly clear. I don't consider *The Birds* to be a great work of art as, say, *French Cancan,* or *Los Olvidados,* or *The Quiet Man* are great—it is too drastically limited by its conception of character to be this—but I do think that pas-

sages of it, and, above all, its final image, are as thrilling as anything I have ever seen. The unifying vision of the film is so
gripping that I realize here, almost as an afterthought, that I've
thus far neglected to mention that, all else aside, *The Birds* is a
technical achievement of astonishing magnitude, and that, with
Kurosawa (when aroused), Hitchcock is probably the most brilliant technical virtuoso making films today; and, beyond that,
one of the most subtle and dazzling talents in the medium. That
the final image of *The Birds,* charged as it is with the accumulated force of all that has preceded it, is the greatest moment in
all of Hitchcock, I am certain. Despite the wit and brilliance of
his best films of suspense, it is in this moment that one sees revealed, unmistakably, the director's true identity. And yet, recognizably of its company are most of *Psycho,* the de Chirico
cornfield of *North by Northwest,* the bell tower climax of
Vertigo, the trauma and snow sequence of *Spellbound,* the recurring waltz image of *Shadow of a Doubt,* the infinite vista of
deserted windmills of *Foreign Correspondent,* the chillingly
empty landscapes of *The Thirty-Nine Steps.* In such passages as
these, as, in fact, throughout *The Birds,* with its persistent imagery of nature's most beautiful and gentle creatures rushing
savagely toward peoples' eyes, in effect, *our* eyes, one sees the
quintessential Hitchcock: an individual in a state of dreadful
intimacy with the terrible, with the terms and the texture of
nightmare. And it is this awful knowledge which has always con-
stituted his closest claim on our attention.

(1963)

POSTSCRIPT, 1966

It would be a mistake to begin by making unjustifiable claims
for *Torn Curtain;* it is decidedly minor Hitchcock. The plot
is slight and unconvincing, and, though Paul Newman manages
to bring more conviction to his performance than has been his
manner of late, Julie Andrews—to be fair, an apposite addition
to that gallery of glacial types which Hitchcock seems to favor—
makes a singularly bloodless heroine. Beyond this, the script,
the words themselves, that is, apart from the conception and

dramatic action, is weak, and both words and images are rather consistently betrayed by a musical score which tends to over-stress them. I seem to be saying then that *Torn Curtain* is with-out interest, and yet it is not. To ask why it is not is to ask again what it means to be a creator in film as against a traffic director; to try to understand how materials of apparently little abstract distinction may be radically transformed in the process of being imagined in the language of another medium.

Yet these questions carry their own pomposity, and need de-flation. For the fact is that one may be a genuine film-maker and still not be good, just as one may be a genuine jazz musician and play music which is truly jazz, which swings, and is still banal; the categories, in both cases, are merely descriptive, and don't, in themselves, denote value. Hitchcock *is* a film-maker in his very essence; watch, in *Torn Curtain,* how he cuts in the close-ups of a book, hand, knife, or other detail without missing a beat; how many other directors are there who can piece film together with such fluent precision as both to direct attention and not distract it by the halting injunction: Look at this! Watch his use of the stop-motion stare during the ballerina's pirouette; at a moment in film history when stop motion has become a new cliché, observe how unobtrusively Hitchcock uses the device to serve the action without calling attention to itself. And look at the quality of light during hero and heroine's en-counter in his hotel room, expressively deepening in gravity as if in sympathy to the dramatic action; expressing in itself, in fact, a depth of feeling the action itself cannot convey. These are the touches which speak of a medium's mastery; one may respond to them or one may not; one may *see* a film or simply listen to it and follow the actors; the fact remains that these things are there. But the fact is also that, though they may impart to *Torn Curtain* a definite artistic life, such things, in themselves, cannot make it good.

And, in fact, they don't; they only make engrossing a film which almost any other director would have left as pedestrian as he found it, as dull as its elements would seem to have destined it to be. But the question then is why did Hitchcock find it?—why *Torn Curtain?*—and why is his whole career so checkered by boldness and timidity? Why are films as dazzlingly audacious as *Psycho* and *The Birds* followed by the feebleness of *Marnie* and the conventionalities of *Torn Curtain?*

The question with respect to *Torn Curtain* is even more complicated, for I have it on reliable information that, in its case, Hitchcock departed from his usual practice of tight shooting (photographing his films in strict obedience to their conception, with almost no room left for altering them in the editing) to have enough footage for virtually two different films, eventually releasing the safer of them. What factors may have gone into such a decision we will probably never know, but, surely, it taxes credulity to believe they numbered *artistic* considerations among them. And I am reminded here that, when he was visited on the set of *Marnie,* a film which holds a very special place in the canon of Hitchcock's failures for being, in addition to all else, botched even in technique, he remarked to one observer that his only interest in the film was in its use of color filters. Perhaps this was just a put-on or simply the alibi of someone who realized his latest work was going badly, but, surely, whatever such things may mean, they are among the problems that must be confronted in any serious critical consideration of Hitchcock, taking precedence, it seems to me, over deep-think inquiries into Catholic guilt, the confession, and moral reversals. The question one needs to ask about *Torn Curtain* is not how Newman's role and relationship with Julie Andrews may be explicated,[4] but why the impact of the film is incommensurate with any such explication, and, finally, why a director as brilliantly capable of the extraordinary as Hitchcock, and in so exceptionally free a position to make the films he wants, could have wanted to make this one. I don't pretend to have the answers; I am frankly baffled. And I say this as a Hitchcock devotee, out of an extreme admiration for Hitchcock's artistry. The artistry is not lacking, but where is the artist?

One does catch glimpses of him at moments, those astonishing

---

4. For how it can be, and most cogently so, see Andrew Sarris' review in the *Village Voice* of September 1, 1966. His argument is persuasive in all but one respect: though everything he cites is indisputably *in* the film, his reading of it is simply not consonant with its effect. Does one perhaps glimpse in Sarris' interpretation the version of *Torn Curtain* that wasn't released?

moments when one is suddenly made to forget how much one has to question. He is there at the opening and in a few other isolated moments of *Marnie,* and fitfully throughout *Torn Curtain.* He is there especially in one long sequence of the latter film that is among the best things he has ever done. It is the kind of sequence which Hitchcock's detractors unfailingly dismiss as sadism: a chase followed by the graphic, prolonged, horrendous depiction of a murder. No detail of this act is euphemistically omitted, and never before have I been given so vivid a sense of the excruciating modulations in the extinction of a human life by violence. The act is committed (with assistance) by the hero upon an extremely unpleasant (though acutely characterized) adversary, but never passed off as derring-do or fun à la *Thunderball.* The murder is dwelt on, yes, but as an antidote to sadism; it is an ordeal the hero and audience mutually suffer, both of them horrified at the persistence of life in the face of this clumsy assault on it. It is dwelt on, but one would need to be mad to feel the experience of it could possibly be enjoyed. Nightmarishly, the antagonist is struck and still holds tenaciously to life beneath the blows. The audience in which I saw *Torn Curtain* laughed, yet there could be no doubt it was the laughter of profound discomfort. Hitchcock gives us nothing in the sequence to make it easy.

Is this, then, why Hitchcock made *Torn Curtain:* to create this single image of murder to remain stamped ineradicably on one's imagination? And is this the most one can reasonably hope for from American films—fragments of excellence seized from the commonplace—art, but not works of art? That this sequence of *Torn Curtain* is art of an exceptional intensity I have no doubt. But is this all there is; is this all Hitchcock can finally be said to be about? Once I thought I was close to some answers about Hitchcock. Now I see that it is still chiefly questions which remain.

RADICAL FREEDOM:
ASPECTS OF JEAN RENOIR

Part of the problem, in attempting any clear understanding of the films of Jean Renoir, is to free him from the claims of his admirers, English-speaking, on both sides of the Atlantic. The object of this admiration is Renoir the humanist, making films which are careless in form but rich in feeling and in an "affirmation of life"; and, apart from some occasional unconscious parodies of the New Criticism, this version of Renoir has held a potent sway. Writing in 1969, one of the most intelligent of Renoir's American enthusiasts can say, "One doesn't want to talk about how Jean Renoir does it; one wants to talk about what he has done"; while another critic, representing the British view, can speak of "the apparent formlessness and imperfections" of *The Rules of the Game* in the course of paying tribute to it. And yet both are critics who would clearly seem to join in the consensus that Renoir is one of the very greatest artists to have worked in his medium, a proposition which would probably be subscribed to by more people of otherwise dissident opinions than any other that one could state in the discussion of film.

But, of course, one *does* want to talk about how Jean Renoir does it, if only better to understand what he has done. Like most plausible misrepresentations, the humanist Renoir does engage a certain half-truth. It is probably true, for instance, that Renoir's films, like Tolstoy's novels, seem, in their oceanic embrace of a world and their evenness of temper in response to it, to overflow formal conventions and to achieve a range and density more nearly that of "life" than "art." And the world of Renoir's films seems distinguished further by its generous compassion and its absence of individual viciousness; perhaps no other major body of fiction has been as lacking as have been Renoir's films in the creation of truly malevolent characters (the publisher, Batala, in *The Crime of Monsieur Lange,* whose villainy is nevertheless seen chiefly from the aspect of his vitality and charm, being possibly the sole exception to this).[1] This characteristic lack of malevolence has, of course, no aesthetic merit in itself, yet it is difficult not to respond to it for its extra-aesthetic appeal, for its transcendence of mean-spiritedness; and, indeed, difficult not to respond to Renoir's work as a whole as the effusion of the artist's humane and expansive personality. And, in fact, the sustenance of the figure of the humanist Renoir demands just this: that one is attentive primarily to the personality of the artist rather than to the character of his art. Yet the ultimate distinction between the two may be expressed in a single question. Why is it that, in a world so free of malevolence as is that of Renoir's films, things seem almost always to end so sadly?

For years, *Grand Illusion,* made in 1937, was (along with the exquisite short film, *A Day in the Country*) Renoir's "official," textbook masterpiece; now, one is more likely to find a unique distinction of this sort being given to *The Rules of the Game* of two years later. On both sides of these two films, however, lies the bulk of Renoir's work, some thirty-six films made between 1924

---

1. One might also except Joseph in *The Diary of a Chambermaid,* but, though brutish far beyond Batala, he is seen essentially as the product of social determinations. Indeed, the very concept of intrinsic, individual evil is subjected to mockery in *The Testament of Dr. Cordelier,* Renoir's black comic version of Jekyll and Hyde, in which the "evil" nature isolated and released in Hyde finds its unprovoked expression chiefly in the commission of "social indiscretions," making faces, purposeless and bungling attempts to snatch babies from prams, and other such banal antisocial behavior.

and 1961, most of which have never been convincingly assimilated in criticism to any general understanding of Renoir's art other than by the touchstone of "personality." In part, this failure is accounted for by the fact that, following *The Rules of the Game,* Renoir spent some ten years in America with the inevitably attendant ascriptions of decline, but it has been only aggravated by the *auteur*-istic rehabilitators for whom, Renoir being great, each Renoir film must inevitably be greater than the last. In some ways, though, the *auteur*-ists carry more credibility than the decline-mongers. Many of Renoir's most famous films of the thirties seem not quite to have found a true subject and to suffer from some fundamental inappositeness between the artist and his material—this most strikingly in the adaptation of *Madame Bovary,* in whose temperamental mismatch Flaubert's hard precision is dissolved into pretty bittersweet, but only somewhat less so in such dramas of low life as *La Chienne, The Lower Depths, La Bête Humaine.* Though the best of these, the peasant drama, *Toni* (which reputedly exerted an important influence on the Italian neo-realists through Visconti, who briefly served as Renoir's assistant), achieves a crystalline, balladlike simplicity, the others, while not without their beautiful passages, all seem somehow cramped by their materials, by their attempt to reconcile melodramatic contrivance with Renoir's tendency to de-melodramatize, cramped even by their humanism. Whatever one can say against Hollywood, Fritz Lang's American remake of *La Chienne* (as *Scarlet Street*), while never coming close to the achievement of those moments of real feeling that distinguish the Renoir film, does nevertheless achieve a kind of success which eludes the Renoir in Lang's giving basically trashy materials the kind of highly stylized, basically trashy treatment they deserve. On the other hand, whatever one can say *for* Hollywood, it is true also that none of Renoir's "proletarian" French films of the thirties, even the adaptation of Gorky's *The Lower Depths* which is probably the least convincing of them, rings quite as false as does Renoir's American film of peasant life, *The Southerner,* with Zachary Scott and Betty Field playing sharecroppers.

In fact, like that of any so Promethean artist, Renoir's career cannot be made to conform to any neat critic's pattern of rises and falls. His first masterpiece (and I limit myself to speaking of his sound films and, obviously, only those which I have seen) came as early as 1932, in *Boudu Saved from Drowning*, with another, three years later, in *The Crime of Monsieur Lange*, a film which anticipates not only Renoir's imaginative transcendence of those naturalistic materials with which he was to continue to struggle intermittently throughout the thirties, but also, and in striking fashion, the modern temper of such works as Truffaut's *Shoot the Piano Player* of some twenty-five years later. In Hollywood, before making *The Southerner*, he made a quite charming excursion into rustic Americana in *Swamp Water*, his first American film (which, based on a Dudley Nichols script that seems tailored for John Ford, could probably pass for long stretches as a Ford film). During the same year in which he made *The Southerner*, he made also the brilliantly fanciful *Diary of a Chambermaid*, which, if less consistent than *Swamp Water*, seems to me nevertheless both the best of Renoir's American films in its imaginative exuberance and the most important in its relation to his most characteristic work. As late as 1956, it was possible for what would seem to be the most congenial materials of *Paris Does Strange Things* (*Elena et les Hommes*) to go almost utterly awry by an indulgent preciousness in the handling, and yet three years later, in *Picnic on the Grass*, a similarly antic farce is developed with a wonderfully unforced playfulness. The main point, however, is not the commonplace one that, like the work of most serious artists, Renoir's encompasses an erratic progression of failures and successes, of problems engaged and eventually solved, but the no less commonplace one that, like the work of most serious artists, it reflects, failures as well as successes, a persistent complex of artistic preoccupations. And these, being *artistic* preoccupations, are, insofar as the two can be distinguished, always as much formal as thematic.

The notion that Renoir's films are somehow formally lax has sprung in part from their structural looseness, a looseness, one should add, that now seems an inseparable part of their self-renewing freshness and modernity. In this regard, it is probably relevant to the favored position long held by *Grand Illusion* that, alone of Renoir's films, it seems slightly held in check by a thesis-bound script, and to the general esteem now accorded *The Rules of the Game* that, though with no sacrifice of Renoir's characteristic sense of mercurial extemporaneity, it is a work so masterly in the orchestration of its intricate parts as to invite comparisons less with other films than with works such as *The Would-be Gentleman* or *Così fan tutte*. It is not, however, his films' looseness of construction that has given rise to the questions of formal carelessness so much as it has been their deliberate rejection of what had for years been virtually axiomatic standards of excellence for a film's editing and photography. As early as in *Boudu Saved from Drowning* one is aware of the sustained development of a style in which the classical criteria of visual composition within a frame are abandoned in an attempt to open up the frame to depth of field and to peripheral fluidity; and a style in which the momentum of the films derives not from a pulse created in the editing but in the realization of those possibilities for expressive movement to be found in the imaginative transformation into movement of their subjects. Already, in *Boudu Saved from Drowning*, one sees a film which in great measure takes its movement from the kinetic thrust of its protagonist, as embodied in an astonishing performance by Michel Simon, a performance reprised no less astonishingly by Jean-Louis Barrault in *The Testament of Dr. Cordelier* of twenty eight years later; both films comparable perhaps only to Chaplin's in the extent to which their life springs directly from that of their ceaselessly animated central figures.[2]

Unlike those of Dreyer or Eisenstein, Renoir's films rarely

---

2. And, though *Boudu* and *Dr. Cordelier* represent extremes, and no Renoir film could ever be lacking in visual distinction as is, for want of Chaplin's presence before the camera, *A Countess from Hong Kong* (the Chaplin film not, however, without some other distinctions), this need of Renoir's films for expressive actors accounts, in part, for the shortcomings of such works as *The River* and *The Golden Coach*. Whereas a Buñuel film may sometimes overcome lapses in performance by the sheer force of its conception, much as some great music can survive almost any performance, *The Golden Coach*, however beautiful it seems as a conception, is seriously crippled by the general impoverishment of its acting, particularly as a work so directly concerned with theatrical styles. (I except, of course, Anna Magnani, who nevertheless, in her occasionally almost rapacious outpourings of Earth Motherly, Italianate charm, can provide problems of another sort.) Beyond this, *The Golden Coach*, in particular, founders in its attempt to introduce as a subsidiary theme what has been a controlling metaphor throughout Renoir's work—the interpenetration of life and theater—and its overstated and awkward failure to manage this.

yield a composed still, yet if Renoir's films reject the ideal of compositional equilibrium—their movement perpetually spilling over the frame—it remains to be said that in their lavish attention to texture, light, and color they are works which must be described, above all, as painterly; even so primarily gray a film as *The Elusive Corporal* being able to find, within its limited range, an extraordinary richness of coloristic resource. The images of Renoir's films almost never achieve the kind of self-contained epiphany that one may find in those of Dovzhenko or Ford—in Renoir's work, the image almost always disappearing into the film—but, though we may not be particularly aware of striking images as a Renoir film unfolds, the films nevertheless remain in one's consciousness as works whose meaning and imagery are inseparable. Renoir's camera is never situated so as to execute any flourish but rather always at the point of maximum expressiveness, and yet this stylistic self-effacement seems finally not only to result in a fluent, beautiful, fully achieved style of its own, but to call into question the traditional concepts of what is style in film and, indeed, the very vocabulary of the medium as it has been traditionally employed.

With the recent translation from the French of a selection of the essays of André Bazin, there now exists, in some language approximating English, a cogent exposition of the theoretical basis of Renoir's style and the cinema of depth of field (or "deep focus"), one which I don't propose to recapitulate here.[3] Yet it must be said that, even in Bazin's sophisticated argument, the defense of depth of field and, through it, of Renoir remains obscured by a certain humanistic piety. For beyond the arguing of a greater subtlety, ambiguity, and visual richness in the cinema of deep focus versus that of montage are Bazin's claims made for the greater democracy of deep focus in its giving the members of the audience a certain freedom to select for themselves with their own eyes from among the elements which the

3. André Bazin, *What Is Cinema?* Berkeley, University of California Press, 1968. In addition, what is probably Bazin's key essay in behalf of depth of field, "The Evolution of Film Language," also appears in a translation into more fluent English in *The New Wave,* edited by Peter Graham, New York, Doubleday, 1968.

image contains, and thus far to participate in the films' creation.[4] One understands what Bazin means—there is, in Renoir's films, the illusion of this freedom, and, watching them, one never senses the visual constriction imposed, as in Eisenstein, by the blackboard pointer of the catechist, or, as in Resnais, by the master plan of the Master Artist. Yet (as Bazin acknowledges) the deep-focus cinema of Orson Welles (and the choreographed, antimontage cinema of Antonioni, and of *Le Amiche* in particular) have demonstrated that neither need be practiced without a meticulous control as extensive and as evident as that of Resnais or Eisenstein (as, conversely, films such as *Breathless* and *Jules and Jim* have demonstrated that fast cutting and fragmentation need not be inimical to subtlety, ambiguity, and visual richness). Here (though, with less misleading result, throughout his argument), Bazin seems not to realize that he is dealing not so much with hard and factual distinctions as with essentially figurative matters, with stylistic tonalities and artistic effects, with resonances and suggestions. Depth of field *does* imply an attitude of the artist toward his subject, a deference of the artist to the rhythms of his subject's autonomous life, as montage implies a subordination of the subject to some aesthetic or conceptual design; yet these divergent tendencies, or, at least, the first of them, can of necessity be realized only to degrees forever falling short of the absolute. For, insofar as the artist's subject is a fiction, the concept of its autonomous life (as, conversely, that of a wholly transparent art) has meaning only as a metaphor, or an infinitely receding ideal. An artist may act *as if* certain figurative things were literally true, but, just as the stories of Chekhov are in actuality no less contrived than those of Maupassant, so, too, is the life of a Renoir film, as much as that of a film by Cocteau, a creation solely of the artist's imagination.

Bound up with this misconstruction of Renoir's films as engaging a world more "real" than that of, say, Eisenstein's (when what one actually means is that it is a more profusely imagined one) is that of Renoir's democratic style by which one's eye is

4. A notion which seems to be given some assent by Penelope Gilliatt's recent writing on Renoir in *The New Yorker*.

given the freedom to see as one chooses.[5] For surely a recognition of the power of Renoir's films is, in itself, an inferential refutation of this; were they merely the discursive anecdotes in affirmation of life that their admirers often make them sound, it would be impossible to account for their oneness of impress. It is not that Renoir lets you look where you will but rather that he gives you more to look at; when one says that he doesn't direct one's eye, one actually means that he directs it with that art which conceals art and with a consummate subtlety. Yet no less than in the films of Eisenstein it is the artist's vision that our eye is finally brought to see.

If, however, one can speak of the subject's autonomous life in Renoir's films only as a metaphor, the force and centrality of this metaphor in the films' impress on us is hardly thus denied. Unfolding in images whose compositional repose has been abandoned to expressive movement, and propelled not by a rhythm imposed in editing but by the rhythmic movement of three-dimensional characters seen in full as they interact in depth of field and integral space, the sense of liberation with which Renoir's films leave us is not only our own but that of those characters themselves.[6] Which is to say that the condition or possibility of being free, in which aspect we typically perceive the characters of Renoir's films, is, at least in part, a purely formal creation; much as, in *The Crime of Monsieur Lange,* Batala's murder by Lange, though unprepared for psychologically, is given all the motivation it needs by the camera's headlong movement downward as it traces Lange's course from a second-floor window to the courtyard where the act takes place. And yet, if it is true that, in a sense, the content of a work of art may be seen from one perspective as an aspect of its form, so, too, may stylistic concerns merge with thematic ones and a work's form

5. Penelope Gilliatt: "He shot in deep focus . . . because he wants to see everything in motion at the same time and because he prefers not to commandeer your eye."

6. Which goes further to explain the almost necessary failure of Renoir's version of *Madame Bovary* even though it is visually the most conventionally mounted of his films. *The Rules of the Game,* in which only the ineffectual Octave and the hapless Jurieu are not bound by the rules, is something of an exception to this generalization about Renoir's characters, but one in which the film's formal freedom is qualified by its tightening web of plot.

be seen as an aspect of its content. As the formal means of Renoir's films combine to convey his work's characteristic sense of artistic freedom, so, too, are the films involved thematically in a continuing reflection on what it means for a man to be free; what Renoir does and how he does it being twin aspects of the same thing. And, having attempted some sketch of the films[1] formal principles, it is in their thematic aspect that I want now to look at them, as their persistent thematic concerns have found expression in two films made almost thirty years apart.

I. | BOUDU SAVED FROM DROWNING

Boudu Saved from Drowning was adapted from a popular play of the period, but (though I don't know the play) it is clear, quite apart from assurances to this effect by several writers, that the film cannot be seen as other than an original creation of Renoir's. Whatever its borrowing from the original, all its elements are directed to what one now sees as Renoir's characteristic concerns, and indeed, from its realization as a film, it is virtually impossible to reimagine as a work for the stage.

Boudu is a tramp; he is saved from drowning when he jumps into the Seine following the loss of his dog. His rescuer is Lestingois, the bourgeois incarnate, complete with shop, wife, and youthful maid who is also his mistress; and the action is that of Boudu's introduction into Lestingois's serenely ordered household, and its progressive disintegration into chaos under the impact of his explosive anarchy.

The film opens with the sounding of the pipes of Pan. We see a man and a dog, looking much alike; Boudu, as we see more of him, having the aspect less, as has been suggested, of a premature Hell's Angel than of some shaggy, atavistic throwback to an antediluvian past. The dog gets lost, and Boudu wanders off in desultory search of him. He approaches a policeman, who warns him to move off and later fusses over a rich lady's expensive lost dog. He approaches someone else to inquire after the dog, and is dismissingly given five francs "to buy bread"; he holds open the door of a limousine as its foppish owner emerges, and expressionlessly gives the man the five francs "to buy bread." At this point, we meet Lestingois in his bookstore as he gives away a volume of Voltaire to an indigent young browser because he "likes youth."

We see Boudu walking along a street facing the Seine, our view of him intermittently obscured, in typical Renoir fashion, by cars as they pass. The maid sings as she dusts, and Lestingois watches Boudu from his window through a telescope: "I've never seen such a perfect tramp!" he exclaims, spying another abstraction. As he watches, Boudu casually jumps into the river, and Lestingois rushes to the embankment, forcing his way through the crowds of spectators who immediately gather to watch disinterestedly as Boudu drowns; crowds and commotion shot with Renoir's characteristically off-centered framing, the looseness and freshness of the scene's images seeming now to capture in them a precious memento of a flurry of life on an actual Parisian street in the sunlight of a particular vanished day. The bourgeois rescues the tramp.

Boudu's entrance into Lestingois's home proves disruptive even before the tramp is fully revived; Lestingois's wife complaining as Boudu is laid down, "And I just reupholstered the sofa!"; Lestingois answering, "I told you it could wait!" Once revived, Boudu declines to play the role of gratefully submissive charity case. Asked why he jumped, he replies, "I'm fed up with life"; eying the maid, he remarks, tactlessly but with a certain grasp of natural fitness, "She's nice. She's your daughter?" Lestingois's wife offers to get him soup and eggs; he complains that he doesn't like soup and eggs; complains that the nightshirt he's been given is too small; and, when the food arrives, complains, "It's about time." Given wine to drink, he spits it out; Lestingois's wife exclaims, "Oh, oh!" and Boudu asks what does "Oh, oh!" mean. Though both wife and mistress are against Boudu's staying, Lestingois determines that he shall, and, as the scene ends, we see him affectionately patting Boudu's shaggy head much as, earlier, we watched Boudu scratching his dog.

If, however, we are left with a suggestion that Lestingois has found a new pet, it is soon clear that it is one which will not be housebroken. That night, as a flutist's sensuous melody issues from a neighboring window, Lestingois is kept from his assignation with the maid by Boudu's presence in the corridor, where, unable to endure the comfort of a bed, he has stretched himself

across the floor. And, in the days which follow, disorder proliferates as we watch (from perspectives increasingly distinguished
by depth of field) Boudu spilling wine, breaking dishes, spitting
in books (*The Physiology of Marriage*), shining shoes (this last
a breath-taking tour de force of wreaking havoc throughout two
rooms!), while earning such mild rebukes from Lestingois as
"You'll have to change your ways, my friend" and "I can only
shun the man who spits in Balzac!" (Boudu: "Which man is
that?") With the young maid who reveres her master, Boudu
derides his benefactor as an old woman; to her question of why
then Lestingois saved him, replying, "Maybe he wants a servant"; and through it all he continues to flirt with her. "Ever kiss
anyone before?" she asks. "I had a dog once," he tells her.

And we watch as Boudu seduces Lestingois's straitlaced, sexually restless wife (he: "Emma!"; she: "Here in an honest, bourgeois home, you act like a cave man!") in an ecstatically happy
scene of sexual awakening, ending with her rising joyously into
frame; and then, immediately after, as, with a hint of that poly-
morphous perversity in which distinctions blur between woman,
man, and dog, Boudu unself-consciously embraces Lestingois,
who has just been decorated for the rescue: "No kidding, Eddie,
you got a medal!" All defenses of the domestic arrangement
crumble before his whirlwind activity; even the business is in-
vaded as Boudu, temporarily in its charge, upbraids a customer
requesting *Flowers of Evil,* informing him that it's not a florist's
shop. Then, as they must, the household's sexual intrigues con-
verge, in a joint confrontation of Boudu caught with wife and
Lestingois caught with maid. "And in a bourgeois home!"

What follows this obligatory scene, however, is, far from being
obligatory, one of the most unexpected, astonishing, and beautiful passages in all of cinema; in its magical feeling, like nothing
so much as the opening of *L'Atalante,* but preceding Vigo's film
by two years. For, having succumbed to the fascination of his
liberated energy, his bourgeois benefactors now discover that
Boudu has attained financial respectability as well, through a
winning lottery ticket which happened to come into his posses-
sion, and it is decided that he is to be married to the maid. And,
from the confrontation scene with which the farcical action traditionally reaches its climax, we move suddenly to Boudu's wed-

ding; a sequence of dreamlike poetry commencing with the image of a gliding rowboat carrying the wedding party, dressed for the occasion and surreal in the natural setting: Boudu sitting erect in suit, bowler hat, and boutonniere, while Lestingois invokes a pagan blessing of the match. The camera, gliding dreamily as the boat, moves to take in an ensemble of violinists on the shore and then again to find the boat. A corsage drifts by; Boudu reaches out for it; the boat capsizes: all in images constantly surprising in their off-centeredness and yet unfolding with the slow gracefulness of some reverie. Boudu floats serenely downstream in his wedding suit to the sounds of the violinists' waltz off-screen in what seems to be the final image of the film, but isn't. Instead, what follows is a breath-takingly sustained climactic succession of shots, each seeming to be the last, and each (but the very last) justifying the sequence's prolongation. Boudu drifting; Boudu onshore, exchanging clothes with a scarecrow; Boudu badgering some picnickers for food; Boudu sharing his food with a goat, singing a song and rolling in the grass; the water, as Boudu's bowler hat floats by; the water; Lestingois with his wife and maid sitting exhaustedly onshore, the maid asking, "Where is Boudu?" and Lestingois replying wistfully, "Drifting . . ."; marching tramps seen against a church spire, and the sound of their fraternal song.

Boudu is a tramp, but, despite the slight sentimentalization of the film's final shot (affecting in itself but something of a lapse from the creative level of what has gone before), the Chaplinesque qualities such a description evokes are rather far from the mark. And, though he jumps into the Seine and is saved from drowning following the loss of his dog, the impulse toward pathos is confounded again, for, rather than signaling some sorrow, his attempted suicide has the character of a gratuitous, even affectless act (and one which, seen in retrospect from his later demonstrated ability to survive a plunge in the water, can hardly be said with certainty to have been a suicide attempt at all). Indeed, the gratuitous act typifies Boudu. Unlike Chaplin's tramp, who consistently acts out a vision of social graciousness which society fails to live up to, Boudu stakes out a freedom which seems based on some presocial, even precivilized model, in which no informing direction can be found other than the slipping of all restraints. He is liberating and admirable, but he seems also dangerously volatile and a bit deranged; turning menacingly on a passing stranger from whom he has requested help in deciphering his lottery ticket when the man exclaims he has won: "What the hell do you care!"; telling the maid of the customer whom he has just turned out with his response to the request for *Flowers of Evil*: "See that customer who just left? I really took care of him. I could really run a bookshop."

This is funny but also slightly crazy, for Boudu seems genuinely to mean what he is saying, and one's impression of him is of someone not stupid but wildly cunning. And, indeed, he probably *could* run the bookshop by throwing all customers out, much as he has thrust the household into exhilarating anarchy. But perhaps the paradigmatic instance of Boudu in action is his shining of his shoes, in which, bedclothes blackened, crockery smashed, a large part of the apartment left a shambles, he casually does a handstand, and, to the wife's query, "Are your shoes shined?" noncommittally replies, "No, I didn't shine them." Surely this kind of behavior could never be socialized, no less domesticated, and that (and not the embarrassment of the bourgeois, who, while often foolish, are nonetheless sympathetically portrayed) is what the film is about. The marriage of Boudu's kind of freedom with society is impossible from the start; society can only aspire to some modified version of his model, and he wander uninvolvedly at society's fringes, drifting affectlessly from dog to a jump in the river to passing entanglements to a jump back in the river to another dog (or goat), and on and on. To us, he may seem somewhat sad in his freedom, though there is not the slightest hint of sentimentality in the film (that of the final shot having a quite different object) to support one's thinking that he finds himself so. Yet, sad or not, his freedom cannot fail to awaken in us the recognition of our lack of it. He offers us a vision of radical freedom, of a kind of freedom attainable only outside society. It is a vision which does not reappear in Renoir's work until *The Testament of Dr. Cordelier,* where it has become the inspiration for the Mr. Hyde liberated by Dr. Jekyll, but it remains a vision which haunts his work, forever hovering about the edges. What now comes to occupy that work's center is another but related vision: that of what freedom can be *within* society. And, though I am now going to skip over the work of thirty years to look at one film which springs from this vision, the intervening work is a subject to which I will return.

II. THE ELUSIVE CORPORAL

If one may call the vision of Boudu's freedom precivilized, then the world into which one is plunged with *The Elusive Corporal* reveals itself immediately as civilized in the extreme. The film opens with clips from World War II German newsreels, confidently predicting victory, and ending, as do all but one of the newsreel inserts used throughout the film, on the image of explosive destruction. From this larger view, we move abruptly into the particulars: a German prisoner-of-war depot inside France, following France's capitulation and the signing of the armistice. The prisoners are being processed, and one of them, a stolid peasant type, learning that the armistice has been signed, steps out of formation to go home. But he is restrained, still a prisoner.

We are introduced to the group of prisoners, and to the corporal, whose repeated attempts to escape constitute the action of the film. The first attempt, following almost immediately on our introduction to the characters, is (the corporal excepted) bungled and apathetic, one of the participants losing his eyeglasses, the rest quickly recaptured. Before it, someone had questioned, "But why? The armistice is signed." "I signed nothing," the corporal replies. The group of prisoners is moved from France to Germany, to a new camp, the quality of life in which is suggested by a name seen fleetingly on a railway station sign that they pass as they are being transported to it. The sign reads: WINTERFELD.

The suggestions soon materialize: not atrocities but dispiriting forced labor; not bestial Nazis but officers, German and French, who cooperate to enforce the values of discipline and *Arbeit!* Existence becomes so mechanically routinized that another escape attempt goes unnoticed, the participants succeeding merely in transporting themselves from one work site to another. (This, incidentally, in a sequence that is hilariously funny; here, as elsewhere, I am scanting the film's comic invention, which is in any case largely not paraphrasable so dependent is it on expressive gesture, for other aspects of the work which are.) And, gradually, the prisoners grow acclimatized to the drudgery, finding in it only an extension of their civilian imprisonments, and even certain fulfillments their life outside denies them. When asked by the corporal to accompany him in a new escape attempt, Pater, his friend and accomplice in the earlier attempts, speaks of being "afraid of going back to Paris," of sinking back, "each in his own rut. . . . Here a comrade is a comrade though the soup may be watery." And, though the corporal assures him, "Back in Paris, we'll share soup from the same pot," Pater declines to go with him, and cries when the corporal has gone.[7]

An elaborate, extended escape sequence follows, both comic and exciting, involving masquerade in female costume and ending as the corporal has fall into his arms a passer-by shot by accident during a chase in a railway station—a moment which epitomizes the difficulties of explicating the film since, though description may not hint at this, it is, as it happens, both wildly funny and emblematic of a universe in which improvisation and chance are in the ascendancy. The corporal is sent to a punishment camp, and then back to the former compound, where he is surprised to find the group as before. "You didn't try to escape?" he asks his friend Ballochet in amazement. "What for?" Ballochet replies. "Freedom's not all the other side of the barbed wire. In Paris, I'm more of a slave than here. . . . I stick to my tower high above the battle and I invite you to join me."

And, for a time, the corporal does join Ballochet in the relatively comfortable and privileged niche he has found, by his cleverness, amidst the unpromising circumstances: playing cards, eating confiscated *pâté*, loafing. For a while this routine continues, interrupted only by periodic supervised trips to town to visit a dentist, a German woman with whose daughter the cor-

7. "I looked at a photograph pinned up over his desk. It showed a cluster of men in cloth caps sitting on the ground and laughing. The scene looked rather like a factory picnic, but not quite. Renoir said that the picture was by his friend Henri Cartier-Bresson and that the men were convicts. 'When their sentences were over, they didn't want to leave the labor camp, so they just stayed. They had their friends, et cetera, et cetera. And also, you see'—he spoke seriously—'I think they'd come to like the work.'" (Penelope Gilliatt, *"Le Meneur de Jeu," The New Yorker,* August 23, 1969.)

poral manages, during the fugitive moments they find alone together, to strike up an affectionate relationship: borrowing books, correcting her French, exchanging tendernesses from his unlikely position in the dentist's chair. When the last of his visits takes place, she invites him to choose one of her books to remember her by, and he chooses a volume of Ronsard. "I love Ronsard," she tells him. "A soldier told me you tried to escape. I like a man who's not a slave." An expression of his recognition of what he has allowed himself to become passes across his face, and, back at the camp, he turns on Ballochet: "You in your high tower! You're fattening on this life, aren't you!" The corporal deliberately gets himself into trouble, and is thrown back into the punishment camp. And there he is soon joined by Ballochet, who has chosen to abandon his tower.

Later, in a scene played in a latrine (like those in the dentist's office and others, its emotional pitch both achieved through and transcending an abjectness of place), Ballochet confesses having lost his eyeglasses intentionally during their first attempt to escape, and declares his decision to attempt another. And that night, after sounding the traditional three blows signaling the start of a theatrical performance, he flamboyantly announces to all, "Good night. I'm taking a little stroll . . . as a nobody in search of human dignity. . . . Fear not. My plan's the best for I've no plan at all." He walks out of the barracks, and, in a scene realized chiefly in the expressions of the corporal's face, we wait as the seconds that Ballochet needs to reach the camp's gate are counted off by the men left behind. Reflected in the corporal's face, we read their growing anticipation as Ballochet nears freedom, and their anguish on hearing him shot. Another newsreel insert immediately follows, this one Japanese, but like the several others, British included, that we have seen, boastful of national prowess and offering only images of destruction.

The last escape attempt follows. Improvising on a sudden opportunity, the corporal, Pater and another prisoner pose as surveyors and measure their way out of the camp. In town, after being aided with changes of clothes at the dentist's office by the German girl, they are almost recaptured when chance rescues the corporal and Pater as, dressed in black, they are mistaken for members of a passing funeral procession and given wreaths to carry in it. (The third prisoner, ludicrously outfitted in the Tyrolean costume which was all the girl could offer, is recaptured, but smiles beatifically as he watches Pater and the corporal walking away.) After passage through fire in the form of a bombing, train wreck, and more newsreels, they reach the countryside, and finally near the French border. At a small farm on the German side, they find a German woman living with a French peasant "prisoner" who has been put in her charge to work, the two waiting for confirmation of the death of the woman's husband to marry. The corporal asks the man, "You never made a dash for it? To the land of your ancestors."

"My ancestors never had any land," the man replies.

"My land and my wife are in Paris, so I'm going back," the corporal says. (It is the first time we hear of his wife.)

"And I follow the crowd. My home's where my friend's is," Pater adds. As he says this, we see in the corporal's face (characteristically, in the same shot, without cutting or emphasis) his sudden realization of Pater's dependence on him and of his responsibility for the companion he has led to freedom.

The woman feeds them, and, as they leave, Pater (who had earlier been distrustful of the dentist's daughter) says of her, "She's a friend. A true friend." Their last view of the couple is, from a distance, of them working the farm. A single newsreel shot is inserted of a lone German plane flying overhead. Then we see the corporal and Pater, having reached the outskirts of Paris, in early-morning grayness on a small deserted bridge. The two men stop, and speak somewhat awkwardly. "Surely, someone has always been waiting for you," Pater says. "Maybe, after you've found the one who's waiting . . . Think you'll tackle them again? . . ."

CORPORAL: . . . Paris is beautiful. . . .
PATER: I can see it isn't over.
CORPORAL: No, it's just beginning. Swastikas depress me.
PATER: Then we'll surely meet again, Corporal. Soon . . .
CORPORAL: Very soon, Pop.

Pater leaves. The corporal turns and, taking the opposite direction, as we watch his receding figure from the camera's position on the bridge, walks away.

This last sequence of *The Elusive Corporal* (which may prove to be the last sequence of all of Renoir's films,[8] and is, in its muted way, quite as beautiful a creation as the coda of *Boudu Saved from Drowning*) concludes a section which seems explicitly to recall the final episode of the escape in *Grand Illusion*, as, indeed, *The Elusive Corporal* in its entirety seems thematically to evoke the main body of Renoir's work in films.[9] For a number of critics, the comparison to *Grand Illusion* has been to the later film's disadvantage, revealing a retreat from the political commitment the earlier film seemed to represent. It is true that the Germans in *The Elusive Corporal* are not seen, according to the conventions of World War II, as bestial, or the camp as monstrous, but it's important to remember that the camp isn't a concentration camp and the conditions are not meant to be unbearable. The film *is* a call to resistance, but it's not so much Nazism or even suffering as it is the very condition of enslavement which the corporal stubbornly resists. And, increasingly, the prison camp comes to be seen as a figurative extension of the imprisonments of the world outside: of the commercial exploitation of *The Crime of Monsieur Lange;* the bourgeois family in *A Day in the Country;* the petrifaction of a social class in *The Rules of the Game;* the bondage of artist to audience in *The Golden Coach* and *French Cancan;* the self's own obsessive superego in *The Testament of Dr. Cordelier;* and, indeed, the naturalistically drawn, actual prison of *Grand Illusion.* Yet, for all this, the possibility of individual freedom remains alive[10]—in the imaginative faculty of Lange; the ungovernable spontaneity of the chambermaid, Celestine; the power of the artist (Camilla, Danglard) to liberate his audience through his art; the biological nature which survives the quasi-scientific attempts at man's "improvement" in *Picnic on the Grass;* and in the inextinguishable

8. Shortly after I wrote this, there was news of the completion of a new Renoir film, *Le Petit Théâtre de Jean Renoir.*

9. The film's original title is *Le Caporal Épinglé* (*épinglé* meaning "pinned"); the English title providing, I think, the rare case of a retitling as good as the original if one bears in mind that it is not simply his captors which the corporal eludes.

10. Other than in the rigid and moribund society portrayed in *The Rules of the Game* and (its dominion more circumscribed) in *The Diary of a Chambermaid,* which might be described as a servant's-eye view of the world of the earlier film.

impulse to escape from actual imprisonment which informs the magnificent final passages of *Grand Illusion*. It finds its embodiment, above all, in the elusive corporal, who, though realized in his individual particularity (in a beautifully modulated and vivacious performance by Jean-Pierre Cassel), remains nevertheless, without psychology or biography, an almost pure expression of the will to freedom. Although there are continual reminders throughout the film that one can *also* be a slave in Paris, the corporal knows that one can *only* be a slave in the world within the camp. Yet one not only escapes *from* something but also *to* something else; and, in this, Pater knows that he has found something in the camp which it will be hard to find again outside. Despite the corporal's promise to share soup from the same pot in Paris, the two men part, and, despite the corporal's parting declaration that they will meet again, the film's underlying sadness and ambiguity rests in our sense that probably they will not.

In Renoir's vision, the impulse toward freedom seems always to lead away from community, and, to the degree that Renoir's personality (which does, after all, enter *artistically* into his work) tends toward a gregarious pleasure in fellowship, this vision of freedom is always of something purchased at a heavy price. Of course, the vision of the individual in conflict with society has become a familiar enough one in art since the romantic movement, but it is Renoir's ability to imagine the claims of both poles which distinguishes his work and gives it its breadth and its fervor. Given Renoir's personality, this conflict might furnish the basis for a conservative stance were it resolved in favor of society, but, insofar as the value of individual freedom seems paramount in Renoir's films, the result is a radical but also tragic (or tragicomic) one. The corporal's almost tropistic movement toward freedom is heroic, but to the extent that it is also a movement away from other men, from the fraternal bond of the men in prison, it seems also to represent some sort of failure (albeit not the corporal's alone): a failure to realize or imagine a relationship between men within society in which individual freedom might flourish.

Perhaps Renoir's most positive image of a socialized freedom, a freedom in society, is that of the publishing cooperative in *The Crime of Monsieur Lange,* which requires the malicious intervention of Batala to jeopardize it, yet the cooperative is so essentially a community of fantasists as hardly to suggest possibilities available in any world but its own, its fragile existence sustained chiefly by the breath of fantasy of the film itself. And *The Crime of Monsieur Lange* ends, as recurringly do the other films, on images of escape. Out of the contrary movements toward freedom and society, Renoir has created both his greatest works, among which I number *Boudu Saved from Drowning, The Crime of Monsieur Lange, A Day in the Country, The Rules of the Game, French Cancan, The Testament of Dr. Cordelier,* and *The Elusive Corporal,* and such others falling just short of these as *Grand Illusion, The Diary of a Chambermaid, The Golden Coach, Picnic on the Grass;* and it is the failure to reconcile the two movements which has given his work, despite its immense gaiety, that sadness and ambiguity which characteristically underlie it. The corporal *must* escape, his doing so is his assertion of his humanity, yet, as he leaves Pater and the fraternity of the camp behind, an aspect of his humanity remains unrealized; he remains both elusive and pinned down. For one not only escapes from something but also to something else. And, though he is both beautiful and noble in its performance, the highest act of which the corporal is capable is escape from imprisonment. Like Boudu, he can only escape, and, reimprisoned, escape again.

(1969)

BUÑUEL

On the simplest level, there is Buñuel the foot fetishist. This is the Buñuel who makes films which freely indulge a complex of private obsessions and fantasies—a figure which extends to include Buñuel the sadist, applying razors to the end of literally opening eyes—and, of all the "false Buñuels," it is probably the most persistent. Following close on this is the liberal's Buñuel, scourge of the clergy and bourgeoisie. (In the account of one mindless idolater: "Any child brought up by priests bears some trace of this upbringing. With normal boys, religious education is transformed in time into a healthy reaction *against*. Buñuel was a normal boy."[1]) Frequently in tandem with this appropriation of Buñuel as political ally is the notion of his observational, "documentary" style. ". . . The art of a master like Luis Buñuel lies in his being not only original and radical but also utterly unobtrusive. He simply uses his camera to look at people, plainly, patiently, mostly in mid-shot, without tricks or illusions or ex-

1. Ado Kyrou, *Luis Buñuel: An Introduction*, New York, Simon and Schuster, 1963. It is ironic that Buñuel, who of all major film-makers has been perhaps the most unfailingly lucid and illuminating in commenting on his own work, should also probably be, of all major film-makers, the object of the greatest amount of dithyrambic nonsense by others.

pectations. Like a man whose gift of silence makes other people talk more and more anxiously, Buñuel's camera waits for the characters to reveal themselves—their obsessions, their perversions, their corruptions. The director, meanwhile, defines nothing, asserts nothing; he remains detached, accepting, sardonic."[2] From this follows, especially for those who would agree with such a description but put a less sympathetic construction on it, the sense of Buñuel as cold, withdrawn, uncommunicative.

This last Buñuel makes a prominent appearance in a piece by Pauline Kael that is virtually a little anthology of "false Buñuels."[3] (As it is the measure of most of what passes for criticism in the specialist film books and magazines[4] that it seems as worthless when capable of being adduced in support of one's own view as it seems irrelevant as something to take issue with, so also is it true that one can often learn as much in disagreeing with the "mistakes" of a good critic as one can from finding one's own and the critic's views in agreement. And, in many ways, Miss Kael's is the most valuable Buñuel criticism in English; a piece worth taking issue with—as I intend to—and worth appreciating for the clarity and conciseness with which it articulates those issues on which a relevant discussion of Buñuel should take place.) Yet, certainly, Buñuel's films cannot be considered cold in the sense that one may speak of the coldness of, say, the later works of Carl Dreyer, with their wintry refusal to entertain the possibility of any emotional transaction with an audience (an intransigence that can, to be sure, have its own fascination). The coolness of Buñuel's films is not in their relation to their audience, since their aim, above all, is to arouse and disturb that audience, but rather in their relation to their subject. It is that subject—human cruelty and suffering—that is regarded coolly, yet *this* coolness, far from bespeaking an absence of feeling, creates tensions which act to intensify the feelings of the spectator, and is at the heart of the films' impact upon their audience. The camera looks coolly at material of a burning agitation; we cannot. But much as a film by De Sica

2. A. Alvarez, *Beyond All This Fiddle*, New York, Random House, 1969.
3. "Saintliness," *Going Steady*, Boston, Atlantic–Little, Brown, 1970.
4. See, for example, *Luis Buñuel* by Raymond Durgnat, Berkeley, University of California Press, 1968, or almost anything on Buñuel in *Sight and Sound*.

(the De Sica of the neo-realist period, to invoke the artistic model
for the critical orthodoxy ascendant in 1950 when, after a
silence of fifteen years, *Los Olvidados,* or *The Young and the
Damned,* suddenly thrust Buñuel again before an audience's
attention) is so completely suffused by the director's own feeling
that ours can only be carried along by the tide, so conversely
does Buñuel's reticence force us to a response; his reluctance to
draw the conclusion presses us to reach ours. And, to the extent
that we are aware that we are unable to respond, or to respond
adequately, we laugh. It is the laughter of black comedy, and
ultimately one may recognize in it the only response a sane
person can make.

It is this stylistic reticence that has given rise to the notion
of Buñuel's documentary "objectivity," a reticence that does
indeed remain intact between *Land Without Bread* (or *Las
Hurdes*), his one actual documentary film, and the fictional films
which precede and follow it. Yet, if the forgotten wastes of Las
Hurdes do actually exist, they are equally a region of Buñuel's
mind; if they didn't exist, he would have invented them, and he
has, before and after. Buñuel's camera does not "wait . . . without . . . expectations . . . for the characters to reveal themselves"
as though these characters were not of his creation, and their
revelation not the measured effect of that artistic creation and
control. If, in that subjective world which Buñuel's camera
"objectively" evokes, some may be disposed to see merely the
expression of an antipathy toward the clergy and the bourgeoisie,
they must blind themselves both to all that is admirable in
Nazarin (displayed most unmistakably in his angry speech to the
colonel) and all that is corrupt in Jorge, the "progressive" son in
Viridiana, with his radio blaring, "Shake your cares away," and
his games of cards. And if, in that world's ubiquitous fetishism,
some can see only the indication of Buñuel's own idiosyncrasies,
they must disregard the fact that the fetish is a perfect physical
manifestation of the principle of functionless or dislocated energy around which that world revolves and of the harvest of
frustration in which that principle has its issue. For what is the
foot fetish but an instance of the concentration of the most
fundamental human energy and desire on an object in which
there can be found no truly satisfactory consummation—unless

it is by a kick. It is useless, and the uselessness it exemplifies lies at the very center of the world of Buñuel's films, radiating outward in such variegated forms as the hallucinatory jealousy of Francisco (in *El*, released in the U.S. as *This Strange Passion*) and the saintliness of Simon upon his pillar, and finding what is perhaps its most ambiguously disturbing embodiment in the incident of the exploited dog which Jorge releases from his master only to have yet another dog bound to a cart in identical enslavement follow in its wake. We laugh, but why? What do we laugh at when we laugh at Buñuel's films, and why?

Far from there being, as Pauline Kael contends, "no way to get a hold on what Buñuel believes in," Buñuel's films constitute, with a singleness of purpose as unwavering as any to be found in art, a continually unfolding fiction in the form of an almost scientifically methodical testing of the proposition that we are living in the worst of all possible worlds—a belief if ever there was one. It is a world emblematized by its dislocations, whether inflicted by the folly of institutions, as in the saintliness of Simon and bourgeois "virtue" of Don Francisco, or the cruelties of nature, as in the hopeless passion of the dwarf for his full-grown inamorata in *Nazarin;* or, as in the miseries of the Hurdanos, by the complicity of both.[5] It is a world evoked by an art in which loathing, a Swiftian revulsion and disgust, is a motive force; but an art in which, if one cannot really discover a recognizable sympathy or compassion in the "entomological" interest out of which a Francisco is explored, neither is there misanthropy.[6] Socially refined man may indeed be the monstrous creature which populates Buñuel's *Diary of a Chambermaid,* but the human needs on which society is based are depicted in Buñuel's *Adventures of Robinson Crusoe,* seen there undistorted by social institutions, as endowed with both dignity and a kind of beauty. If then, as Pauline Kael says, "Buñuel makes the charitable the butt of humor," it is not necessarily the impulse

5. And, in the words of André Bazin: "It does not matter that they [the Hurdanos] are an exception; what matters is that such a thing can be."
6. Neither, however, is there always that "impression of incorruptible human dignity" which Bazin speaks of finding in *Las Hurdes* and *Los Olvidados.* Indeed, chief among Buñuel's charges against the world as it is made is precisely its power and propensity to strip man of his dignity and corrupt him.

toward charity that is being ridiculed. The charitable impulse of Nazarin is never impugned (nor is that of the enlightened reformatory director in *Los Olvidados*, or that of Jorge toward the dog), but the main fact about Nazarin as about them all is that he's ineffectual, irrelevant to the plight of those to whom his charity is directed, *useless*. "You're thoroughly good and I'm thoroughly bad, and neither of us serves any purpose," the thief tells Nazarin in prison. Nazarin is as self-defeating in his charity as Francisco is in his jealousy; he is, like Simon of the desert and Archibaldo de La Cruz, like the young man in *Un Chien Andalou* and the *husband* in *Belle de Jour*, like Don Francisco (and all—church and state—that Don Francisco internalizes and exemplifies), *obsessive;* unyielding in the refusal to compromise with reality. They are not idealists but (like Cordelier, in Renoir's lone Buñuel-like black comedy) absolutists, and it is absurd, faced with a work so richly ambiguous as *Nazarin*, to say, as does Pauline Kael, that Buñuel is "so enraged by the unfulfillment of ideals that he despises dreamers who can't make their dreams come true," or that Buñuel fails to "give in" to the film's final gesture. For, though the specific effect on Nazarin of the woman's gift of the pineapple following his disillusion- ment with saintliness may not be knowable, the affective impact that the woman's mundane charity has on him is unmistakable in every detail of the scene's realization, from his stunned be- wilderment to the final, shattering roll of drums; indeed, it is a case of the final moment of the film (like the last line of Waugh's *The Ordeal of Gilbert Pinfold*) retrospectively transforming everything that we have experienced before. And, though it may be true that one cannot say with certainty that when Buñuel's obsessed characters "lose their faith" they become any more use- ful, it certainly would be false to assert that Buñuel is suggesting that human nature doesn't change, or that he holds a Grand Inquisitor's view of man's basic animality; false to the very es- sence of his films, which are nothing if not a demonstration that we must change human nature and change the institutions that at once distort and reinforce it in its present state; changes to which saintliness is irrelevant. And if it is true that Buñuel's films cannot be made to yield any programmatic definition of what a better human nature might be, it is clearly the implied injunction of his surrealist commitment and of the ribbon of dream which runs through his work that there can be no meaningful change which does not admit and dignify the irrational side of man's nature; this not as a surrender to animality but as a victory for a more whole humanity.

Apart from such things as the mock reformation of Archibaldo and mock damnation of Simon,[7] Nazarin's is the one serious instance of a Buñuel character brought in this world to at least the brink of some fundamental change of nature, though what lies over that brink we cannot know. Yet the importance with which Buñuel invests the critical moment in which that change hangs in the balance, the respect he accords it, is never in doubt. Buñuel's scorn is reserved for such change's substitute and counterfeit: for those anodyne half-measures which serve to make clear consciences, of which the most troubling instance is that of Jorge and the dog. For surely what Buñuel makes us see, and laugh at, in Jorge's act is not the particular kindness but its general inadequacy, and, more specifically, the vastness of its inadequacy in conjunction with Jorge's satisfaction in having acted virtuously. It is not the "saving one Jew from the ovens or one Biafran baby from starvation" that we laugh at, in Pauline Kael's emotionally charged comparison, but ourselves, and our ameliorative checks to the Biafra relief fund, which ameliorate, to be sure, while things go on essentially as before. Is Jorge only a realist

7. Seldom can any sequence in films as straightforward as the ending of *Simon of the Desert* have been met with such obtuseness as that of most of the film's American critics. For, far from revealing to us Buñuel's vision of hell (and its impoverishment), *Simon* ends with a brilliantly insolent joke on the banality of "sin." Simon, unchanged in his "damnation," sits in a discothèque, sipping Coke, mechanically trading formulae ("Devil behind me!"—"Devil above you!") with Satan, both locked no less than before in their mutual irrelevance; it is, after all, the devil who describes the kids' innocuous dance as "Radioactive flesh . . . the latest and the last," and who earlier remarks to Simon, "We're very similar, you and I." Moreover, anyone reading the ending as originally written (published in *Three Screenplays*, New York, the Orion Press, 1969, with interpretive comments one takes on faith and reason not to be by Buñuel) can see that the ending as filmed has been made to emphasize just this joke, and that no shortage of money can, as has been alleged, be held accountable for the differences. But the strongest argument for one's understanding Buñuel's joke as I have described it is simply this: it, and not the moralistic interpretation of the critics, is totally in character with everything in the film (and in Buñuel's work) that has gone before.

who does what he can? But it is just this kind of realism, and the reality that shapes it, which Buñuel exposes to our shamed laughter. Yet Buñuel's scorn for our ameliorist liberalism comes not from the side of a Lawrence or Pound, as Pauline Kael misleadingly suggests, but from that of a surrealist anarchism.[8] And though we may be unable to appropriate him to any congenial reformism, the fact remains that his refusal to make the reformist statements is precisely that quality in his work which, in its denial of feelings to assuage ours, presses us to our own confrontation.[9] Upon our habitual numbness, Buñuel's films exert the terrible pressure of the noncommittal. And we laugh.

We laugh, in black comedy, at a vision of the world so intensely terrible that only our laughter can relieve its pressure; we laugh, at its very extremity, in order to endure it. (And it is no paradox that, but for the unflaggingly witty *Simon of the Desert*, Buñuel's deliberately light or playful films—*The Criminal Life of Archibaldo de La Cruz* or *Belle de Jour* or *The Milky Way* —are actually less funny than the darker ones.) It is the world of Modot in *L'Age d'Or*, the Hurdanos, the forgotten ones of Mexico City, Nazarin, Viridiana and her Uncle Jaime, Celestine the chambermaid and Joseph the fascist brute. It is a world at the very center of which lives Francisco in *El*, like a character out of French bedroom farce except that the farce is being played in his head. Whether prosecuting his paranoid legal suit (whose fortunes are so intertwined with those of his marriage) to redress some ancient grievance, straightening a picture or his wife's shoes, or scurrying around the house in his bathrobe with his queer assortment of implements, he is a figure as preposterous (in his sheer ineffectuality) as he is inescapably disturbing. Francisco is continually creating situations in which all alternatives confirm his suspicions; and it is in our sense of the discrepancy between

8. "... In a world so badly made, as ours is, there is only one road—rebellion." (Buñuel, quoted in Kyrou, *op. cit.*)

9. "I will let Friedrich Engels speak for me. He defines the function of the novelist (and here read film maker) thus: 'The novelist will have acquitted himself honorably of his task when, by means of an accurate portrait of authentic social relations, he will have destroyed the conventional view of the nature of those relations, shattered the optimism of the bourgeois world, and forced the reader to question the permanency of the prevailing order, and this even if the author does not offer us any solutions, even if he does not clearly takes sides.'" (Buñuel, quoted *ibid.*)

things as they are, things as he imagines them, and the elaborate, self-defeating stratagems by which he attempts to deal with things as he imagines them, that the film's comedy lies. And yet, recognizably, his world is ours, and he its creation; almost, one might say, its purest creation. For the madman is also the model citizen and perfect Christian gentleman; the product of the institutions which sanction him. "Don't hurt him! He's my friend!" cries the priest, at the end, of the victim of that "friendship," and it is a cry into which Buñuel has managed to infuse not only his icy rage but also something surprisingly like compassion. If, then, we laugh, what is our laughter, the laughter of black comedy, but a strategy for preserving sanity while contemplating the intolerable? And, if the "entomological" interest can yield this, as it yields also the tortured Modot, the miseries of the Hurdanos and *los olvidados,* the agony of Nazarin, the convulsions of innocence in *Viridiana* and decadence in *The Diary of a Chambermaid,* then one must acknowledge that Buñuel's "coolness" is something which may contain passion; that it is, like the "coolness" of a Brecht or Bresson, an instance of the transformation of passion by art. And the sensitizing effect this coolness produces on us is a testimony to the degree of passion Buñuel's art truly contains.

"What can I do against . . . the idiotic multitude which has pronounced as *beautiful* or *poetic* what in essence is only a desperate and passionate appeal to murder?"[10] Unlike the later work of a Welles or von Sternberg, Buñuel's films are marked by an evolution *away* from pictorial beauty, from richness of decor and what newspapermen are given to calling "poetry" in films, and toward a kind of stripped-down bluntness. Probably, *Los Olvidados* is the last of Buñuel's films to be visually striking in a way that immediately connects with the brilliant imagery of *Un Chien Andalou* and *L'Age d'Or;* thereafter, "beauty" is to be found in the autumnal rotting leaves and deliberately revolting, overripe beauty of *The Diary of a Chambermaid* and (to some degree) *Belle de Jour.* (Indeed, it is a tribute to the resolve with which Buñuel has sought this antibeauty that he has been

10. Buñuel, *L'Age d'Or and Un Chien Andalou,* New York, Simon and Schuster, 1969.

able consistently to impose his own characteristic visual directness
on the work of Gabriel Figueroa, Mexico's most famous cine-
matographer and one notorious for his penchant for lush effects.) The images of Buñuel's films are conceived as those not
of a plastic but a dramatic art, and what they lack in beauty they
make up in strength, a strength which has its own beauty. Perhaps, Buñuel's "Last Supper" from *Viridiana* may be taken to
typify that myriad of indelible images with which his work
abounds, from the severed hand in *Un Chien Andalou* to Simon
on his column; and to typify also that quality of Buñuel's art
which is probably most problematical for an audience bred on
a modern aesthetic: its lack of subtlety. Yet is subtlety an inalterably superior virtue in art? I think not, and think that
Buñuel's films make what is possibly the most powerful argument
in contemporary art for its opposite: one might call it boldness.
Yet if, like much that is great in Buñuel, the "Last Supper" is
unsubtle, it is, for that, no less complex. Beyond symbol or
parody, it fixes itself in our imagination as another Last Supper
to set beside Christ's, and to throw open, by its separate existence,
the values upon which a world is based. Like Francisco's house,
with its mysteriously closed-off, darkened room, and his final
zigzagging walk, both exact objectifications of his convoluted
psyche, like the crucifix which conceals a blade in *Viridiana,* a
common item found throughout Spain,[11] it symbolizes nothing,
if, indeed, anything in Buñuel's work can accurately be called
symbolic. Rather, they are all a surrealist art's autonomous
"found objects"; physical manifestations of the irrational, whose
"meaning" lies not in correspondences but in themselves and is
to be discovered not behind their disguises but in their juxta-
positions.

   ". . . Technique is no problem for me."[12] Buñuel's technical
"indifference" has been remarked on by a number of critics, both
those who, like Pauline Kael, seem unsure whether there isn't
more to admire in it than to deplore and others, like James
Price, who writes:

11. "One day my sister, who is very religious, met a nun who was using one of
these same little knives to peel apples." (Buñuel, quoted in Kyrou, *op. cit.*)
12. Buñuel, quoted *ibid.*

He has an instinctive gift; but sometimes one wishes he hadn't, and that instead he had to grapple with his equipment to make it answer his purposes, that sometimes a technical difficulty would actually *alter* what it was he wanted to do or say. The art and literature we value most very often exhibits the signs of the artist's struggle with his means. But Buñuel's films never do. . . . Mallarmé fought with language, Michelangelo with stone, and Beethoven with the combinations of sound capable of being produced by a string quartet. In Buñuel's case the sense of creative tension which this kind of struggle produces is absent.[13]

No matter how one chooses to construe "indifference," the common judgment on the "indifference" of the acting in Buñuel's films should not be allowed to go unchallenged, given such extraordinary performances as those of Gaston Modot in *L'Age d'Or,* Dan O'Herlihy in *The Adventures of Robinson Crusoe,* Arturo de Cordova in *El,* Francisco Rabal in *Nazarin,* Jeanne Moreau in *The Diary of a Chambermaid,* and Pierre Clementi in *Belle de Jour,* among others. But there is a sense in which what James Price says is true, and also capable of another construction. Buñuel's art *does* evince a struggle, not so much technical as formal—as in the failures to integrate the nonnaturalistic premise of *The Exterminating Angel* to its realistic mode, or adequately to sustain the parity of plot and theme in *Belle de Jour;* both failures aspects of Buñuel's major problem as an artist: that of reconciling his surrealist perception of the world with his fundamental allegiance to an art of narrative realism. Yet I wouldn't wish to defend Buñuel against Price's comment by instancing these failures. I think, rather, that one must situate Buñuel in a different (antiromantic) artistic "tradition" from that of Beethoven and Mallarmé; in that of, say, Cervantes, Haydn, Picasso, Thelonius Monk; artists who, however disparate their technical resources, nevertheless share the characteristic of seeming always to have possessed all the technical means needed for their expressive ends; and the tradition especially of such artists as Swift, Melville, Dostoyevsky, Strindberg, whose imaginative struggle was not primarily with art but with the world. Such prospect as one can see for the out-

13. "The Andalusian Smile: Reflections on Luis Buñuel," *Evergreen Review,* No. 40, April 1966.

come of that struggle which rages through Buñuel's art may indeed appear bleak; it is hard to think of many other artists whose work has offered in such warring combination so dark a pessimism about the world with so great an urgency to remake it. And yet Buñuel's pessimism, far from being depressing, is elating; there is, in films, almost nothing else I can think of which so engages this paradoxical quality save for Kurosawa's *Yojimbo*. In Buñuel's work as in the Kurosawa film, a vision of the world of an almost overpowering blackness is somehow felt to be exhilarating. Our exhilaration is that of watching while someone we sense to be of an exemplary sanity shows us what is, for him, the truth.

(1970)

A PERSISTENCE OF VISION

> ... The frontier is the outer edge of the wave—the meeting point between savagery and civilization.—FREDERICK JACKSON TURNER

The Man Who Shot Liberty Valance is a fascinating film, but a film whose fascination lies less in what it is in itself than in what it reveals about the art of its maker, John Ford. In itself, it is a sporadically imagined work; passages which are fully realized artistically alternating with others which merely point sketchily to what they might have been, with another cast, perhaps, or another budget, or in another time. And yet, in a curious way, the sight of a barrel-bellied, fifty-five-year-old John Wayne heaving himself onto a horse, hopelessly destructive as it is of any suspension of disbelief, does nevertheless evoke feelings which no then thirty-five-year-old actor could summon. At moments such as these and others played out in obvious sets and against painted backdrops, the film as an artistic creation is scarcely even pretended at; rather, the effect is of a lecture-demonstration, or an essay on the Western; a summing up. And it is as this—as a self-exegetical essay—that the film takes on its peculiar but real excitement—even those sets and backdrops charged with their special significance. Despite its bearing on his films before, nothing in John Ford's previous work could have quite prepared one for it, and, faced with the fact of its existence, the stock figure of John Ford, notoriously taciturn interviewee and putative "folk artist," will hardly stand up to further perpetuation.

The film opens on an image of a nineteenth-century railway train, whistling and steaming its way round a bend through a pastoral landscape; an image which, in the serene self-sufficiency of its curves and perspectives, seems somehow to contain a world. The train pulls into a small Western town where an old man is waiting to greet two of the passengers, who, it transpires in the flurry of activity which follows their arrival, are Ransom Stoddard, a United States senator, and Hallie, his wife. Questioned by a reporter on the reason for his surprise visit, the senator replies with a smooth politician's blend of orotundity and evasiveness, but he finally consents to visit the newspaper office to give an interview. His wife and the old man are left in the latter's buckboard wagon, where they sit awkwardly and exchange guarded reminiscences without looking at one another; the moment, as indeed the entirety of the opening and closing sequences which frame the action of the film, photographed in a just sufficiently higher key than the body of the film to impart a slightly bleached or faded quality to the image. The man, Link, tells her that the cactus rose is blooming, and, at her request, they drive out to the site of an old, burned-down house near whose ruins he picks a cactus rose for her.

At the interview, the senator refuses to divulge more than that he has come to attend the funeral of Tom Doniphon, whose name is unknown to the reporters. He is rejoined by his wife and the old man, and together they enter the undertaker's establishment; the three walking stiffly to view the plain wooden box provided for county burials. An old black man sits beside it; slowly, he and the newcomers recognize each other; the black man crying, the woman going consolingly to him. The senator looks inside the coffin, and is angered to see the body is without boots, spurs, and gun; he orders the undertaker to put them on. "He didn't carry no hand gun, Ranse," Link tells him. "He didn't for years." The four sit silently, absorbed in their mourning of the past, when the present breaks rudely in on them in the form of the newspaper editor pursuing his story in the name of the public's right to know—contemporary cant. The wife nods her consent and the senator goes out, leaving the other three to their private griefs. Repairing to a place nearby, the senator discovers the cobwebbed wreck of a stagecoach, and is led by memory into his story.

At once, in a flashback, we are met with a burst of vigorous action in a world seen more vividly than the "present" in its low-key, high-contrast photography. A stagecoach—in a "landscape" that, to strange effect, is recognizably a set—is ambushed and robbed with brutal viciousness by a band of men in long white coats. One of the passengers, the young Ransom Stoddard, protests, as a lawyer, in the name of the law; the gang's leader, thrown by this into a paroxysmal rage, sets upon Stoddard, rips up his lawbooks and takes him off to beat him savagely, shouting: "I'll teach you law—Western law!" Ironically, the bandit's name is "Liberty." Later, the beaten man is found and brought to a house in town by Tom Doniphon and his black "boy," Pompey; Tom treating Stoddard with an odd mixture of roughness and gentleness, a mixture which he manages to impart even to the name by which he addresses him: "Pilgrim." Revived, Stoddard discovers that the robbery has been committed outside the jurisdiction of the town's timorous sheriff, and he declares his intention to bring his assailant to justice—to jail, not kill, him. "Out here a man settles his own accounts," Tom tells him. "You're saying what he said! What kind of community have I come to?" Stoddard exclaims incredulously. But his only answer is Tom's exit line, an admonition, classic Western-hero-style, to remember that: "Liberty Valance is the toughest man west of the picket wire—next to me."

The house to which Tom has brought Stoddard is that of his girl, Hallie, and there, robbed and without his lawbooks, Stoddard is forced to remain, working as a kitchen helper in the restaurant run by Hallie's parents. Soon he has become a competitor with Tom for Hallie's affections, offering her, as Tom cannot, the refinements of "civilization"; among them, teaching her to read and write. When Tom brings her a cactus rose (a symbol, through the film, of his peculiar gentleness in toughness), she shows it to Ranse and asks, "Isn't it beautiful?" "Hallie, did you ever see a real rose?" he asks her in reply. Yet Tom's kind of toughness remains indispensable, and, when Liberty Valance makes a sudden appearance at the restaurant and humiliates Ranse, it is Tom and his (and Pompey's) recourse to a gun which causes Valance to back down. "Now I wonder what scared him off. The spectacle of law and order?" Tom derides Ranse. But "I'm staying, and I'm not buying a gun!" Ranse stubbornly reaffirms.

And he stays, setting up practice not only as the town's lawyer but as its schoolteacher; becoming, in fact, the Promethean bringer of all that is civilization in the frontier community; the sense of this effectively conveyed even in such lapsed form as the naïve lesson in racial equality which Pompey's presence in the schoolroom at one point occasions. But civilization burgeons under the threat of Liberty Valance's return, and, when that return suddenly impends, the classroom is abandoned; Pompey fetched by an irate Tom; and Ranse left alone in it to erase the blackboard motto, "Education is the basis of law and order." Surrendering to his situation, Ranse rides out for a shooting lesson to Tom's place; a ranch (an addition to the house being built in the expectation of Tom's marriage to Hallie) where, alone in the film, we experience a movement out into natural landscape and a sense of expansive space. Liberty Valance's return is for the purpose of taking by intimidation the town's votes as delegate to a statehood convention—to cast his vote against the encroachment of civilization on the frontier wilderness. Yet, despite his fiercest efforts (and he is played by Lee Marvin, in the film's best performance, as constituting virtually a sustained explosion of pure, natural malignity), he is frustrated by Tom, who, declining the nomination himself, secures it instead for Stoddard. But the victory only precipitates the final confrontation, a classic Western showdown between Ranse and Valance, in which, despite Ranse's incompetence with a gun and his being first wounded, he manages to kill his antagonist. Tom arrives to find Hallie lovingly tending Ranse, and tersely steps aside in the contest for her: "Sorry I got here too late. . . . I'll be around." But, once away from them, his emotions erupt violently in a fight with two of Valance's former lackeys and a bout of drinking (during which he is watched over

by Pompey, acting—see Leslie Fiedler—the devoted wife); the
outburst ending with Tom returning home in desperate agitation and setting fire to the house he has built for Hallie, where
he sits insensibly until carried out by Pompey. The unfinished
addition bursts into flame as the entire house and stable are
enveloped by the spreading conflagration. At Tom's command,
Pompey frees the horses. The sense, unmistakably, is of not
simply a place but an entire style of life being consumed by
the fire.

The scene shifts abruptly to the circuslike, recognizably contemporary atmosphere of the statehood convention, in the midst
of electing a man to represent the territory in Washington; one
of the nominees is Ranse, described in the nominating speech
as a "lawyer, teacher, but more important . . . a champion of
law and order." During the course of the oratory, Tom appears
at the back of the assembly hall, looking haggard. Another
speaker attacks Ranse as a man whose "only claim" is "that he
killed a man" (someone shouts: "Do you call Liberty Valance a
man!"). Ranse leaves the auditorium, under attack; Tom follows him, calling: "Pilgrim!" The two seclude themselves to
speak to one another, and Ranse demands: "Isn't it enough to
kill a man without trying to build a life on it?" Then, in a flashback within the flashback, Tom tells Ranse (while we resee the
event from his perspective) that the shooting of Liberty Valance
was actually done by him as he stood in the shadows while
Ranse and Valance fought; declaring, in conclusion, that it was
"cold-blooded murder . . . but I can live with it." Tom urges
Ranse to go back and take the nomination, and take Hallie,
too; "You taught her to read and write." Ranse returns to a
gala welcome, the band playing; Tom leaves alone; and the
flashback which is Ranse's story to the editor comes to an end.
But the editor declines to publish the story. "This is the West,
sir. When the legend becomes fact, print the legend."

Ranse rejoins the others still gathered around the coffin, upon
which a cactus rose has been placed. Later, back on the train
which is about to depart, Ranse sits stiffly next to Hallie and
asks her if she'd like to return home to the town to live. "If
you knew how often I dreamed of it," Hallie replies. "My roots

are here. I guess my heart is here. . . . Look at it. It was once a wilderness. Now it's a garden."

He asks her who put the cactus rose on Tom's coffin. She tells him that she did.

But the conversation is suddenly interrupted by the intrusion of the train's conductor, fawning ostentatiously on the senator, who responds by resuming his public face and unctuous politician's manner. The conductor leaves them, declaring, "Nothing's too good for the man who shot Liberty Valance!" and they sink again into a silence resonant with a sense of loss and sadness. The train pulls away from the station. The film's last image is the same as its first but for the reverse of the train's direction as it traverses the landscape, winding through the garden that once was a wilderness: a world.

The world that *The Man Who Shot Liberty Valance* makes manifest is, in fact, that contained by all of John Ford's most personal and deeply imagined films, and the uniqueness of *The Man Who Shot Liberty Valance* consists in its bringing into explicitness what has for so long lain covertly beneath the surface. It is a world not our own but parallel to our own; existing in a relation to our world not that of a mirror but of an analogy; and, though couched most appositely in an historical past we may think we recognize, finally independent of any historical reality and wholly self-contained. That world's archetypal drama is the winning of the West, and the Western the most natural form for its embodiment. Yet, as one watches this archetype being fleshed out imaginatively throughout Ford's work, one gradually comes to see that the winning of the West is ultimately a metaphor for something else, and that the vision which informs Ford's most personal work persists undiminished in films outwardly as diverse as *Young Mr. Lincoln, They Were Expendable,* and *The Quiet Man.*

What the winning of the West means in the context of Ford's films is the conquest of wildness by civilization; the remaking of wilderness into garden; the progress toward union and community. Yet, while it is a relatively simple matter to identify the elements of this drama in such early works as *Drums Along the*

Mohawk or even others as late as *Wagonmaster,* it is not quite so easy to get one's bearings toward the more complex distribution of conceptual values in *The Man Who Shot Liberty Valance.* I don't mean to suggest that these earlier films are slighter works than *The Man Who Shot Liberty Valance;* they are both far greater. And already in the earlier films there is that complex network of cross-reference, of variation and elaboration, which so distinguishes Ford's work and enriches it: the Indian friend of *Drums Along the Mohawk* reappearing to say a last farewell to Nathan Brittles in *She Wore a Yellow Ribbon;* the Indian's handing of a switch to Gil for him to beat his wife in the earlier film and Mary Kate's handing her husband a stick with which to beat her in *The Quiet Man* sounding echoes of each other across a distance of thirteen years; while the Clegg family in *Wagonmaster* seem both the unmistakable heirs of the Clantons in *My Darling Clementine* and the progenitors of Liberty Valance as personifications of an elemental savagery. Nor is it yet that the earlier films are any more conventional than the later; on the contrary, *Wagonmaster* is the film which, in its dispensing with an individual hero for a communal one and with a dramatic structure for the more open, epic form of narrative, spectacle, dance and song, has been characterized by Lindsay Anderson as an avant-garde Western. Yet in both *Drums Along the Mohawk* and *Wagonmaster* the archetypal drama of the progress toward community is played out with a confident balance and a tranquil acceptance of the values that the polarities of wildness and civilization are assumed to possess. Artistically, these works are complex creations; in their meaning, they are whole and beautifully simple. But, by the time of *Liberty Valance,* the scheme of values within which the film's meaning is contained has become so fragmented and ambiguous that one may wonder if it is not that very complexity which accounts for Ford's unwillingness or inability to make of it a wholly satisfying artistic creation. In any event, were a satisfying artistic creation to be made of so ambiguous a clash of values, it would, one feels, be of necessity a drastically different kind of work than those serene and harmonious creations his greatest films have always been.

What is wildness and what civilization in *The Man Who Shot Liberty Valance?* At first, the answers may seem easily come by.

Liberty Valance, his name one letter away from the nomenclature
of allegory, is the incarnation of the frontier's savage wildness,
and he is conquered by Ransom Stoddard as the agent of civilization. Yet it isn't Stoddard but Tom who is the man who shoots
Liberty Valance; and Tom, too, represents wildness—the expansive liberty of the frontier; indeed, he alone in the film is
associated with a sense of unconfined space. (Though, for all I
know, the film's use of sets as its use of black and white may have
been dictated by budgetary considerations, the effect obtained by
both is of a stricter measure of control by the director over the
work's formal and conceptual scheme. This control to some extent
represents a failure of imagination; it would have been possible
and certainly well within Ford's powers to have linked Tom's
presence with spaciousness in a less abstract and artificial way.
Nevertheless, what I wish to stress here is the intention, both
clearly conscious and unmistakable.)

Nor is the film's vision of civilization any less divided. It is, to
be sure, embodied in Ransom Stoddard, the pilgrim, who comes
in the name of the law and nurtures a community in the wilderness; but again it is Tom whose power and sacrifice make the
civilizing process possible; who is able not only to confront and
use violence but to accept the moral responsibility for this: to
"live with it." Yet in what balance is his sacrifice weighed? At
the end, he lies, without guns, stripped of his power, his way of
life vanished into extinction. And Hallie, whom he has given
over to civilization, seems to look back longingly, with no
evidence of her having found happiness, on what she has left
behind. Only Ranse, or the public person he has become, seems to
have flourished in the garden he has cultivated, and even he shows
visible signs of an awareness that it is not Eden.

If Liberty Valance incarnates the furthest extreme of the
frontier's wildness, a wildness taken by its extremity to the borders
of abstraction ("Do you call Liberty Valance a man?"), it is also
true that there is an element of this wildness in Tom, and that,
in killing Valance, he kills also something of himself. This element—the appropriation to the individual of the sole power to
determine the content and contours of his life; the claim, as it
were, to an unbounded moral space—cannot coexist with civilization; nor is it something we, the civilized audience, find congenial

to our own sense of moral style. Probably, apart from Ford, there is no other film-maker fundamentally within the community of liberal sentiment (excepting, that is to say, such cryptofascists as Samuel Fuller) who is able to draw a character so offensive to the liberal sensibility as Tom Doniphon with so great a responsiveness to the heroism and even beauty of his nature. I think there can be no doubt where Ford's sympathies lie in the tendentiously egalitarian sequence of Pompey in Ranse's schoolroom, and yet Stoddard's relation to Pompey smacks unmistakably of paternalism while between Tom and his "boy" one senses a bond of something like love. It would be wrong to suggest, as I may have, that Tom is the sole hero of the film, although he alone is indisputably at its center. The heroism is divided between the two men, and, at least in the earlier sections, one is kept keenly aware of both the gentleness and decency of Ranse and of the moral crudity of Tom's world, across the precarious terrain of which a Liberty Valance can maraud unchecked but for Tom's individual authority. In that world, whatever survives must be able to grow wild; there are no roses but the cactus rose; it is a wilderness. Yet, if Ranse's values are admitted to be both necessary and inevitable, *The Man Who Shot Liberty Valance* is still an elegy to the cactus rose. The future, which is to say the present, belongs to Ranse; yet, for all the gain in stability, a certain grandeur has gone out of it, and even the pilgrim has given way to the politicians. And, though the present may legitimize itself with edifying legends, the film remains a dissenting tribute to the stature of the man who "really" shot Liberty Valance.

John Ford has been making films since 1917, and his work has come, in its entirety, to resemble one vast fiction of such breadth and limpidity as virtually to make it seem a creation of the art of another age. (In speaking of Ford's work, I exclude of necessity his silent films, only one of which I have seen, and have in mind chiefly those of his films dating from the mid-thirties.) More specifically, I think that period of Ford's activity extending roughly from *Stagecoach, Young Mr. Lincoln,* and *Drums Along the Mohawk* in 1939 through *The Sun Shines Bright* in 1953 comprises a body of work constituting an efflorescence of artistic creativity unparalleled in the American film but for the work of

Chaplin and Keaton. Moreover, it seems to me that, again but for Chaplin and Keaton, Ford is the only American director of films whose body of work has the formal beauty, richness of imagination, thematic unity, and wholeness of vision which we associate with artistic greatness as it is commonly understood with respect to the traditional arts. In order to see this, I believe one has to accept and reject several things; to accept, for instance, the Hollywood system in which Ford has had to function and which has required his continually having to buy again the freedom to make a film of his own choosing with others that were commercial successes (a system, however, in which Ford, like Chaplin, could thrive because of having by nature the gifts of a truly popular artist); and accept also Ford's imperfections of nature—his penchant for low comedy and his occasional inclinations toward sentimentality (good Shakespearean and Dickensian faults, respectively). I believe one has to reject, or at least have serious reservations about, such a textbook classic as *The Informer*, which bogs down in a middle-brow artistic pretentiousness that—Ford's characteristic flaws being of another kind (as witness *Three Godfathers*)—seems in retrospect to be more the contribution of Dudley Nichols than of Ford. And one must reject as well the cult of Ford; whether taking the form of Andrew Sarris and *Sight and Sound* hailing a potboiler such as *Seven Women* as a masterwork, or of thirty years of "Fordolatry" restricted to gauzily impressionistic tributes to his masterly visual style; both, in their insularity, confining to the dimensions of a ghetto an art whose reach encompasses a world.

The great theme which runs like a current through Ford's major work is that of the civilizing of wildness; on the largest scale, in the settlement of the West; on the most intimate, in the domestication of his heroes by his heroines through their union. Thematically, the two are twin manifestations of the same process. Through their experience of love, Ford's heroes become civilized; the personal love story becomes a kind of microcosm of the myth of winning the West; the individual instance of the coming of civilization; the entrance into the community of human feeling. Yet, ultimately, the macrocosm is also reciprocative, and the myth of winning the West an external symbolic representation of the individual's initiation into that state of communion. In both instances, there is the same dramatic clash of values: natural values versus civilized ones, to oversimplify—because Ford's women, the agents of civilizing values, certainly possess a natural force as well. And, in both, the process is envisioned as always entailing a loss with the gain: a loss in power and freedom, a gain in insight and humanity.

It has been said that the degree of one's responsiveness to Ford may be measured by whether or not one prefers *Stagecoach* or his subsequent Westerns, and I suppose it is true that, if, like Manny Farber or Robert Warshow, one conceives of the genre as essentially unvaried ritual, *My Darling Clementine* can seem, in Farber's phrase, "a dazzling example of how to ruin" a Western. I think *Stagecoach* is a fine film, and virtually a model of narrative cinema; yet, if it is also a model and perfection of the genre of the action Western, it seems to me still a species of dogmatic rigidity to fail to appreciate the extent to which Ford was able subsequently to create variations on the genre and increasingly to imbue it with a personal content. *Stagecoach,* Ford's first Western in sound, is, of course, already rich with details of sentiment and portraiture that mark it as his own, and, technically, it is a splendid achievement and an announcement of the consolidation of Ford's control over the formal resources of his medium. Yet, in *Drums Along the Mohawk,* made later the same year (and a Western in all but the literal sense, its frontier being New York's Mohawk Valley during the time of the Revolutionary War), one is aware, as one is not in *Stagecoach,* of an imaginative thrust born of the artist's discovery in his materials of the theme which is his own.

Drums Along the Mohawk is a simple film; a narrative of the settlement of a wilderness, with a married couple, the partners relatively undifferentiated in their thematic roles, at its foreground; the two seen against a developing community in which they come to take their place; and the struggle waged between the settlers and their hostile environment (of which Indians, inflamed by a mysterious British agitator, are a virtually abstracted expression) providing its action. It is also a beautiful film; tender in its depiction of new marriage and burgeoning community, heroic in its description of the settlers' determination, and fierce in its portrayal of pioneer suffering and sacrifice. But, by the time of Ford's next Western, *My Darling Clementine*, seven years later, the simple elements of *Drums Along the Mohawk* have been elaborated into a vision as wholly charged with meaning and as distinctively personal as any in films; a vision refined throughout a seven-year period of intense and prolific creativity.

Between *Stagecoach* and *Drums Along the Mohawk*, Ford, in fact, made one other film, *Young Mr. Lincoln*, and, before *My Darling Clementine*, two others, *How Green Was My Valley* and *They Were Expendable*, that are all among his finest achievements. *Young Mr. Lincoln* relates an incident from Lincoln's early life imagined as a legend of his bringing justice to a frontier town, and manages, with lyricism and humor, to evoke both the Lincoln of folklore and the shrewdly practical, inexhaustibly interesting person that the folklore usually obscures; the two Lincolns merging in the astonishingly austere, climactic image of Lincoln, following his first courtroom triumph, framed in the doorway of the courthouse, stiff and awkward against a flat background in a shaft of blinding sunlight, as he steps out into the world to accept the crowd's acclaim. *How Green Was My Valley* is a loving remembrance of a child's coming of age set against the dissolution of a family and community in a Welsh mining village; a sweet and poignant work marred slightly by a tendency toward prettification. *They Were Expendable*, with Wellman's *The Story of G.I. Joe*, one of the two great films of World War II, is Ford's tribute to the gallant last stand of MacArthur's troops in the Philippines in 1941; an epic of valor in defeat realized in a majestic succession of images of PT boats cutting through the sea and straggling lines of men on beaches whose heroic poetry seems to me to justify an attempt to rescue "Homeric" as an adjective with a meaning; and a work, as much as *Young Mr. Lincoln*, having as its imaginative center the establishment of a community at the edge of civilization. It was also in this period between *Stagecoach* and *My Darling Clementine* that Ford made *The Long Voyage Home*, a vividly atmospheric adaptation (photographed by Gregg Toland) of four short sea plays by O'Neill, and *Tobacco Road* from a stage adaptation of the novel whose grossness would defeat any attempt at reclamation, as well as *The Grapes of Wrath*, which, however one may now regard it as a work of social conscience, remains alive in the extraordinary expressiveness of Ford's (and Gregg Toland's) great figures in landscapes.

My Darling Clementine marks the resumption of Ford's work as a maker of Westerns, five others following between it and The Quiet Man in 1952. Of these, My Darling Clementine, Wagonmaster, and Rio Grande seem to me Ford at his best, and the rougher She Wore a Yellow Ribbon (in which John Wayne quite movingly plays an old man twenty years before True Grit) for long stretches not far below this; all of them, with the exception of the bathetic Three Godfathers, engaging with greater or lesser directness the thematic materials made explicit by The Man Who Shot Liberty Valance. Though She Wore a Yellow Ribbon and Rio Grande are often grouped with Fort Apache as Ford's "cavalry trilogy," their combined effect is less that of companion pieces than of a progressive reworking and revision of common materials, the crudeness of the last named (and first made) eventuating in the refinement of the third; such elements as the soldiers' serenade passing from the awkwardness of Fort Apache to the off-screen song of She Wore a Yellow Ribbon to be rewoven into the texture of Rio Grande, whose whole fabric is rich with a sense of ceremony and tradition. Rio Grande seems equally, in the relation between its principals, a preparation for Ford's last great film, The Quiet Man, and, almost as much as that work, tremulous with a pervasive sexuality. Ironically, Ford spoke of The Quiet Man at the time of his making it as his first love story; it is his last. It was followed by a nostalgic and charming return to the desexualized pastoral of Judge Priest and Steamboat Round the Bend in The Sun Shines Bright and by a lightweight erotic entertainment in Mogambo. Apart from one occasionally grand and inconsistent work in The Searchers, it is not until The Man Who Shot Liberty Valance, ten years after The Quiet Man, that one encounters another Ford film with a thematic charge comparable to that his work from Young Mr. Lincoln to The Quiet Man almost invariably bore; and, by the time one does, it is the differences as much as the similarities of which one is aware.

Earlier, I mentioned the special qualities which John Wayne brings to The Man Who Shot Liberty Valance, his association with Ford as long and as fertile as any between actor and director in films. I think there is no need to exaggerate Wayne's capabilities as an actor to appreciate how wonderfully right he is for Ford's films, with that suggestion of both physical bravery and moral crudity his presence now almost iconographically conveys —the icon very much of Ford's creation. Ford's films with Henry Fonda, a much finer actor than Wayne but also a more gentle kind of presence (and, in the context in which Ford tends thematically to see the encounter between male and female, a more androgynous presence), tend to be less dramatic, more lyrical than those with Wayne, and, when they fail, somewhat static. As realized by Fonda, the Ford hero suggests the self-sufficient embodiment of both masculine and feminine grace; in the terms of the Platonic myth of love, needing no complement; an essentially lyrical figure remaining outside the action which he affects but by which he remains largely unaltered. Even in Ford's two masterpieces with Fonda, *Young Mr. Lincoln* and *My Darling Clementine,* the hero remains essentially a figure of undifferentiated sexuality, responding fraternally to the devotion of the young girl in the former and extending his love alike to Clementine and Doc Holliday in the latter. In *My Darling Clementine,* Victor Mature's is really the dramatic role, and his more nearly than Fonda's the figure which, in Wayne's performances, the Ford hero was to become. But it is not really until the succession of films after *My Darling Clementine* through *The Quiet Man* that the Ford hero is consistently imagined as a dramatic one, and Ford's major theme finds its place decisively at his work's center. Yet the effect of these films, revolving so steadily about their thematic polarities, remains not one of repetition but rather of incessant variation and diversity; though the thematic elements remain constant, their imaginative embodiment embracing both the communal hero of *Wagonmaster* and the role reversal of *The Quiet Man,* in which it is the hero who presses the claims of civilization and the heroine who is brought from wildness into domesticity; the idea of the frontier itself proving capable of exerting its figurative power despite a removal to rural Ireland.

Given the unusual degree to which Ford's films have required certain "natural" qualities of the performers in them, the decline in their thematic intensity soon after *The Quiet Man* surely owes in part to their lack of apposite casts due to the loss of some of

Ford's favorites through death or aging. A Richard Widmark or
Carroll Baker may be a better actor than a John Wayne or
Maureen O'Hara, but they are unable to suggest those special
thematic attributes which the screen presences of Wayne and
Maureen O'Hara in Ford's work project so perfectly; which may
explain, in part, why *Cheyenne Autumn*, one of Ford's few attempts to come to grips with actual Western history (the history
of injustice to the Indians) remains so static a pageant. But, if
most of Ford's films since *The Quiet Man* seem almost deliberately
to step aside from the kind of material which might engage his
major theme (though it insistently reasserts itself, if only periph-
erally, even in such minor works as *The Wings of Eagles* and
Donovan's Reef), the appearance of *The Man Who Shot Liberty
Valance* ten years after *The Quiet Man* is testimony to the hold
which that theme continues to have on him, and the extent to
which his work's excitement is bound up with the centrality of
his theme's place in it. But it is testimony also to the extent to
which that theme's elements have been reconceived in a new
relationship. For no longer is the Western conquest imagined in
the instance of the individual's progress toward community. Already, in *The Searchers*, one could see the beginning of a withdrawal of the hero from the center of the personal drama. In
The Man Who Shot Liberty Valance, the love story is gone, and
the "woman's" role (Hallie being merely a passive trophy in the
contest for predominance) taken by Stoddard; he acting as the
agent of civilization, and seen as the custodian of the future. And,
with this shift of emphasis in the values whose tension is sustained
through Ford's major work of more than a decade, the balance
of that work is drastically altered. The finest of Ford's films remain among the few great Apollonian creations in the art of this
century. *The Man Who Shot Liberty Valance* is a sad and bitter
postlude to them: an old man's reverie on the glory of a vanished
wildness.

I have stressed, in this piece, the thematic unity of Ford's work;
the presence throughout it of a persistent imaginative vision; and
have concentrated so much attention on *The Man Who Shot
Liberty Valance* because of the way it retrospectively throws that
vision into a sharper focus. Yet I would be unfaithful to what is

best and what I value most in Ford were I to pretend that *The Man Who Shot Liberty Valance* is more than a half-created epilogue to his finest achievements; or to seem to say that his best work's greatness is experienced through an apprehension of its thematic unity. That Ford's work, like the work of all great literary and dramatic artists, has a thematic unity has been insufficiently stressed,[1] so I have stressed it here. But the experience of that work's greatness remains largely of its sweep and color, its narrative vigor and visual beauty. Ford's films are easy to enjoy; the difficulty to which I have addressed myself is that of properly appreciating them. Above all, however, they are not texts to be explicated but sensuous creations in which to take pleasure. And yet even that immediate pleasure which Ford's work offers so accessibly seems increasingly to lie beyond the pale of the cultivated modern sensibility. At a time when all sentiment has become suspect, is there any basis left to us for appreciating or understanding the work of an artist capable in his greatest films of responding with so unambiguous a strong, simple feeling, such wholeness of spirit and normality of temperament, to the fundamental human virtues of manly gallantry, womanly grace, love, heroism, gentleness? It may be that there is none, in which case the loss is ours.

(1970)

1. Peter Wollen's section on Ford in his mainly jargon-clogged *Signs and Meaning in the Cinema* (Bloomington, Indiana University Press, 1969) is a worthy exception to this, and particularly good in analyzing the range of antinomies that Ford's theme may contain, but a case in which the author's assumption that the continuity of theme in Ford's work is in itself the measure of the work's artistic achievement renders him seemingly incapable of distinguishing Ford's failures from his successes.

FOR AND AGAINST GODARD

> When one says that something is not "real," one is actually saying that
> the author doesn't believe in it.—JORGE LUIS BORGES

Seven years ago, I published a long piece on *Breathless* which
may well have been (and, apart from brief reviews, was almost
certainly) the first serious criticism in praise of Godard in English, and, during the course of which, I invoked comparisons with
A Portrait of the Artist as a Young Man and *Les Demoiselles
d'Avignon*. A short while ago, I was present at a lecture by a film
critic on Godard at which the critic, and he is an intelligent one,
compared Godard to Picasso, called him "*the* artist of the second
half of the twentieth century," and declared *Weekend* to be about
"the history and prehistory of the universe." Before the lecture, I
had asked the critic if he liked *Weekend*. No, he said, he didn't
actually *like* it, but, in the course of seeing it numerous times,
he was starting to.

This is about par for the course. Even Homer nods, but not,
to judge from current cant, Godard; and, in such ardently
Godardite camps as *Sight and Sound* (in which ardor flamed after
initial coolness), one often feels no more is needed than the

242

latest title and synopsis to prepare the ritualistic rave. The sense of ritual is quite real, and twofold, for so far has Godard come to be seen as the film-maker as exemplary figure, ushering in the New Sensibility, rather than as an individual artist of (naturally) inconsistent achievements, that a point granted against Godard now seems to carry with it a loss of ground for all of cinema from its new-found eminence. Godard is the one film-maker about whom one must have a position, and usually an extreme one, and one would need to have something like superhuman confidence in one's own powers of judgment not to feel pressured onto the bandwagon by one's awareness that all the intelligent critics, Susan Sontag chief among them, are already there, passionately on Godard's side, leaving it for people like John Simon and Stanley Kauffmann to attack under a flag of outraged philistinism from the rear. Yet to have mixed feelings, to admire some things in Godard's work while rejecting others, is not to have no position, but only an unhistrionic one. I have now seen thirteen of the fifteen feature-length films he has completed as I write, and I have deeply divided feelings about Godard, feelings bordered on their extremes by the highest admiration and an intense aversion but mainly falling somewhere in between. When I wrote about *Breathless*, I had seen no other of Godard's films (none other, at that time, having been released in the United States). Recently, I saw *Breathless* again, and, despite the complicated reservations I now felt about Godard's art, I found it no less a masterpiece than I had at first, its freshness undiminished by the extent to which its innovations have been cannibalized by commerce, much as Brando's performance in *On the Waterfront* has withstood all onslaughts of imitation and parody. Nor was the renewed excitement of it, so strong as to take me by surprise, simply a case of being bound by my previous critical investment in the work; though I have, in fact, seen only one Godard film which I admire as much—his second full-length film, *Le Petit Soldat*—I saw *Le Petit Soldat* for the first time only after having seen all but a few of the films Godard has made since.

Even if it cannot quite persuade one to join the committed, the *ad hominem* scatological vituperation of a John Simon does provide a chastening illustration of the folly of ignoring their argument that it is foolish to criticize Godard for not doing what he nowhere intends to do. The lecturer I heard described Godard's style as essayistic, a word I thought taken aptly until I realized that it was being extended to validate every inconsistency of the films as imaginative fictions in the name of the freedom of direct address. It is true that Godard is not a narrative artist though he makes extensive use of narrative fictions in his art; Godard's art *is* essayistic in that he has innovated the most supple, lively and brilliant expository style in the history of films, but one needs to remember in this that an expository style is no less (and, in many respects, more) bound by canons of coherence and integrity than a narrative one. Unless, of course, one is appealing to the New Sensibility and the future, in which case, anything goes, because who can tell that it may not?

There is, of course, another word which has been used to sanction everything in Godard's work which is digressive, jarring of tone, "unreal," unbelievable, and self-conscious in calling attention to the films as films, and that word is "Brechtian." It would be interesting, I think, to trace the progress of that word, especially in its application to films, from description to sanctification, but that subject is beyond my scope here, nor is it my intention to denigrate Brecht. Brecht is, I think, a great artist (who, like Homer, nods, as witness *Galileo*), but, unlike Godard, pre-eminently a narrative artist and a poet, whose celebrated theatrical devices were intended to cool off plays of great dramatic fire for didactic purposes, and, contrarily, to enhance their power by the tension created between style and substance (with the contradictory effect possibly not an intended one). Godard is an artist of essentially cool temperament, in whose work Brechtian devices function, at their best, as paradoxes and conceits, and more often as mannerisms; his most self-consciously Brechtian film, *Les Carabiniers,* being not only, to my mind, by far his least successful one, but also the most advanced case of Brecht in the head—of Brecht as a lifeless concept—that I have ever seen. Among films, only Kurosawa's *Yojimbo* has seemed to me truly Brechtian, and this not in any of its trappings but rather in its ironic view of "human nature"—it was Brechtian in spirit, in the way in which such affinities become truly meaningful. In *Les Carabiniers,* characters and events in which there has been not the slightest investment of imaginative energy are endistanced by Brechtian devices. It is like a distance taken on empty space.

Les Carabiniers is, admittedly, an extreme case; a work aping Brecht in its totality, like a bad dream of *Mother Courage*. Elsewhere, in Godard, devices which might be called Brechtian, such as the use of titles and of the actor turning to the audience in direct address, are employed to brilliant effect, but also to strikingly different effect from that to which similar devices are put in the work of Brecht. Though the plot-revealing titles which serve as chapter headings to the episodes of *My Life to Live* may superficially resemble such features in Brecht, their effect in Godard's film is not to diminish suspense but rather to intensify pathos in being a formal equivalent to the deterministic universe in which the prostitute heroine is enmeshed without her comprehending it.[1] Similarly, the profusion of interpolated "titles" from billboards, magazine advertisements, etc., in *The Married Woman*, although frequently providing a commentary on the action in a sense that might be described as Brechtian, provide far beyond this a context, an ambience, for the heroine's affectless dislocation; indeed, becoming, in this film, an element as tangible and animate as the characters themselves. And when the actors in *Masculine Feminine* turn to the camera and begin to speak to us, the action is interrupted and our interest in it temporarily distracted, but the sense achieved is of a *cinéma-vérité* interview in which the subject reveals itself, and, while the critics may go on about the paradoxes of art and life thus embodied as they will, the immediate effect is of an *increased* involvement with the characters' "reality."

If one would be foolish to ask Godard to be what he essentially

---

1. This reading of the film is at considerable variance with that of Susan Sontag in *Against Interpretation,* who takes the heroine's words—"I think you are always responsible for what you do. . . . And free"—at something like face value although they are contradicted by all the events of the film, culminating in the heroine's stunningly abrupt death during a casually violent quarrel between two pimps about who owns her. Indeed, the film's main force and extreme poignancy derive, I think, from just this contradiction between how the heroine conceives herself and what happens to her; this intensified by our being deliberately deprived, in the manner of the *nouveau roman,* of any psychological interpretation of character and event through which this contradiction might be reconciled.

is not, and if he is not Brecht, then what is he? Essentially, a film by Godard is a patchwork of action held together by an intricate, tensely strung network of ideas and associations and by the urgent charge of the technique. Even in his best films (as I noted in writing even of his first), the action seems somewhat randomly distributed through the work as a whole, lacking in that sense of structural necessity which one traditionally apprehends in most great films and works of literary and dramatic art, however episodic in character, and through which one perceives the work's essential unity. In part, this is only to say in a more descriptive way what I have already said: that Godard is not a narrative artist, something which most of his admirers and even Godard himself have been quite willing to concede. My films have a beginning, a middle and end but not necessarily in that order, Godard has said, though, like many of his recent pronouncements, this tends to sound more impressive the less one attempts to look into it.

Yet Godard's best work does have a unity, a unity of theme and of thematically interwoven ideas. The life and energy of a Godard film are pre-eminently conceptual, and this, despite the great vividness and brilliance of detail, in a way that tends always toward abstraction. Godard's films have been frequently contrasted with Antonioni's, and usually to make a point the reverse of which I think is true; for, though it is easy to discuss Antonioni's films with reference to large generalities about the failure of communication (and despite the fact that much of *The Red Desert* does conform to just such a stereotype), a film such as *Eclipse* seems to me marked rather by its extreme concreteness, by the way it resists the attempt to abstract some generalization from the materiality of the characters in their shifting relationships to one another and to the objects they imbue with their emotional resonance.[2] *Eclipse* is *about* its two principal characters; *Breathless* is about the styles of life its chief characters embody and the destinies these styles imply to the extent that one is hardly aware that its climax is psychologically implausible so

2. Which is to say, with respect to my previous observations about the meaning of *L'Avventura*, that Antonioni's films have become much less novelistic than that earlier work.

much is it conceptually necessary and inevitable. Pauline Kael has somewhere spoken of Antonioni as a director of surfaces, and, though the phrase was intended pejoratively, it is possible to extend its meaning to describe one of his films' most impressive qualities—their fidelity to the texture and solidity of the material world. In this sense, Godard might be called, not always happily, a director of depths; at least, he could not be said to be concerned with surface verisimilitude. Where his films attain the abstract power of a *Breathless,* this lack of concern scarcely matters and, indeed, can be felt as a strength and a freedom, as in *Le Petit Soldat* when the protagonist, walking along a crowded street with a gun in his hand to commit political assassination, goes unnoticed by the passers-by in a way that is superficially incredible but given a metaphorical rightness by the film's accelerating thematic movement (and, paradoxically, happens to have been filmed with a hidden camera recording a real street, real people, and their actual failure to react to what was happening). And, conversely, when this power is lacking, Godard's films have seemed debilitated even when most successful as straightforward narrative, as in *Band of Outsiders,* in which the abstract rigor is sacrificed to a failed lyricism, or *Alphaville,* in which the intellectual complexities and great plastic beauty of the film's surface are unable to redeem the Luddite tract at its core.

If it is true that the richness of Godard's best work derives, in great part, from its density of ideas, it must be added that the ideas, too, move toward their furthest limits of abstraction; to that point where, abstracted from argument or context, they can be employed for their poetic reverberations. (The play of ideas in *La Chinoise* is, perhaps, an exception to this.) I have in mind, especially, the use Godard makes of literary ideas and of the quotations from literature with which virtually all his films abound. Like everything else in Godard, these do not always work, but when they do, as in the quotation and paraphrases of Cocteau's ruminations on death from *Thomas the Impostor* in *Le Petit Soldat,* the effect achieved is of both a crystallization and a prismatic dispersion of the theme. But beyond their particular resonance within each individual film, the literary quotations and allusions become cumulatively an expressive parallel to the recurring attempt of Godard's protagonists to arrest something sustaining, however fragmentary, from the chaotic flux of their culture, both high and low, the latter represented by the repeated references to other movies.[3] Much like Pound, Godard ransacks and appropriates all culture to serve his immediate ends, and, though the effect of this can descend at its worst to mere pastiche, it is, as in Pound, almost always accompanied by a freshness of technique and an innovative excitement of a kind probably unmatched in his medium since the days of the silent film masters. Indeed, Godard's films have come increasingly to take on the aspect of a compressed stylistic history of his medium in their combination of natural settings and natural lighting with a revival or, rather, reinvention of the two lost traditions of the silent film: of montage, freed from didactic rigidity in the expressive collages of *Breathless* and *Le Petit Soldat;* and of expressionism, given a new sensuousness in the flattened space and primary colors of *Contempt* and *La Chinoise.* In fact, in the prolific impact he has had in revolutionizing and synthesizing ideas of film style, there is probably no one in his medium to whom Godard can be compared since Griffith. There is, however, another comparison of a different sort which Godard seems almost consciously to be inviting in his most recent work, and through which one may see, in part, what Godard is not.

I have spoken of the essence of a Godard film as a patchwork, and Godard has himself subtitled one of his films, *The Married Woman,* "Fragments of a Film Shot in 1964," though, ironically, these words are used to characterize what is perhaps the most symmetrically structured of all of the films he has made. In the course of a strenuous defense of Godard in *Partisan Review,* Susan Sontag has attempted to justify the fragmentariness, form-

---

3. Apart from their use in *Breathless,* the references to other movies seem to me among the least assimilated and weakest elements of Godard's films, as in such things as the flash title, "Arizona Jules," in *Weekend*—a meaningless transposition between the "Arizona Jim" of Renoir's *The Crime of Monsieur Lange* and the title of Truffaut's *Jules and Jim.* Since those who don't "get" such allusions may feel defensively that they have failed to penetrate to some level of profundity and those who do are invited to self-congratulation, these things have tended to be praised as wit by the only persons who might be capable of knowing better.

lessness, and disunity of Godard's films head-on, without denying the accuracy of these words as description, and again with the determination to meet Godard on terms confined by his intentions. But there is a point beyond which such argument cannot go: the point at which one must attempt to appraise the intentions themselves, and, with this, to understand that, even if it were true that traditional concepts of artistic unity are no longer viable, it does not necessarily follow that disunity is endowed with aesthetic worth. Yet, even short of arguing this, one may feel Miss Sontag's terms do not define the issue precisely. Where Godard's films fail is not in formlessness; *Breathless* is structurally weak yet a spectacular achievement in its more than compensating virtues, whereas *The Married Woman* achieves something like formal perfection at the exorbitant cost of the earlier film's vitality; nor is it in what Miss Sontag has called their "intermittent" plots, a less unprecedented phenomenon in films than she seems to believe. Films as diverse as *Eclipse*, Dovzhenko's *Earth*, Vigo's *L'Atalante*, Renoir's *French Cancan* and Ford's *Wagonmaster* have used plots more or less as pretexts, to be intermittently taken up and abandoned, while their main developmental movement lay elsewhere. When, in *Pierrot le Fou*, a violent cops-and-robbers plot is intermittently grafted onto the study of an intellectual's disaffection, one is troubled not so much by the intermittence as by the grafting; by the failure of the plot to relate organically to the theme.

It is not intermittent plot but intermittent imaginative energy that seems to account for the peculiar impoverishment of so many passages of Godard's work; that gives his work its fitful, partially uncreated quality. In part, this may owe to Godard's improvisatory methods, though the extent to which he actually relies on improvisation has never been made clear; no one expects that even a great improvising artist—Sonny Rollins, for instance—will not on occasion perform erratically. Of Godard's films, only *Breathless* and *Le Petit Soldat* seem to spring from a unifying vision which infuses all their parts, however discursive, with an equal power; despite their narrative intermittence and stylistic fragmentation, possessing a unity of conceptual movement which is beautifully shaped and modulated; and probably *Contempt*

alone, though more seriously flawed a work, has a coherent, over-
arching action capable of containing the film's ideas and feeling.[4]
Where this organic power wavers, there may substitute an application of force as in the violent interludes of *Masculine Feminine;*
and where it is largely lacking, a Godard film might be redefined
as a patchwork of anecdote and unassimilated references held
together by will and marked by the director's personal intrusive-
ness. For it is almost unvaryingly true that Godard's films are at
their most powerful wherever the director is furthest from addressing us in his own voice, the voice that is so insistently present
in the Third World harangues and hippie-guerrilla agitprop of
Weekend.

In *Weekend,* as perhaps never more clearly before, one sees
together what Godard is, what he is not, and what he is in the
act of trying to become. The opening section, with its Swiftian
conceit of modern civilization finding fulfillment in a riot of
horrific highway carnage, is brilliantly stunning; both typical in
the way it has its life as idea and atypical in the way it derives its
intensity not from a complex of associations but rather from the
relentlessness with which a single idea is pushed to its furthest
extremity, incidents escalating from the frustrations of minor col-
lisions to ever bloodier and more casually regarded spectacles
of orgiastic destruction.[5] To this point, the film's meaning is fully
made metaphor, but the director has intentions which take him
beyond, and increasingly we hear Godard's own voice articulating
them; first, in the twin monologues on the Third World, which,
more than anything else, evince how quickly the *cinéma-vérité*-
like interviews which seemed so fresh and vital in *Masculine
Feminine* and only slightly less so in *La Chinoise* have hardened
into stylistic mannerism; and then in the depiction of the new
life of guerrilla warfare in which we are confronted finally with

4. Though this action may be taken over from the Moravia novel from which
Contempt is adapted, it is clearly made Godard's in all its details, the film's
failure stemming from the burden that is placed in it on one's sharing
Godard's conviction that Fritz Lang is a great artist and one's being able to
believe that the film within a film suggests art, both of which elements exist
in the work as imaginatively uncreated assertions.
5. As my language may indicate and is strikingly announced by the long
erotic monologue with which *Weekend* begins, the film's identification of
destructive with thwarted sexual energy is unmistakable.

Godard in his new role of propagandist for the revolution, making films toward the end of remaking the world.

Speaking on the Berkeley campus shortly before he made *Weekend,* Godard remarked, "I think an idea is a theoretical weapon and a film is a theoretical rifle"; soon after *Weekend,* he was advocating art by group, and urging his audience at the premiere of his new film in London to demand the refund of their ticket prices so as to send the money instead to the Eldridge Cleaver Defense Fund, having only a few weeks before announced his last-minute cancellation of a speaking engagement with the message: "Go out into the streets, find the poorest man, pay him my fee, and speak instead to him of sounds and images." My point in mentioning this is not to belittle the particular causes or sentiments involved nor to argue in general the internal inconsistencies and futility of such postures—Eric Bentley has done this better than he apparently now wishes he had in the first part of his essay, "The Pro and Con of Political Theatre."—but rather to note the extent to which such commitment has its palpable effect on Godard's art. For, if the notion that art is a weapon has never demonstrably altered the world, it has altered the art of its adherents. And what one sees in the direct addresses on the Third World and hortatory depictions of life among the new revolutionaries, quite beyond their naïveté as actual politics, is the propagandist's traditional impatience with art itself in Godard's deliberate rejection of those elements of his art from which it drew so much of its richness. Where were once the vivacious character-revealing monologues of *Masculine Feminine* are now monologues which reflect a reluctance to imagine character at all; where were once the complex meditations on the inescapability and inescapable tragedy of political involvement in *Le Petit Soldat* are now recruiting posters for the new life punctuated by titles like "Arizona Jules." Where was once Godard is now neo-Eisenstein.

Perhaps nowhere is this development in Godard's work more strongly sensed than in the images of death which pervade his films, and on which almost all end. Stylized as those images are in *Breathless* or in *My Life to Live* or *Contempt,* they are invested still with the impact of death as an actuality in a sense that is increasingly lost to such later work as *Band of Outsiders* and

Pierrot le Fou, in which death is conceived directly as an abstraction or conceit, unmediated by any imagination of it in its reality. I have spoken earlier of the abstractness of Godard's films, but, in his best work, the pull toward abstraction is always exerted against some element of concreteness. *Breathless* is dense with ideas about death, but when, early in it, a man is killed by a car and Michel walks over to see what happened, crosses himself, and continues on his way, the thing itself seems, here as throughout, never far away. When Arthur dies with exaggerated gestures in *Band of Outsiders,* there are elaborate, echoing cross-references without a compelling embodiment. We are given the depths, but deprived of the surfaces.

With *Weekend,* this tendency comes full circle, for, as though unwilling to trust that the harrowing black comedy of the film's first section is sufficient to arouse his audience, Godard goes on to stage a real slaughter of real animals. Again there is the application of force in the absence of power; and again, despite Godard's incomparably greater intellectual complexity and suppleness of style, one is reminded of Eisenstein. As with Eisenstein, art is sacrificed to the exigencies of didacticism, but, as with Eisenstein, an exigent didacticism becomes both a virtuous armor and an alibi. For one needn't feel repelled by such activity as a failure of humanity to see that it is also an artistic failure: reality by default of the artist's imagination.

There is a sense in which, as Robin Wood has suggested in a piece in *New Left Review,* all of Godard's films until *Weekend,* strikingly different from each other as they are, can be seen as embryonically present, both stylistically and thematically, in *Breathless.* In all, alienated protagonists attempt to wrest for themselves a coherent identity and an epistemology from the fragments of their culture and its debris. "A person ought to feel unified," says Belmondo as Godard's alter ego in *Pierrot le Fou.* And, as in the case of Resnais, different as he and Godard are in almost every particular, one sees in such moments an epitome of how the artist, especially one practicing self-consciously an art of highly developed technique, can make, of his own artistic weaknesses, his subject.

Godard is, I think, an artist with serious weaknesses. He is also one of the handful of stylistically innovative geniuses to have worked in films, and an artist whose first two works are among the masterpieces of his medium. None of Godard's subsequent films (and, of the full-length films he has made before *Weekend,* I have not seen *Made in U.S.A.* and *Deux ou Trois Choses*[6]) seems to me quite as consistently good as these, though *Contempt* falls just short of them and my admiration for *Masculine Feminine,* and such intentionally lighter works as *A Woman Is a Woman* and *La Chinoise,* is considerable. In writing on *Breathless,* I tried to show, in detail, how a particular Godard film works; in this piece, I have rather been concerned with what seem to me the general tendencies of Godard's work seen in its entirety. Inasmuch as current writing on the subject seems mainly to divide into the passionately pro or con, this piece has been against Godard; against, at least, the unqualified adulation of him. Otherwise, even where I take exception to a number of the characteristics of his work, I would like not to think of it so. There is much, especially in Godard's most recent films, which I reject or dislike, but nowhere, apart from *Les Carabiniers,* are these feelings unmixed with admiration. I go now to each new Godard film with a certain skepticism, even an anticipatory resistance, as well as with some anxious expectations of the work's difficulty, but never without an anticipation also of immense intellectual excitement of a kind that Godard has virtually introduced into films singlehandedly. For this achievement, one must have admiration, even while acknowledging what may be the defects of its virtues. To eulogize indiscriminately both defects and virtues is only to bring all praise of Godard into disrepute.

(1969)

---

6. I have since seen the latter, and admire it greatly.

SATYAJIT RAY: AN APPRECIATION

Satyajit Ray has, as of my writing, directed seventeen films, some half-dozen of which have been commercially released in the United States. His first film, *Pather Panchali,* achieved a certain success in this country, in part due to its image as a kind of "UNESCO cinema" and of Ray as the heir to De Sica (though the UNESCO phrase was coined by a detractor to whom the De Sica linkage would doubtless be equally damaging). *Pather Panchali* was the first film of a trilogy, the second of which was *Aparajito* (which tended to bear out ascriptions of a De Sica influence), and the third, *The World of Apu;* shown as a triple bill, the trilogy as a whole also achieved a measure of success in the early sixties with the college audience. Even such success, however, was never to be repeated. Though most new Ray films manage to make a dutiful appearance at the New York and San Francisco film festivals, where they can usually count on cross-cultural pieties and unsold tickets, it is almost invariably to be swallowed up afterward by a silence as inviolable as that from which they suddenly emerged; Godard makes conversation, and, meanwhile, the campus crowds have discovered more congenial pleasures in double bills of Richard Lester. In the midst of the hippie-rock-raga boom, I have sat in a San Francisco theater during a rare Ray booking, and found myself barely shouting distance from the nearest person to me in the audience.

Why this should be so I cannot with certainty say, though certainly it is not that Ray's films themselves are inherently inaccessible. On the one occasion when I had an opportunity to program a public showing of a film by Ray (at an art museum, for an audience which mainly subscribed to an entire film series and thus did not have to be lured to the Ray film in particular), it was the most warmly received work in a company of those by filmmakers almost all of whom are able to attract a larger American audience to any one of their films than has attended all of Ray's films together. Not the least of the reasons for the way popularity has eluded Ray has been, I would guess, the unmysterious one of the absence in his films of "stars," even of the more highbrow sort (Belmondo, Karina, Léaud, etc.) that has been featured in the films of Godard and has accounted perhaps more than generally acknowledged for even such limited popularity as Godard's films have attained (though by now their director, cool smile and inseparable shades, has himself achieved this sort of stardom). Ray has tended to favor the use of nonprofessional actors in his films, and, at least in the West, the failure of his principals to attract a following has been intensified by what might be called the wog syndrome, in which a Soumitra Chatterjee is virtually indistinguishable from a Madhabi Mukherjee. For the Western audience, one Ravi Shankar probably taxes recognitory faculties to the full.

In any event, this is not likely to be true of Ray's forthcoming work, for which one may at last expect some general exhibition in the West as it has been announced as an English-language film to feature Peter Sellers; and, though it seems hardly credible that any Ray film could do for its director's reputation what *Blow-Up* has for Antonioni's, some larger public seems assured. In fact, whatever effect Ray's new film may have on his reputation, I think it can have none on his actual stature; and this, given his existing body of work, even if it should be a virtually unmitigated disaster. And that stature, to put it bluntly (and judging from the eleven of his films I have seen), is quite simply of being one of the half-dozen or so greatest artists ever to have worked in films.

Despite the UNESCO label, which, once applied, has tended to stick, perhaps the most remarkable aspect of Ray's body of work is its range and versatility. Even within the trilogy, each of the films is strikingly different from the others: *Pather Panchali,* a Dovzhenko-like poem of the earth and of human lives coming to definition against the anonymity of nature's cycles; *Aparajito,* owing less perhaps to De Sica than to Zavattini in the latter's call for an open form; and *The World of Apu,* in which a narrative of spiritual questing that reminds one of Hesse in its largeness of gesture is given an embodiment whose critical detachment and admittance of a natural world are as different from the emotional posturing of Hesse as they are again from any of the stereotypes of a film by Ray. Before completing the trilogy, Ray made two other works, *The Philosopher's Stone,* a comic fantasy and the only one of Ray's films I would characterize as slight, and *The Music Room,* a Gothic study in obsession and decay that more nearly evokes the fateful cosmos of a Kleist (and of his "St. Cecilia, or The Power of Music," in particular) than it does any world of a perfectable human nature. Despite its backdrop of societal transformation, the essential force of *The Music Room* resides in the extent to which we are drawn into its protagonist's proud madness; the extent to which we are brought even to admire the declining aristocrat's compulsive sacrifice of all else to the thrall of a more perfect music.

Now I mention names like Hesse and Kleist not to ascribe influences nor even less to provide dignity by association for an artist I regard, in both cases, a richer one than those to whom I make comparisons; rather, to suggest succinctly some sense of the effects, and the variety of effects, which Ray's art encompasses. Nor have I come close to exhausting the range of character there is to be described in it. For what is the longer story of *Two Daughters* if not the classic "Jewish mother" joke taken beyond this to become a joyous celebration of sexual awakening, and *Mahanagar* (or *The Big City*) but a Hollywood of the thirties-style sophisticated comedy of the emancipated female and sexual role reversals, which, once deftly achieved at this level, unobtrusively extends itself to work at quite another. *Mahanagar* is probably also, quite apart from Hollywood comparisons, one of the least typical of Ray films in being one of the most visibly

plotted. As in those farces it resembles, the action develops with
a kind of independently propellent comic logic; when the wife
is forced by family economics to go out into the world and get
a job, we know her husband will eventually lose his; the logic
of the situation demands it. But, even as this comedy of situation
is allowed to run its traditional course, the characters in it are
so fully fleshed out as to create of their relations a comedy of
character that is both remarkably interactive with the farcical
action and yet developmentally independent of its motoric drive.

Mahanagar has been judged a relative failure in Ray's work
(its farcical plottedness measured against a Zavattini-like norm)
by several of those critics favorably disposed toward him, who
often seem as unresponsive as those disposed against to the formal
and temperamental variety with which Ray's work abounds; for
my own part, such distinctions as I would wish to draw between
Mahanagar and Ray's best work are fine. Elsewhere, though the
action of *Kanchenjunga* is no less plotted, it is done so rather
through the more oblique interaction of a large number of characters in their shifting combinations that reminds one of the plays
of Chekhov in the way its nuanced movement conceals its dramatic strength and its drama is conceived through the chemistry
of reacting characters. Yet *Kanchenjunga,* too, is a film that has
disappointed several of Ray's admirers, and one is reminded again
in this how ill served Ray has often been by even his admiring
critics, whose writing is often full of a praise for Ray's "humanism" which succeeds only in making his work sound like the
hopelessly dull UNESCO cinema its hostile critics have claimed
it to be.

Whatever qualities talk of "humanism" may actually refer to
in Ray, it seems to me that the salient quality of his work is its
almost intoxicating sensuousness, its all but overwhelming apprehension of a physical world of flesh and fabrics, textures, tangible
surfaces, material presences, odors, sexual vibrations, body heat;
probably no other films convey to one as do Ray's the sense of an
actual temperature emanated from the screen. What one can say
critically of such an accomplishment, I do not know; perhaps one
can only attempt to appreciate it. Ray's films defy analysis in the
literal sense of being entities which it seems virtually impossible
to separate into their component parts—that is to say, theme,

style, etc.—even for purposes of discussion. They are narratives, stories about people, of such lucid simplicity that even art itself seems to disappear into their general transparency. I do not mean to give the impression that all of Ray's work is equally achieved and of a constant perfection. *Aparajito* may be lacking in focus; *Mahanagar* may evidence some excess of manipulation; there may be fleeting moments in *Devi* when the sexually charged atmosphere thins long enough for one to glimpse a trace of that thesis on religious superstition about which a paraphrase of the work can make it sound. But of those film-makers whom I would unhesitatingly call great (and, to qualify what I am about to say fairly, there is none of these who has made as few films as has Ray) there is none other whose total body of work is so preponderantly at the level of the best of it.

Ray's films are perhaps the supreme instance in film of a purely narrative art; one—like Chekhov's, in his stories—in which all abstract meaning is merged into a narrative whose reality seems to be confluent with our own; whose characters seem as fully alive, and whose events seem as wholly independent of artistic arrangement. Possibly one can say that much in Ray's films is touched by a sense of the primacy of life's natural rhythms over any plans which individuals may try to impose on them; but, if this sense does enter into the films, it is not as an abstract idea, or theme whose working out may be explicated by the action, but rather as something which the action is exactly equivalent to and which it celebrates. "Usually this happens naturally. If not, we must make it happen," the young husband in *Two Daughters* pontificates to his reluctant bride after her forced marriage.

"You just got married," he reminds her.

"I didn't!" she cries.

". . . I mean you did but you didn't want to."

And later, when, after runing away and their long separation, she returns to him: "You came here! Why?"

Because, she answers, "I wanted to."

And the film itself, like all of Ray's films, is no more and no less than a celebration of those forces in life which, in their own time and fathomless mystery, bring things together, and rend them apart.

(1969)

FOUR | **SPECTATORS**

ON AGEE ON FILM

I | NOT QUITE ON PAPER

As one of the book reviewisms put it, James Agee, for a number of years, has had an underground reputation as America's best film critic. The phrase may be slightly redundant—after all, what but an underground considers such reputations worth establishing?—and the sense of an underground tends to go a little fuzzy when one finds it includes people like the man from the Saturday Review Syndicate. But one can hardly blame Agee for this; he is no longer free to choose his company. How we love our dead artists!—perhaps we even like them better that way. Scott Fitzgerald, Dylan Thomas, Charlie Parker: these are our cultural folk heroes, deities of self-destruction and defeat. And so it satisfies our morbid sentimentality to award posthumous prizes to those we hardly knew when they were alive, hoping always that next year we may again be so lucky.

There is something depressing about reading James Agee's collected film criticism,[1] but it is an effect for which he cannot be

1. *Agee on Film,* Volume One, New York, McDowell Obolensky, 1958; republished by the Universal Library, Grosset and Dunlap, in 1969.

held responsible. It is simply that, despite the wit and intelligence
with which Agee deals with them, it is dispiriting to see memorial-
ized so many appalling movies otherwise mercifully forgotten,
and, with this, a record of the hours of one's own life misspent
with them. It arises necessarily that much of his criticism owes its
interest to the extent to which the writing illuminates the mind
of the critic rather than the work criticized. After all, movies
like *And the Angels Sing, Bride by Mistake,* or *Roger Touhy,
Gangster* have to be less important than what any sensitive and
intelligent person can say about them. And so, if much of Agee
on film contributes more to an understanding of Agee than of
the movies, there are only the movies to blame. He, I am sure,
didn't want it that way, and despite the highly subjective tone
of his criticism it is, finally, remarkably self-effacing.

Still, a general sense of Agee's basic attitudes toward the medium does emerge from his particular reviews. The movies must
work for, and through, the eyes.

> . . . there is only one rule for movies that I finally care about: that
> the film interest the eyes, and do its job through the eyes.

> Most movies are made in the evident assumption that the audience
> is passive and wants to remain passive; every effort is made to do all
> the work—the seeing, the explaining, the understanding, even the
> feeling . . . pictures are not acts of seduction or of benign enslave-
> ment but of liberation, and they require, of anyone who enjoys
> them, the responsibilities of liberty. They continually open the
> eye and require it to work vigorously; and through the eye they
> awaken curiosity and intelligence. That, by any virile standard, is
> essential to good entertainment. It is unquestionably essential to good
> art.

The experience of seeing a movie should appear to be an immediate rather than a reflected one.

> . . . the two primal requirements of the camera, in whose neglect or
> dilution you might better not use a camera at all: living—rather
> than imitative—visual, aural, and psychological authenticity, and the
> paralyzing electric energy of the present tense . . .

> The movie . . . has its chance to be born in front of the camera,
> whereas the general run of screen plays force what takes place be-
> fore the camera to be a mere redigestion of a predigestion.

[Huston] has a feeling about telling a story on a screen which sets him apart from most other movie artists and from all nonmovie writers and artists. "On paper," he says, "all you can do is say something happened, and if you say it well enough the reader believes you. In pictures, if you do it right, *the thing happens, right there on the screen.*" . . . At his best he makes the story tell itself, makes it seem to happen for the first and last time at the moment of recording.

His preference is for the fiction film.

Nearly all of the most talented people in moving pictures work in fiction, and most of the greatest possibilities lie within fiction.

The most important work in films is likely to be done by amateurs, but must not be amateurish.

I . . . put my deepest hope and faith in the future of movies in their being made on relatively little money, as much at least by gifted amateurs as by professionals. . . .

. . . plenty of people realize a point that many others will never understand and that there is no use laboring: some professional experience is exceedingly useful and perhaps indispensable, but most of the best movies could be made on very little money and with little professional experience.

Though . . . the picture is streaked with . . . amateurishness . . . I am forced more and more to the narrow, dismal hope that if good movies are to be made any more at all . . . they will have to be made on shoestrings, far outside the industry, and very likely by amateurs or at best semi-professionals.

And, with this, goes his preference for the nonprofessional actor.

To use non-professionals well . . . is a rare and potentially very important kind of creative faculty, called for by movies . . . as by no other kind of art.

The Hollywood traditions of acting . . . when there is any pretense whatever of portraying "real" people . . . are painfully out of place.

The people in this film . . . do and *are* things, over and over again, which are beyond acting and utterly different from it . . . a blending of reality and imagination. . . .

Above all, there is his absolute commitment to the thing in itself, to the unaltered stuff of reality incorporated into an imaginative fiction.

My heart goes out to the people who reproduced the Brooklyn streets—I could probably lose every other interest in life in the love for such detail—but try as they will, they only prove . . . that the best you can do in that way is . . . dead . . . compared with accepting instead the still scarcely imagined difficulties and the enormous advantages of submerging your actors in the real thing, full of its irreducible present tense and its unpredictable proliferations of energy and beauty.

[Rouquier] realizes that, scrupulously handled, the camera can do what nothing else in the world can do: can record unaltered reality; and can be made also to perceive, record, and communicate, in full unaltered power, the peculiar kinds of poetic vitality which blaze in every real thing and which are in great degree, inevitably and properly, lost to every other kind of artist except the camera artist.

The films I most eagerly look forward to will not be documentaries but works of pure fiction, played against, and into, and in collaboration with unrehearsed and uninvented reality.

Upon such general commitments was based Agee's performance as a practical critic, but one need not necessarily take issue with them to have some reservations about the practice itself. He had a tendency to reimagine material which both attracted and disappointed him, and most of his comments on films such as *Lost Angel, National Velvet, The Human Comedy, The Lost Weekend,* and *Farrébique* consist of suggested revisions, often to the point of suggesting totally different films. Yet, for all that one might argue against this as a valid aspect of criticism, the chief concern of which is with the given, to begin this way is to get nowhere, for, finally, it is impossible wholly to divorce Agee the critic from Agee the would-be film-maker.

More subject to question is his inclination toward a good deal of allusion and comparison to the other arts which often appears as little more than a meaningless and futile attempt to impart dignity by association. Thus René Clair is compared to Mozart and declared to be "one of the few great artists of this century"; Hitchcock shows "qualities of judgment and perception which . . . bring him abreast of all but the few best writers of his time." In discussing *Farrébique,* he invokes Hesiod, Vergil, Homer, and Mozart; *Ivan the Terrible* and *The Treasure of the Sierra Madre* both invite comparisons to Shakespeare, *The Story of G.I. Joe* to Whitman, *Man's Hope* to Homer.[2] Some of his imputations of literary devices to movies are a good deal less than clear. What can he mean by the "internal rhyming" of a film like *Desert Victory?* And, occasionally, his rhetoric goes obscure just when it appears to be most clear and technically exact, as in his observation that the shots in Huston's films are "cantilevered, sprung together in electric arcs, rather than buttered together." Perhaps his most specious tendency is to overestimate the mass audience, and overvalue the virtues of popular art. Thus he believes that "most though not all good films get much of their vitality and resonance by being designed for a broad mixed audience," and claims of a film he likes that it approaches "the global appeal, to the most and least sophisticated members of an audience, which the best poetic drama and nearly all the best movies have in common." Occasionally, Agee on the virtues of the Forty-second Street audience reminds one of nothing so much as Count Tolstoy idealizing the peasantry.

Lionel Trilling has observed, in discussing *Let Us Now Praise Famous Men,* that: "Agee has a sensibility so precise, so unremitting, that it is sometimes appalling; and though nothing can be more tiresome than protracted sensibility, Agee never tires us: I think this is because it is brilliantly normal and because it is a moral . . . sensibility." It is certainly true that Agee's vocabulary as a critic is throughout a singularly moral one. Writing, as he did, during the war years, he grew intensely concerned with the moral consequences of the war films in brutalizing and degrading the audience by allowing it, "at an incurable distance from participation, hopelessly incapable of reactions adequate to the event," to "sit in comfort and watch carnage." Much of his harshest criticism of films derives from what he senses to be their moral blindness, cowardice, evasion, and deceit. And occasionally he slips into some alarmingly theological terminology: a particularly trashy movie derives from an empty "soul" when an empty mind would seem more just, and Chaplin's tramp is the "most nearly complete among the religious figures our time has evolved."

Yet, in a sense, all this is still only further to pose rather than

2. This tendency seems to me no less dubious when, as with *The Story of G.I. Joe,* I share his esteem for the work in question.

answer the question of Agee's merit as a critic. Perhaps as much
to his credit as against it was the fact that he was not in the
least methodical or systematic. His criticism is discursive and impressionistic, rarely analytical. Except for his three-part article
on *Monsieur Verdoux,* his longer pieces are simply expanded im-
pressions rather than tightly organized critical essays. What Agee
succeeds in doing, more perfectly than any other film critic I
know, is to communicate a sense of the experience of actually seeing the movie. Whether by a ruthless exclusion of literary description or by an attempt to formulate a verbal equivalent, he is
capable of conveying, about as well as words can, the sense of
the film image.

Of *The Navigator:*
> . . . a ghostly, unforgettable moment . . . when, on a deserted, softly
> rolling ship, all the pale doors along a deck swing open as one be-
> hind Keaton and, as one, slam shut, in a hair-raising illusion of noise.

Of *Meet Me in St. Louis:*
> . . . a mother and four daughters, all in festal, cake-frosting white,
> stroll across their lawn in spring sunlight, so properly photographed
> that the dresses all but become halations. . . .

Of *The Story of G.I. Joe:*
> The sudden close-up . . . of a soldier's loaded back, coldly intricate
> with the life-and-death implements of his trade, as he marches away
> from his dead captain . . .

Of *Monsieur Verdoux:*
> . . . some wonderful loose group shots, full of glass, gravel, gray sky,
> pale heads, and dark clothing, at the garden party . . .

Of *Man's Hope:*
> The descent of the broken heroes from the desperate stone crown
> of Spain, as from a Cross, to the maternal valley, a movement so
> conceived that a whole people and a whole terrain become one
> sorrowing and triumphal Pietà for twentieth-century man . . .

Of *We Were Strangers:*
> . . . what seems to be hundreds of young men and women, all in
> summery whites, throw themselves flat on the marble stairs in a
> wavelike motion as graceful as the sudden close swooping of so many
> doves.

Yet it remains to be said that at the more vital concern of criticism—that of illumination—Agee succeeds but rarely. He is able brilliantly to communicate the immediate sensation of seeing the film, but only rarely does he enlarge our understanding of it. I refer, of course, to those films he discusses which leave anything to be understood beyond the sensation of a nearly perfect boredom and enervation. That Agee rarely achieves more than a scattered impression of film images owes less, perhaps, to the critic than to the patchwork quality of most of the films he is dealing with, in which the only value, if it exists at all, exists in fragmentary moments.

But while Agee is firm on the grounds of what, visually, makes a successful movie, he is often less secure on those of what constitutes a finished work of art; the two, of course, no more the same than fine prose is great literature. And, too often, Agee never goes beyond reviewing at its best into criticism, a distinction I will not make much of here. In his two pieces on *The Story of G.I. Joe* and *Man's Hope,* he suggests what, with sufficiently rigorous organization, might have been his own, exceptionally valuable approach to the criticism of films. In these pieces he is able to pursue the films' imagery with such systematic intent as to make it demonstrably synonymous with the films' meaning. His long article on *Monsieur Verdoux,* after a false start, turns into his most sustained performance in the writing of a patiently developed, firmly organized piece of criticism. It is analytical in nature, and unique among those pieces on the films Agee most admires in that it relies on no justification in terms of the other arts. Perhaps it is that, with Chaplin alone, has he a subject about which he can feel free to write for a nonspecialized audience without taking defensive measures.

In *Let Us Now Praise Famous Men,* Agee wrote:

> If I could do it, I'd do no writing at all here. It would be photographs; the rest would be fragments of cloth, bits of cotton, lumps of earth, records of speech, pieces of wood and iron, phials of odors, plates of food and excrement. . . . A piece of the body torn out by the roots might be more to the point.

In this furious impatience with words and art, he saw in the film the possibility to go directly to the thing itself, to deal imaginatively with concrete reality. The dialectical tension between

what he *could* see as potentiality and what he *did* see as actuality
informs all his criticism and gives it its characteristic tone of
despair. In another context Agee wrote, ". . . socially . . . the most
dangerous form of pride is neither arrogance nor humility, but
its mild, common denominator form, complacency," and his most
characteristic disposition as a film critic was toward a cry of desperation against the mammoth complacency of the industry.

> . . . you have only to compare the best of last year's films with the
> best that have been made or in your conception could be made, and
> the best that have been made with the best work you have known in
> any other art you choose, to know that those who make or care for
> moving pictures have great reason to be angry, for all that is
> frustrated, and still greater reason to be humble, for all that is fallen
> short of, frustration or no. And if you foresee how few years remain
> before the grandest prospect for a major popular art since Shakes-
> peare's time dissolves into the ghastly gelatinous nirvana of televi-
> sion, I think you will find the work of this last year or any recent
> year, and the chance of any sufficiently radical improvement within
> the tragically short future, enough to shrivel the heart.

> When an art is in good health, mediocrity and amorphous energy
> and commercialism and hostility toward disinterested men become
> more than forgivable, as lubricants and as stimulants, and the men
> of skill, or of affable or gentle or charming or for that matter venal
> talent, are more than welcome to exist, and to be liked and rewarded.
> When an art is sick unto death, only men of the most murderous
> creative passion can hope to save it. In either condition it is generally,
> if by no means always, this dangerous sort of man who does the
> great work. I wonder whether it is any longer possible, anywhere on
> earth, for such a man to work in films. I am almost certain it is not
> possible, and is not ever going to be, in this country.

In a sense, even his wit, at its most characteristic, was a function
of his moral despair.

> I could not resist the wish that Metro-Goldwyn-Mayer had topped
> its aquatic climax—a huge pool full of girls, fountains, and spouts
> of flame—by suddenly draining the tank and ending the show with
> the entire company writhing like goldfish on a rug. But MGM
> resisted it.

This is not simply withering—it is *annihilating*, as are his several
suggestions that the only effective remedies for bureaucratic complacency are bullets and dynamite.

Agee seemed always aware but never sure of his audience. It is apparent in his criticism that he was motivated by a constant sense of obligation to inform his readers. It comes as something of a shock to come across his occasional reviews of ten, fifteen, or twenty-five movies, all safely forgotten, in a single column. For six years this immensely gifted man was in the movies, suffering for us! And it is saddening to note the number of films he wishes to discuss at further length but never does. For he was constantly in action, reporting on all he could see in the space allotted, and then back for more. There simply wasn't time for the considered, permanent statement, the critical essay. Almost every time Agee mentions a film for the second time it is to revise his opinion of it, and one feels that were he to mention it a third time there would be still a different opinion; indeed, it is a mark of his honesty that this is so. In constant motion, there simply wasn't time for patient reflection.

I am sure that Agee could never have imagined the possibility of his criticism being collected in a single volume under so simple, yet so imposing a title. He wrote for the moment, to direct his audience to films of merit and rouse its anger at every cheap failure. And behind all his criticism, manifested chiefly in his wit, is his own sense of impotence and failure at having declined the role of critic for that of active influence.

> Although, as is perhaps immodest to point out, the whole of the movie world waits trembling from fortnight to fortnight to learn from this column what should or should not be done next . . .

Is it peculiarly significant, or just peculiar, that the publishers of his criticism saw fit to use as its foreword the praise of a man whose first admission is, "I do not care for movies very much and I rarely see them . . ."?

II | NOT QUITE ON FILM

Perhaps the best means of approaching the odd, perplexing volume of five scenarios[3] which comprises, except for some narration, Agee's writing *for* the film is by way of a few tangential observa-

3. *Agee on Film,* Volume Two, New York, McDowell Obolensky, 1960; republished by the Universal Library, Grosset and Dunlap, in 1969.

tions. For one, the fact that John Huston's brief foreword, with its mixture of showbiz-heaven pieties and subtle patronizing, constitutes an unpleasant footnote to all that he seems to have come to as a director; that it should serve as preface to the work of a man by whom his talents were once so highly valued makes it all the less felicitous. For another, there is the fact of this book as a book, surely an exemplar of casual mismanagement even among books on film, wherein mismanagement clearly is the rule. So we are given five scenarios assembled in such fashion that the first written appears last and the others wander in with no apparent order; so we are not given any source for *The Bride Comes to Yellow Sky* although all others are dutifully cited; so we are given an occasional line of screen direction from the mouth of one of the characters: I happen not to think such carelessness as trivial a matter as it is generally inclined to be treated, but this is a point I won't labor here. And then there is the work's oddness itself—how different it is from what, on the basis of Agee's criticism, one might have expected. But to say this is already to find oneself in the midst of it.

All but one of the five screenplays are drawn directly from literary material, and even *Noa Noa,* his ambitious life of Gauguin, has its literary sources; and all of them are much involved in artifice. By this I don't mean fiction, for Agee's preference was avowedly for the fiction film, but rather the scenarios' ubiquitous trappings of exotic locale, historical setting, and colorful costume. It is *Noa Noa,* I would imagine, on which one must base a serious judgment of Agee's contribution to writing for film; obviously, for his publishers, it is the *pièce de résistance,* heralded by them with suggestions of revolutionary experiment; and, certainly, freeing Agee for the only time in the collection from the demands of a direct adaptation, it presents him, or should, at his most distinctive. And yet it seems to me, in almost every way, the weakest work in the collection, another working of the clichés of the Noble Savage with an occasional obeisance toward some more familiarly those of an all-suffering Christ. Of course, it is true that probably no artist's life conforms more neatly to the theme of the Noble Savage than does Gauguin's; but when truth apes cliché, why embrace it?

The problem inherent in using the artist as hero of a work of art is that of legitimately establishing his genius: if, as in the case of Mann's Leverkühn, the artist is imaginary, one may even have to invent his creations; but, if your subject happens to be Gauguin, or Van Gogh, one has the plausible alternative of simply demonstrating what has already been proven. Thus Van Gogh (as a created character), in *Lust for Life,* is merely Kirk Douglas with problems, except for the inescapable evidence of those actual paintings. And, although *Noa Noa* is considerably more adventurous and daring than *Lust for Life,* it seems to me scarcely more successful than that film in creating, on the basis of internal evidence, the figure of a great artist, or in illuminating the process of his art's creation. Agee's most ambitious attempt to get under the skin of a work in creation—the sequence detailing the painting of "Where Do We Come From? What Are We? Where Are We Going?"—seems to me almost painfully futile in its laborious effort to penetrate the inscrutable surface, and, finally, as dazzlingly superficial as Clouzot's film of Picasso painting with light. When Agee's Gauguin most closely resembles an artistic genius, Agee most closely resembles a devoted curator, and his film a gallery hung as for some great, retrospective exhibition. Otherwise, what we have is *The Adventures of Paul Gauguin, Artist:* this is the appropriate context for that penultimate sequence in which Gauguin petitions the governor for a restoration of the natives' rights, a morally uplifting episode composed with great fidelity to the fact and little to the truth of Gauguin's life, as that truth might properly find embodiment in a work of art. If such a sequence derives from some too simple notion of the way in which art imitates life, there seems to be at work elsewhere, in the specifications that the backgrounds at Arles be patterned after Vincent's landscapes, some equally inadequate conception of life imitating art. Bound up with this confusion is a kind of schoolgirl idealization of the artist, and his indomitable courage:

METTE No: you must do what you must. But—*why,* Paul! Painting is all very well, and I want you to be at peace with yourself, but—*why?*
GAUGUIN *(tenderly)* My dear, I'm afraid that's something you'll never understand. And for that, I revere your bravery all the more. We'll be well, I can promise you—so long as we both keep faith with our courage.

And again:

> METTE *(near tears)* O *please,* Paul; I can't bear to hear it all again!
> GAUGUIN *(quiet, intense)* Now stop it, child: You're a woman of
> courage: I'm a man of courage. . . .

This sort of throbbing emotionalism has, I think, little if anything to offer us of any genuine understanding of either Gauguin
or the artistic temperament, in which, I would guess, courage plays
a subordinate role to necessity. As an attitude toward the artist as
subject, I find even this somewhat naïve reverence immeasurably
more likable than such alternatives as the vulgar condescension of
a *Moulin Rouge.* Yet, if courage and integrity *are* the issues, I
only wish Agee had paid heed to the very words he gives, at one
point, to Gauguin, in response to the ascription of bravery: "If
I were sufficiently brave, I'd have said nothing about it."

Agee's two adaptations from Stephen Crane seem to me almost
entirely successful in the accomplishment of their more modest
intentions; yet what a collaboration of opposites: Agee with his
disposition to elaboration and Crane with his passion for concentration. *The Blue Hotel* is a story in which Crane finally
violates his own aesthetic by some supererogatory moralizing;
Agee goes somewhat further in this direction, and adds a virtuoso
death sequence of agitated editing. *The Bride Comes to Yellow
Sky,* in its cameolike perfection, is perhaps Agee's finest piece of
writing for the screen, and a work of genuine charm, that all but
vanished and, I think, undervalued quality in art; the kind of
charm one finds in a film such as *The Sun Shines Bright,* a work
of which, in other ways as well, Agee's puts me in mind. I have not
seen the short film made of his script, but I would guess its
single defect might be one of point of view; that, I suspect, of the
sophisticated stranger, regarding the newlyweds from a distance
and finding them quaintly picturesque. Which is to say the
material dangerously skirts, as Ford's film never does, a self-
consciousness of its own charm.

   It is difficult to say how much of the published version of *The
African Queen* is Agee's since, although the publishers maintain a discreet silence on the subject, screen credit for the film
was shared by Agee with John Collier and Peter Viertel, as well

as with Huston. It was very much its director's film, I think, and, again, a charming one. The problem with *The Night of the Hunter* is of another nature. Here the script is all Agee's, but the film is to great degree Laughton's, and it is often far from certain where the one leaves off and the other begins. One is at something of a disadvantage in distinguishing the two in having seen Laughton's film before having read Agee's scenario for it; the all but irresistible tendency is to "see" the scenario in the images in which the film realized it. As a film, *The Night of the Hunter* was a work of such magnificent ambition and intransigence as almost to attain success by virtue of such qualities alone. But ambition and intransigence are, finally, not enough. *The Night of the Hunter* is the kind of work which depends for its very existence on the sustaining of a mood and a style, the mood of magic and the style of magic realism; instead, as directed by Laughton, the film is of such a clattering eclecticism as occasionally to resemble a textbook compilation of styles in the medium, from flat-lit naturalism to Germanic expressionism, from Griffith lyric to Welles Gothic. One can imagine Laughton, like Welles, having spent a year just seeing movies in preparation for making his own; unlike Welles, instead of then making his own, he seems rather to have decided to remake everybody else's. Probably, the kind of controlled stylistic unity that such a dreamily fantastic work demands is achieved with less difficulty in literature, in which all events may be estranged from us by a veil of language; to sustain this style of gauzy unreality in film one has constantly to resist the camera's natural propensity for the real, the concrete object, or else, like Cocteau, imagine the fantastic in the form of the concrete. I have not read the novel of *The Night of the Hunter;* the film, despite such beautifully realized passages as the flight down the river, is most often groping awkwardly for that apposite style it only intermittently achieves. And Agee's screenplay seems to be caught in some limbo between the two of them.

And there it is, that is all: *Agee on Film* complete, and yet unfinished. There was, for me, something extremely difficult, even painful, in the experience of reading Agee's screenplays, and I think that there must have been some painful difficulty in the experience of writing them. It is a difficulty beyond that merely in the effort of visualization which every directorial description imposes on both writer and reader, requiring one not only to see the image but to see it in context, as an element of rhythm, contrast, analogy, total effect. I mean rather that troubled sense which one sometimes gets even from Agee's criticism, that sense of watching a man attempting the impossible feat of somehow making a film out of language, attempting almost feverishly to force words to leap from the page and miraculously transmute themselves into that wondrous entity: the visual image. And, for Agee, whose love for language was second only to his love for the visual image, what suffering there must have been in seeing words lose their own beauty in a mass of necessarily functional description (pan camera 1s, etc.) and still not attain that beauty of the state desired. The publishers' blurb for the scenarios has a tendency to argue that they are actually more perfectly realized than could be any possible film of them, and, in a sense, this is true. The scenarios are as fully detailed as any such work could be; every nuance has been already indicated by the writer, and any director wholly respecting the scripts' intentions would merely be going through Agee's preordained paces, performing solely as his alter ego. The scenarios, as they were written, were also directed . . . directed and yet not filmed. For the actual, terrible truth is that, complete as they are, these scenarios do not exist at all; they have no more independent existence than an unperformed score of music. A scenario's only proper life is that of film; just as a film's editing corresponds to the writer's final act of revision, the analogue to the original act of literary creation is filming. Certain sequences in Agee's screenplays seem, on the basis of their description, quite remarkable, and yet one can only say what they *seem* to be, never what, in fact, they *are*. For much as Eisenstein "proved" on paper unprecedented beauties which he was never able to achieve on film, so what is best in Agee's writing for the screen remains less part of the history of art than that of suggestion, speculation, aspiration, passionate desire, and the ephemera of dreams.

So there it is: Agee on film; six years' notes on the run and five scenarios, three of them filmed, none of them filmed by their author. And hovering about all this activity—one cannot honestly call it achievement—a terrible pathos; the pathos of potentialities unrealized, the pathos of unfulfillment. Indeed, it is the pathos of our movies themselves. For six years, Agee sat in the semidarkness of movie theaters and bore witness to the dying of a light that had never really shone. His criticism is the personal record of a search, the search for an ideal—that movie which existed in his imagination, wedding art and life and renewing the possibilities of both, and which he hoped one day to discover for us; that movie of which he found only imperfect approximations, and which only he who imagined it could really make. Agee not only didn't find what he was looking for, but, along the way, could often be curiously unresponsive to what was there to be found; and I include, in this, some actual masterpieces; *They Were Expendable,* for a start. I said earlier that he suffered for us, yet I should add that, for someone else, the identical provocation might not have caused suffering.

The impact of Agee on film is something very like that of a spiritual quest, a quest which failed. It is only that kind of failure which can account for the kind of feeling contained in his despairing cry against the complacency of the industry I have quoted earlier, and in the many other passages from his criticism like it; indeed, for the cumulative feeling of Agee on film, which, for all the wit and what I'd call a desperate gaiety, approaches something akin to anguish. Yet, finally, one cannot wholly divorce Agee's sensibility from his subject; he didn't write theology but movie reviews. And, loving the movies for what he thought they might be, despising them for what they usually were, perhaps he went to them for the wrong reasons. Whatever the interest of Agee on film as a kind of open correspondence to us from this immensely gifted, immensely attractive, intensely vivid man, I think its value as criticism is slight. It burns with a passionate idealism, but only rarely does it illuminate that astonishing intermingling of junk, vulgarity, vitality, and greatness which is the reality of the movies.

                                                                    (1960)

THE ART OF THE FILM (CONT.)

Once, I began a long, eventually unfinished essay comparing James Agee, Robert Warshow, and the handful of other persons who have been responsible for the writing of a serious film criticism in America. I found that, although I had a good deal to say about Agee, whom, as a critic, I regard as Warshow's inferior, there was almost nothing I wished to say *about* Robert Warshow. I kept wanting to quote him, and at length, and, in the end, I did little more than indulge this inclination. Yet, really, Agee is much more quotable; his most valuable writing often in the way of a flashing insight, Warshow's always part of a carefully ordered and integral essay, difficult to remove from context; and, compared to the richness of Agee's language, Warshow's prose seems rather dry and plain. Earlier, however, there was an additional justification for my quoting Warshow in quantity in that I conceived of an audience not very familiar with his work, scattered, at that time, through a small shelf of yellowing periodicals. Then, seven years after his death, Warshow became available in a book,[1] which, at its first appearance, seemed to me destined for the

1. *The Immediate Experience*, New York, Doubleday, 1962; republished by Atheneum in 1970.

remainder tables, though I was wrong; anyway, I would have predicted the same fate for the collected criticism of Agee, and, instead, he has acquired a reverential following encompassing people as far apart as the judges of the highest-brow book club and the Luce intelligentsia. Or is that far apart? In any case, though still unremaindered, Warshow has yet to be quite so . . . lucky.

Perhaps the most curious thing about the curious book in which Warshow has finally been given to us is what the editors have decided to leave out, rather than the often peculiar ways they have seen fit to assemble what they have left in. (I speak of editors, although the book credits only one, as I have it on reliable information that the actual editing was not done by the individual so credited.) That anything at all of any interest has been left out of so slim a posthumous volume is surprising enough, but among the missing, in a collection which purports to present Warshow largely as a movie critic (as I propose primarily to treat him), is what I consider to be a really essential little piece on the movies. It is a book review, but, surely, this cannot be the grounds for its exclusion, since several others are included. The title of the piece is "The Art of the Film," and it appeared in *Partisan Review* of October 1948; since it required no heroic feat of scholarship on my part to unearth this information, I can only assume the editors' neglect to have been intentional.

Here is the substance of that absent piece's conclusion:

> . . . in the films, though it is obviously desirable to respond as fully as possible to the aesthetic complexities of technique, these "pure" values are at least equalled in importance by the medium's immense power of communication, which always raises aesthetic problems that go beyond the boundaries implied by the idea of "appreciation"; the film "connoisseur" tends to go wrong in so far as his concern with the "cinematic" causes him to ignore . . . the essential *aesthetic* importance of film content.

Implied in this, it seems to me, is everything that defines and distinguishes Warshow as a critic in his relation to the movies. If, in the United States, "serious" film criticism has mainly been the production of a few cranky ideologues, in England it has traditionally been the province of those innocent of ideas altogether. I think of *Sight and Sound*–style anonymously curatorial tours of the development of this or that trend or movement and the progress of such and such a director, etc.: this Buñuel dream sequence echoing that and foreshadowing this other; and all with but the vaguest intimations that these things may have some *meaning*. Films become merely something like race horses. In lieu of any real criticism, one can always trace their lineal descent; in lieu of criticism, one can always substitute expertise.[2]

Listen, instead, to the voice of Robert Warshow:

> The force of *Paisan* is in certain images of danger, suffering, and death that remain in one's consciousness with the particularity of real experience. Like the stacked dry corpses of Buchenwald or the clownish figure of Mussolini hanging by the heels, these images have an autonomy that makes them stronger and more important than any ideas one can attach to them. . . .
>
> In the Florentine episode, there is a moment when a group of partisans captures two Fascist snipers. A confused knot of men bursts around a corner into the sunny street and moves rapidly toward the camera, growing larger and clearer. One man is dragged along by the shoulders, kicking and struggling; another, erect, is propelled by blows that force him to move ahead as if he were part of the group, rather than its object, and shared the general desire to bring matters to a quick conclusion. Just in front of the camera, the men are thrown to the ground and left for a moment inside a small circle, the camera pointing downward at their backs. One of them cries, "I don't want to die!" There is a burst of machine-gun fire, and the scene is over.
>
> This scene moves so rapidly that the action is always one moment ahead of the spectator's understanding. And the camera itself remains neutral, waiting passively for the action to come toward it and simply recording as much of the action as possible, with no opportunity for the variation of tempo and the active selection of detail that might be used to "interpret" the scene; visually, the scene remains on the same level of intensity from beginning to end, except for the increasing size and clarity of the objects as they approach the camera—and this has the effect of a "natural" rather than an interpretive variation. The speed of the action combined with the neutrality of the camera tends to exclude the possibility of reflection and thus to divorce the events from all questions of opinion. The political and moral distinctions between the snipers

2. See John Russell Taylor's *Cinema Eye, Cinema Ear*, New York, Hill & Wang, 1964, for an epitome of this in book form.

and their captors do not appear (even the visual distinction is never very sharp), and the spectator is given no opportunity to assent to the killing. Thus the scene derives its power precisely from the fact that it is not cushioned in ideas: events seem to develop according to their own laws and to take no account of how one might—or "should"—feel about them.

My choice of passage is more or less at random; I could, as easily, have chosen one from any essay in the book; it is typical. A work is being looked at closely; it is being seen, but with the kind of seeing which ends in understanding. James Agee is able admirably to give us a sense of how a film such as *The Best Years of Our Lives* looks; Warshow is able to make us see how the way *The Best Years of Our Lives* looks is related to what the film means. And, whereas even so morally engaged a writer as Agee can dismiss the defects of *The Best Years of Our Lives* as unimportant next to the perfection of its surface, Warshow is able to show us with a fine discrimination just how that surface mastery is used to falsify what is going on beneath it; much as, in the quite different case of *Paisan,* he can make us see the way the handling of the camera may radically affect and even express the film's meaning. He can—in the larger sense—make us see.

What does a film mean? How does it mean? These are the questions Warshow continually asks, and makes us ask with him, and one is stunned to realize how few other critics have got around to asking them. I think a major reason for Warshow's attraction to the movies was the way they gave themselves so naturally to meaning, despite the indifference or even resistance of their makers. Warshow advanced no argument for any single conception of the medium, but he certainly understood it to be, regardless of the disposition of any individual artist, always, at least at the core, a realistic one; this in the sense of its retaining some irreducible ability to make things real. For the film, even the so-called "art" or "experimental" film, is pre-eminently a photographic medium, and stubbornly persistent in its tendency to give its subject a certain palpable reality and vivid life.

. . . the picture [of *Death of a Salesman*] has a certain power which for me at least . . . was lacking in the play. No film ever quite disappears into abstraction: what the camera reproduces has almost always on the most literal level the appearance of reality; that is one reason why the movies can afford to be so much more banal than the theater: when we complain of their "unreality" we do not mean exactly that they fail to carry conviction, but more probably that they carry conviction all too easily. In the blankest moments of *Death of a Salesman* one sees, if not Willy Loman, who is always more a concept than a human being, at least the actor Fredric March, brought so close and clear that his own material reality begins to assert itself outside the boundaries that are supposed to be set by his role. On the stage, this would be a fault, for it would mean that the actor was seeking to impose himself on the play; here there is no need for him to put himself forward: he need only be present, a passive object merely available to the camera's infinite appetite for the material. This is not to say that the actor's "real" personality replaces that of the character he portrays—though that may happen— but only that the actor as an object of perception is real and important irrespective of whether we believe in the character: the screen permits no vacancies, it will be filled one way or another.

It is not necessarily *the* real world (what might be called the Kracauer Fallacy), but, of necessity, *a* real world which the film presents to us; even a world as strange as that of *The Blood of a Poet* acquires a certain reality simply by its existence as a visual fact; in Warshow's phrase, it is *there*.[3] There is no analogue in films to the novel of sensibility, the work purely an essay in style. The "pure" film is made all but impossible by a medium which constantly inclines toward impurity, toward meaning; in which image irresistibly moves into meaning.

Carl Dreyer's basic problem as an artist is one that seems almost inevitably to confront the self-conscious creator of "art" films: the conflict between a love for the purely visual and the tendencies of a medium that is not only visual but also dramatic. The principle that the film is a medium based on movement has often been used to justify a complete preoccupation with visual patterns, as if the ideal film would be one that succeeded in divorcing movement from content, but it is this principle itself that raises the problem, for the presentation of human beings in movement necessarily leads to the creation of drama; thus the maker of "art" films, unless he limits himself to complete abstraction or to generalized poetic symbolism,

3. Cf. Cocteau: "The strength of a film resides in its 'truthism,' I mean, in its showing us things instead of telling them. Thus they are made to exist as facts, even if these facts rest upon the unreal. . . ." (*Cocteau on the Film*, A Conversation Recorded by André Fraigneau, London, Dennis Dobson, 1954.)

tends to raise aesthetic demands that he cannot satisfy within the framework he has set. . . .

Dreyer's initial impulse, in his deliberate exclusion of the historical and dramatic, is to deprive events of the quality of reality; it is this, indeed, which accounts for his concern with the past: since the past can be contemplated but not changed, it exists from one point of view as an aesthetic object ready-made—one can experience it "pure." But he practices his aestheticism on events that possess *a priori* an unusual emotional importance, and in one of the most realistic of all mediums. In the screen's absolute clarity, where all objects are brought close and defined unambiguously, the "reality" of an event can be made to inhere simply in its visible presence; so long as the internal structure of a film remains consistent, all its elements are in these terms equally "real"—that is, completely visible. Thus at his best—which means, in [*Day of Wrath*] . . . when he is creating his own images and not imitating the creations of seventeenth-century painting—Dreyer is able to give his aestheticized vision of the past all the force of reality without impairing its aesthetic autonomy; in the absence of a historical-dramatic reality, the purely visible dominates and is sufficient: the witch is an object of art, but she is also—and just as fully—a human being (she is *there*), and she is burnt; the burning is so to speak accomplished by the camera, which can see the witch without having to "interpret" her.

The effect is something like a direct experience of the tension between art and life. In a sense, the image *as* image becomes a dramatic force: the issue is not, after all, good against evil or God against Satan, but flesh against form; stripped as it is of all historical or social reference, the spectacle is of a woman burnt to serve beauty. It is a spectacle not to be understood—the image itself is all the meaning—but to be endured; and the enormous excitement that surrounds it, the sense almost of a prolonged assault on one's feelings, results largely from the exclusion of all that might be used to create an appearance of understanding.

But I am quoting again; and Warshow is—almost—available.

I have relied thus on quotation for several reasons, among them, the virtual impossibility of condensing such closely reasoned argument, and the obvious superiority of such a reproduction to any paraphrase. I see no possibility of saying better those things which Warshow said, and I have no better things to say. It seems to me unimaginable that one could read those passages I have excerpted without acknowledging the singularity of their insight into the art of the film, and yet I am forced to recognize what I cannot imagine. For there, in the initial reviews, was the odd spectacle of literary intellectuals like Leslie Fiedler, and others, telling us assuredly that Warshow, whatever his virtues, was not really a movie critic, and didn't actually know very much about his subject. And in a sense, of course, they are right, if by knowledge one means some specialized province of professional competence, the graduate-school notion of knowledge; Warshow's kind of knowledge is simply that available to anyone of a first-rate intelligence confronting the full possibilities of his chosen subject, and it is communicated to us in a tone characteristically not knowing but inquiring. Warshow's criticism is utterly free from the manipulation of that technical jargon and those elaborate and impenetrable apparatuses by which our high-brow film critics have managed to cow and bully us into validating their credentials, and to convince us that movie criticism is a branch of metaphysics or a practice akin to black magic. (I think here particularly of Parker Tyler;[4] the reader may think of whomever he wishes.) Have we become so conditioned to these paraphernalia that we have learned to require them? Have we come to identify intelligence by its unintelligibility?

Warshow speaks to us without benefit of such occult advantages, and yet it seems to me obvious enough that anyone who has described as he has exactly how the film image works in movies as disparate as *Paisan* and *Day of Wrath,* *Limelight* and *Earth,* brings to the subject a knowledge which subsumes a profound understanding of the subtleties and complexities of the medium, of all but, perhaps, the most technical aspects of film's techniques. The fact is that, but for Warshow, there is probably no critic of film who has not been primarily a formalist, preoccupied with questions of craftsmanship, with the techniques of editing, and camera angles, and the composition of beautiful or striking images, as though these were not what their analogues are in any

---

4. ". . . my merger of psychoanalysis, myth, free plastic analogies, unconscious syndromes in the film industry and straight technical criticism, has already won recognition precisely for establishing new criteria of integrity and coherence" (Parker Tyler, from a letter published in *The Hudson Review,* Winter 1961–62). (See, also, *Myra Breckinridge* by Gore Vidal, Boston, Little, Brown, 1968.)

other artistic medium: the means. For Warshow, the movie camera, employed with aspiration toward art, was, finally, either an instrument of art, another, different kind of means to art's traditional ends, or that film an artistic failure in which it was anything less. Were the art of the film really only an arrangement of beautiful visual images in motion, then *The Birth of a Nation* would be a work of art instead of kitsch with pretty (or magnificent) pictures, which it is.

". . . sentimentality and vulgarity in a work of art are aesthetic defects. . . . I should say that Griffith's genius as a moviemaker was combined with limitations of mind and sensibility that kept him from being a truly great artist. Here, I think, it is [one who extols Griffith] . . . who fails to respect the medium; if the films are an art among the other arts, then a great film artist must have something like the stature of a great novelist or a great dramatist, and Griffith is not to be excused for his sentimentality (or John Huston for his intellectual shallowness) because of his genius in "workmanship."

Robert Warshow speaking, in print,[5] on the movies, but, if you think that fact might be discovered from *The Immediate Experience,* forget it; it is not in the book.

The end of criticism is, I believe, the enlargement of our understanding of its subject; at its best, it serves as a means of discovery. In this sense, Agee is almost never a critic, whatever else of value he may be. He is able brilliantly to describe to us the appearance of a film, and to communicate his immediate response to it, from excited enthusiasm to angry contempt. He is, above all, a guide: go to this, he tells us; stay away from that. I doubt that anyone coming to Warshow's essay on Dreyer in order to find out whether to go to see *Day of Wrath* of a Saturday night will leave it bringing away any uncomplicated answer. From Agee, one often gets the impression that movies exist simply to be seen; that our eyes are sufficient to the experience of them. Warshow engages the movie image, not on that level at which it is merely striking or even beautiful, but on that at which it becomes meaningful as well. One last time, I must permit myself a long quotation. Here is Robert Warshow on *Limelight,* in a recreation of a sequence of film imagery at the point at which what it contains becomes

5. From a letter published in *Partisan Review,* October 1948.

demonstrably equivalent to its meaning. Here is a description of
what can happen on a movie screen, in its totality:

> It remains to be said, nevertheless, that the famous scene near the
> end of the movie when Calvero performs on the stage as a comic
> violinist, with Buster Keaton as his accompanist, represents a
> kind of success far beyond the complex and unsteady ironies of the
> earlier parts. In this there is no longer any problem of interpretation
> and choice . . . only a perfect unity of the absolutely ridiculous.
> Perhaps the Tramp's adventures with the automatic feeding machine
> in *Modern Times* is as funny, but there it is still possible to say that
> something is being satirized and something else, therefore, upheld.
> The difficulties that confront Calvero and Keaton in their gentle
> attempt to give a concert are beyond satire. The universe stands in
> their way, and not because the universe is imperfect, either, but
> just because it exists; God himself could not conceive a universe
> where these two could accomplish the simplest thing without mishap.
> It is not enough that the music will not stay on its rack, that the
> violin cannot be tuned, that the piano develops a kind of malignant
> disease—the violinist cannot even depend on a minimal consistency
> in the behavior of his own body. When, on top of all the other
> misfortunes that can possibly come upon a performer humbly anxious
> to make an impression, it can happen also that one or both of his
> legs may capriciously grow shorter while he is on the stage, then he
> is at the last extreme: nothing is left. Nothing except the deep,
> sweet patience with which the two unhappy musicians accept these
> difficulties, somehow confident—out of God knows what reservoir of
> awful experience—that the moment will come at last when they will
> be able to play their piece. When that moment does come, it is
> as happy a moment as one can hope for in the theater. And it comes
> to us out of that profundity where art, having become perfect, seems
> no longer to have any implications. The scene is unendurably funny,
> but the analogies that occur to me are tragic: Lear's "Never, never,
> never, never, never!" or Kafka's "It is enough that the arrows fit
> exactly in the wounds they have made."

Well, there is Warshow, and here am I, and there is everybody
else telling me that Warshow was not really a movie critic at all,
but a writer on politics and sociology. Yes, Warshow was concerned with politics and sociology; he was concerned, you see,
with ideas, and with actuality; and how better is one to write
about a work such as *Paisan,* in which the politics *are* the ideas,
or *The Best Years of Our Lives,* in which they are the evasion of

them? But it is perfectly plain that Warshow's interest in our
mass-produced entertainments, our "popular culture," and,
especially, the movies, was not as raw data for sociological observations, and, although I shall not quote again, certainly he several
times makes this point explicit. Rather, he went to these things for
what might be salvaged from them, for what might be brought
back that was of value to a serious art and culture. This is what,
in part, he meant when he spoke of his wish to "legitimize" the
movies, for, in them, art is to be found at the place where its
existence has become most problematical, at the nexus of culture
and commodity; where, when least expected and in the most surprising guise, one may discover art, but, only rarely, a finished
work of art. But it was that art, not the epiphenomena, which
Warshow was after.

I can think of only one instance in which Warshow may be said
to have allowed a general idea to get in the way of, rather than
arise from, his response to an individual work; this in his most
generally admired and anthologized essay, "The Westerner,"
which, of all his criticism of the film, I find the least successful.
It begins with a description of the pattern common to the typical
Western film, but, at some point, description slips into evaluation
so that films such as *Shane* and *My Darling Clementine* are dismissed because of their deviation from the pattern, whereas I
should say that their interest derives, in the first place, precisely
from this deviation. But this is the essay in which Warshow is
able to write of *Shane* that its action is "so deliberately graceful
that everything seems to be happening at the bottom of a clear
lake"; and what is lost to judgment is rescued by language; a
language at once modest and extraordinarily vivid, not decorative
but functional, entirely in the service of meaning. It is the
language of the essay, and what I have earlier described as its
plainness is, as the book's introduction rightly observes, the mark
of its elegance; the one point in an introduction otherwise pointless. It is also the mark of what Leslie Fiedler has mentioned, but,
I think, failed properly to value: Warshow's remarkable sanity.
Sanity in literary criticism is rare enough, but sanity in film
criticism!—this is almost incomprehensible in a domain in which
the lunatic fringe has attempted to fill the vacuum at the center.
In an enterprise notorious for its ax-grinding, Warshow grinds no

axes. To the extent that Warshow's sanity made him so aware of
what was best in even the worst of films and worst in even the
best of them, he will always seem, to *cinéastes*, to be "unsympathetic" to the medium. We want our critics (I should say "critics")
to be "generous"; we praise Agee for his "generosity." But "Here,
I think, it is [one who extols Griffith] . . . who fails to respect the
medium." What Warshow said of *Monsieur Verdoux* might
be taken as his standard of excellence for a film: that "it requires
of the spectator that he should constantly reflect upon what he
sees on the screen and what he discovers in his own mind." To
ask this is, it seems to me, a gesture of the ultimate respect.

Having spoken about Warshow, I would now like to say a few
words about the book which will eventually be the basis for whatever there is of his reputation once old *Partisan Review*s and
*Commentary*s have turned to dust, and the generation of the
forties passed on to a world without book introductions. What is
a book? Here is a book: it would have been easy enough for those
responsible to have made a good job of it, but surprisingly, with
a few efficient touches, they have managed to make a bad one.
May I suggest how, simply, it might have been done well? The
total length of Warshow's published writing is not great; there
isn't much, and none of it is redundant. Each of the subjects he
chose to write about was somehow exemplary; of the movies, for
example, *Paisan* and *October* and *Monsieur Verdoux* are not
only different films, but different kinds of films; beyond their
individual interest, they represent alternative ways of working
in their medium. There is no waste motion in Warshow's writing;
a brief book review, even published correspondence, served continually to define and redefine his relation to his subject. Collect
all these pieces then, publish them as they were written, in
chronological sequence, and title the book, say, *Collected Essays;*
a title which might be appropriate enough for a writer whose
own tastes in these matters were such that he would title a piece
on *Paisan* simply "*Paisan,*" and a writer pre-eminently an essayist.
Here is how it has been done badly. Seven years after the first
announcement of its publication, we were given this book, reprinted intact two years later; I do not know what legal difficulties may have accounted for much of the delay, but I do know

that more than one year was spent in waiting for the completion of the slight (auto)biographical memoir which is employed as the book's introduction. Over an orange and blue, simulated-cloth (or paper, take your choice) binding of appalling ugliness, the cover announces a title which, although taken from a phrase of Warshow's, manages to seem uncharacteristically histrionic thus wrenched from context. But the dominant note is struck by the blurb beneath it: "MOVIES, COMICS, THEATRE AND OTHER AS-PECTS OF POPULAR CULTURE." Get the picture? Just in case you don't, the first of the book's four factitious sections is headed "American Popular Culture," and the variety of subjects in-cluded under this topic is wonderful to behold.

"Popular Culture"—is it perhaps significant that the first use of the phrase by the author has it placed inside quotation marks? Now the truth is that Warshow was a writer, and a critic of art and of culture (popular and otherwise), and only in a culture as sick and fragmented as our own could one feel some purpose was served by disposing of him with the label of sociologist or popular culturist or anything else, other than what he was. He was a writer of a kind now virtually extinct: the nonspecialized essayist; the essay his natural form, the varieties of our cultural experience his subject. (Edmund Wilson, encompassing his much wider range, comes to mind as another example of the type. Both he and War-show share the characteristic of being able to discuss events with the seriousness and complexity to be found in the best kind of literary criticism, whereas most literary critics who turn toward the actualities of our experience tend to treat events as though they *were* literature.) As it happened, Warshow was attracted to the movies, and wrote about them, and became our best movie critic, among other things. But the fact is that, dead, he is a commodity like any other, and this is how dead writers are being merchandised this season. Of course, in order to enforce this catchy image, it was necessary to leave a few things out: included among the missing are pieces on Hemingway and Kafka, the latter one of the finest critical appreciations of Kafka I know; omissions presumably made on the grounds that such pieces might be taken for a criticism of literature, which is not "Popular Culture." But far more challenging to editorial ingenuity than the prob-lem of what was to be left out must have been that of how consistently to misrepresent what was to be left in; to this challenge, above all, person or persons unknown have risen heroically; would that I had the name(s), that I might bestow the credit. And so an essay concerned with the attempt of American fiction to deal with the liberal intellectual's experience of Communism in the thirties, dwelling particularly on Lionel Trilling's *The Middle of the Journey*, is strait-jacketed into the section on "American Popular Culture." And so an essay on the Rosenbergs is given to us under the identical rubric; surely, whatever opinion one may have of the Rosenberg case, only a monster could understand it as being merely this. So an essay on the death of Warshow's father, an essay as supple and moving as a work of fiction, turns out to be only another aspect of . . . I can't go on, or, rather, I could go on almost indefinitely. Everything, finally, turns out to be an aspect of "American Popular Culture"—surely, the most potent reductive mechanism yet devised by literary man—except what may be even more falsely categorized. Thus a discussion of Arthur Miller's play, *The Crucible*, a piece which Eric Bentley once called the best analysis of Arthur Miller yet written, is presented to us in a section entitled "American Movies," presumably because the drama, unlike the movies, might be taken for literature, or, worse, art; which is not "Popular Culture." It is only in the case of the two superlative Chaplin essays that the editor or editors seem to have been defeated; these two together compose a section entitled "Charles Chaplin." The whole damn thing is then supposedly legitimized by having been preceded by a statement taken from Warshow's application for a Guggenheim fellowship, describing a work he did not live to complete, presented to us as the "Author's Preface." Surely, since the author wrote a preface, he must approve of it all. But, you see, the author is not in a position to disapprove.

The situation, then, is this. After seven years, we are given an unattractive, cheaply made book, bearing an arguably inappropriate title, and heralded on the cover by a salvo of misleading information. Out of a by no means extensive body of work, some actually unidentified hands have managed to cull a less than adequate selection, and assemble it unsatisfactorily; the whole thing outfitted with the author's preface to another work. The entire project was then allowed to gather dust on the shelf for a matter of *years* while waiting for an Important Name to be attached to it via the gossipy reminiscence which now serves as its introduction. It is a Name which, sad to say, no longer signifies much in the way of present consequence. It is a case of the show being held up for years so that a fading and tardy master of ceremonies can arrive in order to put in a few paternalistic words (the literary world's Good Housekeeping Seal of Approval) about the guest of honor, a figure, by this time, rather overshadowing his own; so that a Name can ramble on about what once was a man. Here is a book, and, with it, all the books which this book typifies. What is a book if not the material symbol of a culture? This is our situation, then, and I put it to you bluntly: in the face of all this . . . this—shall we call it madness?—can any of us, tacitly acquiescing in it, truly be said to be alive?

(1964)

FIVE | **THEORY**

TOWARD "FILM APPRECIATION"

> It's something like the old movies. You had to get the wide screen and stereo to get the truth of the matter.—FLOYD MCKISSICK, in a television news interview

I'd like to begin with a modest anecdote, which, not being amusing, is at least true. Mr. X, a film critic, is presently at work on a book about the art of the film; "From Griffith to Godard," as the tag goes. Informed of this, Mr. Y, an art critic and acquaintance, castigated him for raking up all that old Griffith stuff again, and advised instead to begin with what was really interesting: Godard—"That's art!"

Well, who is the hero and who the villain of this exchange, on the face of it a paradigmatic confrontation between sober responsibility and a shallow variety of being with-it, between moderation and excess? As it happens, Mr. Y is a critic of considerable brilliance while Mr. X has all the responsibility which work of diligent dullness can simulate—which is still not necessarily to have answered the question I asked. Let me get to my own sympathies this way: in 1960, I wrote an extremely antagonistic essay questioning the "genius" of Eisenstein which, alone among the film criticism I've written, I had wanted to see

appear in one of the magazines specializing in films. The piece
was rejected by both *Film Quarterly* and *Sight and Sound,*[1] the
editor of the latter stating in a letter to me that, "I think Eisenstein *was* a genius . . . and I think any useful critical article has
to come to terms with the genius as well as the rest."

That was 1960, of course; there was no Godard (to know of) .
then; only Bergman; and I was by no means prepared to say
start there—that's art! Nevertheless, I *was* prepared, if anything,
to write off even more of the world's so-called Film Classics then
than now, and, since I am about to be severe with a number of
them still, I think it only proper to declare my bias from the
start. I grew up on the films (mainly American) of the forties,
was first excited by the film as an art by *The Treasure of the
Sierra Madre* perhaps more than by any other single film (first
seeing *Citizen Kane* only much later), and then started reading
all on the subject I could find, and tracking down the "classics"
and the rest as I shuttled between Forty-second Street and the
Museum of Modern Art Film Library. But my progress soon
became one of a growing disillusionment; even *The Treasure of
the Sierra Madre,* revisited some years later, looked less good
than it once had. For that disillusionment, I could find no
adequate justification in anything I read, which furnished a
collection of towering masterpiece upon masterpiece. So I
attempted to provide my own justification, and started with
Eisenstein. In that attempt, this piece is another part.

I

Conveniently, for almost anyone who wishes to advance some
argument on the nature of the film, the beginning makes a
good place at which to begin. Though the invention of the film
remains an undecided question still—with claims made variously
for Paul and Friese-Greene in England, Edison and Dickson in
the United States, Le Prince and Lumière in France—there is
general agreement that the first public screening was given by
Louis and Auguste Lumière in 1895. Almost immediately

1. And subsequently published in *The Kenyon Review,* where it no doubt
appealed to a general antifilm snobbery.

after, when, in 1896, Georges Méliès showed his first film, the
medium was already plunged into its major aesthetic dichotomy.

According to an apocryphal anecdote which I recently saw
in print, Méliès, working as a cameraman for the Lumière
brothers, was sent one day to photograph the *n*th train coming
into the station. On inspiration from the muse of boredom, he
shot the train arriving at a distance, turned the camera off and
on again once the train had arrived, and then off again until the
train's departure, when he photographed it dwindling from the
again empty station. *Voilà!* he exclaimed as he revealed the results
to his employers. *Voilà!* they replied as they viewed his mad
deviations from actuality and threw him out. In actual fact,
Méliès' contact with the Lumières was that of having become
interested in making films of his own through attending an
exhibition of theirs; they refused either to rent or sell him
their *cinématographe* and declared his infatuation would ruin
him, which it eventually did. The Lumières went on shooting
trains entering and leaving stations and the like, while Méliès,
obtaining equipment from Paul in England, made his *A Trip to
the Moon, The Conquest of the Pole,* and others (including, one
tends to forget, such different works as *The Dreyfus Affair*). And
though film *theory* has been almost overwhelmingly pro-Lumière,
it is the films of Méliès which are alive for us today with their
wit and invention, and which provided the influence, direct and
indirect, or at least the climate, for the trick films and comedies
of Ferdinand Zecca, Émile Cohl, Jean Durand, the comedies to
follow by Max Linder, the mystery serials of Louis Feuillade,
and, eventually, such works of the French avant-garde as *Entr'acte,
Paris Qui Dort,* and *The Blood of a Poet.* The enthusiasm of
Apollinaire for Feuillade is an indication of the seriousness which
film in France was early accorded, but it wasn't long before the
French film was suffering from another kind of seriousness, that of
respectability, and the flowering of invention which had sprung
from Méliès was to be stifled for years by embalmed theater—the
photographically recorded performances of Bernhardt and Duse
—the so-called Film d'Art.

Meanwhile, in America, the Lumière/Méliès antithesis was
being synthesized (i.e., fictional stories in actual settings) with

nationally characteristic lack of concern for theory in films such as *The Great Train Robbery* which Edwin S. Porter made for Edison. Before long, an actor in Porter's films was making films of his own; his name, not to prolong nonexistent suspense, was D. W. Griffith; though, in a sense, this is where the suspense begins, for, with Griffith, one is asked for the first time in the film's history to make a serious aesthetic judgment—to accept or challenge the received opinion.

What are we to make of Griffith then? Showing *Broken Blossoms* in a course entitled "Film Appreciation" to a class of bored and restless students, though none more bored and restless than I, it occurred to me that we would really do a service to Griffith to show his films, as so much else that comes to us under the rubric of Film Classics, in excerpt form: to distinguish between the good and bad in them, and ask, even of the good, whether it is the work of an artist or innovator. In fact, I think Griffith's stature as an innovator unassailable even if it could be shown (as it can be of the films of Orson Welles) that few of the techniques he is given credit for inventing had not been used elsewhere. As it happens, James Card, curator of the film archives at Eastman House, has reported of a 1915 Francis X. Bushman film in his collection, *The Second in Command,* which antedates *The Birth of a Nation* and is filled with close-ups, intricate follow action, tracking shots, apparent zooms and other such devices the achievement of many of which is unexplained to this day. The fact remains that, in the films of Griffith, as in those of Welles, devices not necessarily new were assimilated for the first time to a sustained and original narrative style.

But to what is this style assimilated? Magniloquent accolades to Griffith's genius as a technical innovator plainly beg this question for, surely, the technical devices have no *artistic* value in themselves. Cross-cutting or close-ups are not in themselves (any more than, say, a monologue) either good or bad: they become so only through the uses to which they are put. And, in Griffith, these uses are almost always the service of trash, from the preachy bombastic melodrama of *Intolerance* to the morbid bathos of *Broken Blossoms,* and clearly neither of these is exempt from the chief vice of the other any more than is *The Birth of a Nation* or Griffith's work as a whole.

The issue has been put as directly as possible by Robert Warshow in his comment on Griffith that I quoted earlier: if the film is an art among the other arts, can we call Griffith a great artist and dismiss his crippling artistic defects because of his technical genius? The answer, of course, is No; and yet institutionalized film history (as well as most film criticism) plods on without evidence of even having heard the question.

Now, if I've said the worst about Griffith, as I feel compelled to, I feel compelled also to add that there is more to be said: that Griffith's genius as a movie-maker was more than simply an innovational one; that it was, in fact, though only in a very limited sense, an artistic genius, if not precisely the genius of an artist. Griffith's films aren't works of art, but they are masterly achievements of stagecraft, and, it seems to me, once one accepts the fact that these achievements are more of the nature of a Stanislavsky (though a nontheoretical Stanislavsky) than a Chekhov (or, to choose less neat but more apt examples, more those of a Belasco than a Dickens), one need immediately be far less defensive in appreciating him. One gift he had in superlative measure: that for the creation of spectacle on a plane of visual grandeur; and this is by no means something we should let ourselves fail to value. Nor should we fail to value it as art when, at its best, as in the battle scenes of *The Birth of a Nation* (and it was usually at its best when most independent of the dramatic constructions Griffith attempted to impose upon it), it becomes an imaginative creation of extraordinary power and beauty.

I want to say something about one other aspect of Griffith's genius, an artistic aspect of a sort but one which I think has as much to do with the nature of his medium as with Griffith. So let me get at it via another film-maker and a protégé of Griffith's, Erich von Stroheim. Stroheim's name is usually linked in the histories with the word "Realism," and is often used as a contrast to Griffith, but it's worth remembering that Stroheim continued to pay respect to Griffith as the man who taught him the director's responsibility for authenticity in his films. The Stroheim of *Greed,* albeit a *Greed* drastically altered from Stroheim's conception of it, we generally know, but *Greed* remains, in many ways, a film apart from Stroheim's other work. What are his films like?

The life history of a young girl, Kitty Kelly, brought up in a convent-school in one of the Duodec States of Imperial Germany . . .

The cousin of the Queen the beloved enfant terrible, "Wild Wolfram"—and the Queen's fiancé—is punished by her for one of his escapades with some extra duty with his escadron of cuirassiers outside of the little capital where he encounters the convent girls herded by their nuns. As the girls curtsy before the Prince one girl's panties fall to the ground. They are Kitty Kelly's. He laughs to the dismay of the girl who throws in her rage her pants into the Prince's face. He keeps them as a souvenir. He falls madly in love with her. He kidnaps her from the convent, brings her to his apartment in the palace where he is surprised by his cousin the Queen. She puts him under arrest and whips the girl out of the palace. After an unsuccessful attempt at suicide Kitty is brought back to the convent where a cable awaits her. It is from her aunt in Dar-es-Salam in German East Africa, who has paid for her niece's education and who suffered a stroke. Kitty is shipped to Africa. On her arrival she finds that her aunt is the proprietor of a saloon–bawdy house. At the death bed of her aunt, she is married to an old but very rich degenerate and inherits the establishment. After the death of her aunt she declines to live with her husband but takes charge of the house. On account of her regal ways and carriage everybody nicknames her "Queen Kelly". The Prince had been sentenced to Custodia Honesta and on his return from the fortress finds out the whereabouts of Kitty. He has himself transferred into the Imperial German Schutz-truppe in Africa. He meets Kitty in her saloon but finds that she is married. After harrowing experiences during which the husband dies, he marries Kitty. The Queen, meanwhile, has been assassinated and he is recalled to ascend the throne. He refuses to come unless his wife, a commoner, would be accepted as Queen. She is accepted and Kitty becomes now really "Queen Kelly" residing in the palace from which she had been forcibly ejected.

This, I hasten to add, is not my paraphrase, but a synopsis, in Stroheim's own words, of his unfinished film, *Queen Kelly*.[2] Are these the raw materials of realism? Perhaps. Perhaps one re-members that it was under the influence of having seen *Foolish Wives* ten times that Renoir came to make his *Nana*. And then, behind the legend of meticulous authenticity—the complete electrical wiring system throughout the set of a palace, the ten

2. As it appeared in the first issue of *Film Culture,* January 1955.

thousand dollars invested in pressing special medals for one of his fictitious kingdoms, the royal crest embroidered on the extras' underwear (legend that is probably just a publicist's dream)— there is the fact of *Greed* and its remarkable fidelity of surface to that of the real world. (Though this fact has its own legends of actors living in the houses of their actual prototypes, a murder re-enacted where it was originally committed, and the duplication of near-murderous passions under the scorching sun of Death Valley.) If I say that this fidelity of *Greed* is more properly called naturalism and then sidestep hoary realism/naturalism distinctions, it is not to depreciate Stroheim's achievement. For it seems to me that, though *Greed* may rightly be called a monument of naturalism on the screen, the achievement of Stroheim rests at least as much elsewhere—in such extravagant fantasy as that of *Queen Kelly* and, especially, *Foolish Wives* and *The Wedding March*—and I think the case might well be made for the essential feculent and algolagnic fantasy of *Greed* as well (think of McTeague's devotion to his huge display gold tooth and Trina nude beneath her money), in which the surface verisimilitude serves primarily to flesh the dream. Yet, while appreciating the prodigal imagination which invented Count Vladislav Sergei Karamzin, the monstrous seducer of Monte Carlo in *Foolish Wives,* or Baron Sadoja, the "aged shoe fetishist who dies of uncontrollable excitement and locomotor ataxia at the jeweled feet of his wife on his wedding night,"[3] and, yes, even Erich von Stroheim himself, fraudulent son of a Colonel of the Dragoons and lady-in-waiting to the Empress Elizabeth (in a fiction not unmasked until five years after his death)—while appreciating this, one must also remember that, though it may all paraphrase like Frank Wedekind (with a dash of Sternheim), it isn't. For what these fantastic creations finally lack is just that quality of objectification which Wedekind's are given, that quality which transforms them into art. In Stroheim's films, the fantasies are not something given artistic form but rather something dwelled upon, and at often staggering length; one is supposed to feel terribly righteous about MGM's cutting job on the ten-hour *Greed*

3. Gavin Lambert's description of a character in *The Merry Widow,* a film I haven't seen.

Stroheim presented to them (and so one should), but one can also at least appreciate that ten hours of *Greed* did constitute a real problem.

It is, I think, the hallucinated fantasy of Stroheim's films that remains their chief fascination for us today, the meticulous detail only the means by which these fantasies could be embodied, and I think it is this that Stroheim shares with Griffith. In both Griffith, the Southerner, with his morbid sentimentality, his fixation on suffering, his obsession-horror with miscegenation, and Stroheim, the self-invented quasi–nobleman, one sees an extraordinary genius for neurotic self-dramatization, and a genius equally for the dramatic projection of their fantasies on a gigantic scale. I use the word "genius" without irony; it is one thing to be neurotic and quite another to externalize one's neuroses into a *Broken Blossoms*. And I find that, despite the foreground trashiness of *Broken Blossoms,* the world in which it is placed, the tormented Limehouse streets, exists for me with a nightmare persistency which is testimony to the force of its realization. But, though the genius of these film-makers *is* extraordinary, at least as extraordinary is the receptivity of the silent film medium to what they made of it. It was a medium which used to attract epithets like "Magic Shadows," and I submit that the extent to which it became this in the hands of a Griffith or Stroheim has yet to be sufficiently considered.

Let me make it clear that I am not claiming that consideration to be sufficient here, or that these remarks constitute a revaluation of Griffith, Stroheim and others beyond an urging of the need for such revaluation. And, if I have been making much of their peculiarities, it is only by way of saying that they worked in a most peculiar medium, one to which the canons of the film historians will poorly serve as any guide. Yet neither would I wish to seem to be saying that Griffith or Stroheim can be seen as representative of all who worked in the medium of the silent film. For, if Griffith and Stroheim may be said to exemplify the artist as servant to his unconscious, then, surely, the comparison to Eisenstein and Pudovkin is inescapable: in them, one sees incarnate the ideal of artist as master, everywhere in control. One wonders in vain as to the shape of the film's history had Griffith accepted Lenin's offer in 1923, after *The Birth of a Nation* reached the Soviet Union, to undertake supervision of the nationalized Soviet film industry. My guess is he would have lasted even less long than Eisenstein did in Hollywood.

The textbooks like to recall to us the story of Kuleshov's experiment in editing, first recorded by Pudovkin, in which the same shot of the actor Mozhukin was intercut with shots of a plate of soup, a coffin and dead woman, and a little girl and toy, each eliciting from the audience its appropriately different response. This experiment is meant to show something scientific about the properties of the film image, but, surely, in it an aesthetic is also implied: that of the artist's domination of his material rather than his deferring (if only as ideal) to its autonomy; and, whatever their differences, it was this kind of domination to which both Eisenstein and Pudovkin aspired.

Now such domination needn't be didactic in nature, and, in Pudovkin's case, often it wasn't. I think the contrast traditionally made between the temperaments of Pudovkin and Eisenstein an essentially sound one and will express it here by saying that Pudovkin was interested fundamentally in manipulating one's feelings to serve his story, Eisenstein to serve his ideology, and, resenting both, I resent the former less. Pudovkin had a real melodramatic-narrative gift, and, if he manipulates, it usually is simply in the interests of excitement. But, in Eisenstein, the manipulation is always judgmental: there is nothing in his films that is allowed to exist apart from the meaning he assigns to it. Again let me quote Robert Warshow from an essay written upon seeing again a number of the most famous Russian silent films in a retrospective showing of them in 1955.

. . . For pathos there must be victims, and in [these] movies the glare of triumphant righteousness is so blinding that one can't see any victims at all, only a few martyrs of the working class, their lives well expended, and a few bourgeois or monarchist anachronisms, swept properly into the dustbin of history. No death is without meaning; even that baby hurtling in its carriage down the Odessa steps in *Potemkin* is part of the great plan, and the spectacle is exciting but not saddening. Of course it could be said that Eisenstein and Pudovkin and Dovzhenko were the real victims, ultimately betrayed by the revolution they celebrated; but that idea, if it is important at all, becomes important only on reflection. It is hard to feel the pathos of their lives when you see them playing with corpses; if they had got the chance, they would have made a handsome montage of my corpse too, and given it a meaning—their meaning and not mine.

If this sounds like political criticism, and, in part, it is, let me make Warshow's criticism another way. When an artist imposes meaning on his subject, the aesthetic question is whether or not this meaning, this point of view, enlarges our understanding of that subject; and the *artistic defect* of Eisenstein's most famous silent films is that the answer to this question is No: his dogmatized vision unyieldingly constricts and diminishes the materials on which he imposes it. Politically, this goes both right and left; both in the "Down to feed the maggots" title appended to the disposal of the ship's doctor in *Potemkin* and in the slaughtering of a bull intercut with the massacre of the workers in *Strike*. But, as Warshow suggests and Stalin suspected, for Eisenstein, this— the meaning—wasn't really all. I have previously quoted Eisenstein on the sequence of the Odessa steps. It is difficult to read (or see) such things without recalling Warshow's characterization of Eisenstein's films as "a triumph of art over humanity."

The Soviet cinema was both the most programmatic and the last national school to come to prominence before the arrival of sound, and thus has served in the histories as basis for both panegyric and theoretical speculation on what the silent film might have gone on to be. Though I cannot similarly rise to the occasion, I would wish to make it clear, before myself turning to the subject of sound, that the silent film, for all its limitations, did encompass more than can be seen in the work of Eisenstein and Griffith. I too, like every good American, prefer a happy ending, and I believe I can produce one.

For there was another Russian film-maker, Alexander Dovzhenko, who came to films a few years later than his famous colleagues; came to the medium from painting and brought to it, as a painter need not have, a supreme painterly sense—by which I mean that rare gift for making films in which the meaning is expressed fully by the imagery rather than by drama, character, plot. Which is to say that Dovzhenko's films, as, for quite different reasons, those of the great silent comedians, seem unconfined by the silence of the silent film—that silence whose character I shall come to momentarily. His films are not unmarred by those characteristics which Warshow has pointed to in Pudovkin and Eisenstein—he can be as rigid as the latter when the dictatorial mood strikes him—but the main impetus of his films is elsewhere; and it is there—in their Chagall-like folk fantasy, their dreamy evocation of peasant life, and their passionate response to the Russian landscape—that they have their life. In 1930, three years after the advent of sound and one year before Chaplin made his silent *City Lights,* Dovzhenko made *Earth.* Together, the Chaplin film and that by Dovzhenko remain two of the enduring masterpieces of the silent film.

II

I have, in the first part of this piece, devoted myself to being as hard as I feel it necesary to be on some of the major figures of the silent film, and now I feel it necessary to engage in some qualification. My strictures on Eisenstein, Pudovkin, Griffith, Stroheim *et al.* have perhaps given the impression that I simply hate the movies; I don't, of course, and hope it hasn't seemed so, but I must acknowledge that movie-hatred can be something for which even a lover may find the proper occasion. A well-known movie critic once wrote: "While in Hollywood, one must often be a snob; in avant-garde circles one must often be a philistine." To this I would add: when faced with the official Classics of the film histories, one must often simply say No. No, for a start, to Griffith as a great artist, though with regret that we are not yet past the point of this No needing to be said. A healthy art can afford to appreciate the contribution to it of a figure such as Griffith (as the novel has Richardson) without defensive and preposterous exaggerations. He gave the medium its language and created of it, at his best, a virtual symphony of extravagant gesture and eloquent movement. Others would speak that language better, have better things to say, bring to the film a greater refinement of intellect and imagination and more consistent kinds of talent, but there would be few without an incalculable debt to him, and his films would still retain an inimitable stylistic sweep and splendor.

Some qualifications then, but mainly apologies for omissions.

Even in so highly selective a view of the development of the
medium as this, some mention should be made of Robert Flaherty;
in the terra incognita between fact and fiction, he found his
métier, and has perhaps confused our judgment of him by the
fact that he considered himself a documentarist. I would suggest,
rather, go to such films as *Moana* and *Man of Aran* with the
reflection that another poet, Synge, also thought himself a
naturalist. Missing, too, is mention of the film in Germany, where
it was early bound up with activity in the theater and early
produced, in Robert Wiene's *The Cabinet of Dr. Caligari,* an
isolated masterpiece of fantasy objectified as Stroheim's or
Griffith's never was. It was not Wiene, however, but the triumvi-
rate of Murnau, Pabst, and Lang that came to dominate the
German film; and, according to the schoolteacherish amenities of
the film histories, Murnau gets his mark for development of the
moving camera and Pabst his for his use of camera angles, with
Lang lagging slightly behind as the mounter of massive Nibe-
lungen sagas, *Metropolis,* and the Dr. Mabuse thrillers. According
to my own responses, tempered by being unfamiliar with several
of their important works, Pabst looks irretrievably dated, a crafts-
man of pedestrian sensibility, while Murnau's work survives on
the strength of a quite splendid visual imagination, his limitations, to my mind, inextricably bound up with those of his
medium itself. Lang, on the other hand, is, I believe, best understood from the perspective of a close individual attention to each
of his films in theme and style. Like Murnau, he has been deified
by the *Cahiers du Cinéma* circle of film-makers and critics, but
given, in Lang's case, a much more extensive body of work about
which to make distinctions, his reputation has been a somewhat
more erratic one. He appears as himself in Godard's *Contempt,*
in which a writer of *Cahiers*istic inclinations declares to him his
admiration for the potboiling *The Tiger of Eschnapur (Journey
to the Lost City).* "I prefer *M*," Lang dryly replies. Likewise, I
have said little about the film in France beyond some mention of
that country's claims to invention and the stultifying effects which
followed with the Film d'Art. By the mid-twenties, the main
movement in the French film had become that of a varied avant-
garde out of which several commercial film-makers were subsequently to emerge. Notable among them was René Clair, whose

Entr'acte remains for me the most exciting of this work with the exceptions of the films of Cocteau, Vigo, and Buñuel; my feelings about the films of these latter as distinguished from most of the other, rather aestheticized activity of the French avant-garde is perhaps best expressed in Vigo's comment on *Un Chien Andalou*: "Beware the dog. It bites."

Before coming to the subject of the medium's transformation by sound, I want to add a note on the subject of silent film acting. I don't know what word exists exactly to name that extraordinary thing which is a performance by, say, Lillian Gish, but certainly acting as we commonly know it is not it. The art of the great silent film stars was as abstract in its way as that of a dancer, and one of the abiding fascinations of a film such as *Greed* is in its incongruous juxtaposition of the director's passion for naturalism with this stylized artificiality of the performers. It was an art often able to evoke certain basic emotions with incredible intensity but as often seemingly incapable of delineating the more subtle or complex ones, so that many of the main characters of the silent films seem to exist solely at emotional peaks or depths. But, whatever its name, the art of the silent film stars was something incapable of surviving the transition to spoken language; where individual stars like Gish managed to go on into the sound film, it was with the abandonment of those qualities which had peculiarly defined their art in silence. The stylization of silent film "acting" and spoken language were soon discovered to be incompatible; the effect of their combination as evidenced in the many suddenly destroyed careers, not all explained, as they usually are, by inadequate vocal equipment (Janet Gaynor, with a voice described as that of a wind-up doll, became one of the earliest favorites in the talkies), was ludicrous. Only the work of the great silent comedians—Chaplin, Keaton (and, to a lesser extent, Langdon and Lloyd)—inasmuch as it alone was truly acting, in the classic pantomimic tradition (in Chaplin's case) or of a prophetic naturalism (in Keaton's), remains from the period as alive and contemporary as it ever was.

If I can say this, couldn't I say equally that neither could one call the silent film itself, excepting that of the comedians, drama as we commonly know it—is it not perhaps more like opera, some mute opera in which movement has adopted the transforming role of music? Of course, this is largely hyperbole; especially when one acknowledges that increasingly in its last years the silent film became reliant on the written titles, the actors in the shots immediately preceding them frequently doing no more than mouthing words which then themselves were seen. But what the silent film was, what it might have become, is something we shall probably never exactly know—why should one assume that the medium had fully explored its artistic possibilities when, in 1927, Warner Brothers, on the verge of bankruptcy, invested in a gimmick, and Al Jolson said, "Hey, Mom, listen to this!" and sang two songs? For the silent film died suddenly and died, as it was born, not of any artistic necessity but of a mechanical invention.

In this, though then contemporary intellectual enthusiasts of the film, and it is those people from that period who have given us most of our accounts of film history, saw but the death of an art corrupted by impurity and only gloom to follow, it must be remembered that several of the most important film-makers of the time saw no such prospect. These were as diverse as Lubitsch and Eisenstein, who, with Pudovkin, immediately hailed the coming of sound and advanced to meet it armed with manifestoes and new theories of sound montage, contrapuntal effects, and a "compound cinema" based on "noncoincidence." But, in fact, the new medium tended, unlike the silent film, to resist their manipulative treatment of it, and Pudovkin's *A Simple Case (Life Is Beautiful)* remains a strange monument to this mismatched wedding of theory and practice. In fact, with some notable exceptions, the new medium did quickly degenerate into one of dialogue with picture accompaniment, with such celebrated tableaux as that of all the actors sitting around a table and speaking into the vase of flowers which contained the microphone. If there is a fitting point in this piece for me to pay tribute to the richly various visual imaginations which informed the silent film, it is now, at the moment of noting their disappearance.

What kind of medium had film become? How was sound to be used in films? To these problems no quick solutions were to come; no Griffith was to appear to invent the syntax singlehandedly; and what one saw instead were graceful acts of balancing. The most adept performers of these were film-makers such as Clair and Lubitsch, who in such films as Clair's *Sous les Toits de Paris, Le Million, A Nous la Liberté* and Lubitsch's *The Love Parade, Monte Carlo,* and *The Smiling Lieutenant* early found ways of liberating the camera from the microphone via postsynchronous and asynchronous sound, recording the sound separately or matching sounds nonnaturalistically as in Clair's blast of trumpets for a trumpet-decorated clock in *Le Million.* Clair and Lubitsch were probably the types of artists best equipped for this kind of inventive flexibility; directors working essentially in extremely artificial, highly stylized genres, and directors of an essentially decorative temperament. By which I mean that the films of both, and especially those of Clair, are distinguished by a very pure concern for visual style: for movement, decor, lightness, grace, and speed in themselves; the imagery of their films tending to be given form independently of considerations for the demands of an expressive communication of content, and their work's independence of this enabling them to achieve—as in *Le Million*—a kind of formal perfection not generally available or even possible to a more serious and complicated art. Their films are dedicated to charm and beauty, and their freedom from what, without meaning them any derogation, I would call more serious (or, negatively, more ponderous) concerns gave them freedom also to experiment.

But though the films of Clair and Lubitsch and some others demonstrated that the sound film was not necessarily static, this was still not to demonstrate what it was. Instead, they pointed to the kind of accommodation or *modus vivendi* that was to prevail in the sound film through its first decade. The films became what Hitchcock called "silent talkies," withdrawing from dialogue and returning to the emphasis on visualization and dynamic movement—I refer, of course, to the best of them—which had characterized the silent film. Sound became something which "punctuated" the visuals; and this concept of sound, by which I mean both sound effects and dialogue, as punctuation became one of the shibboleths of that commentary and criticism being written by those mourners for the lost silence who still remained. The effect of this worked, in fact, two ways: in looking at a number of, say, Hitchcock's films of the thirties today, one is strongly impressed by their immense visual dynamism, and yet the thinness or rudimentariness of their dialogue seems to be a distinct artistic deficiency. The kind of dialogue which flourished in the thirties was pre-eminently that of wisecrack, from *Top Hat* to *The Thin Man*, and what is wisecrack if not dialogue styled upon the very principle of conversational punctuation; beyond that lay the Marx Brothers and W. C. Fields, great comics all, whose films revolve chiefly around their words and their explosive physical presences. Otherwise, it remains true that the best and most vigorous films of the thirties tended toward this kind of style, this punctuation, in their use of sound; tended to avoid taking more than quite limited advantage of sound as a resource; and one thinks of *M*, *The Public Enemy*, *Ruggles of Red Gap*, *Scarface*, *Freaks*, *The Thirty-Nine Steps*, and such others. And so, for roughly a decade, the medium (as a medium) effected a somewhat uncertain compromise between what it had been and what it now might be.

Of course, I specify the medium as a medium for certainly there were individual film-makers who found for themselves in that decade a style which drew from the new medium all the resources they seemed to need. Chaplin immediately springs to mind as one who had already found in the silent film the basis for an enduring style; not until *Monsieur Verdoux* in 1947 do we have a Chaplin film which *required* the use of sound. Frank Capra comes to mind as another, a director of comedies whose technical mastery is probably unmatched in the American film during his period, and a film-maker whose style was based principally on a classic conception of editing. This is perhaps another place at which to note some names of those whom I am otherwise letting go more or less unmentioned: film-makers like John Ford in America; Jean Renoir, Abel Gance, and Jean Vigo in France, the latter, in *Zero for Conduct* and *L'Atalante*, permanently establishing for us a definition of poetry in film; Cocteau, who made *The Blood of a Poet* in 1930 and no film again until 1945; Buñuel, who early made two unique masterpieces of the sound film in *L'Age d'Or* and *Land Without Bread* and did not make another film until 1947; Leni Riefenstahl in Nazi Germany; Mark Donskoi in the Soviet Union; and those I leave unmentioned because unknown —among them, the Japanese film-makers of the time before the forties, a period still largely unfamiliar to the West though we know it was one which contained the work of men such as Ozu and Mizoguchi, the latter known in the United States all but solely by his great *Ugetsu*.

The development of these individuals is one encompassing a great diversity, but their individual development is not here within my scope, which is rather that of the general development of their medium, and, in their relationship to their medium, none of them, though most remain incomparably greater artists, stand in the same position as Griffith to his. Unlike that of the silent film, the development of the sound film is not really evolutionary; there is no Griffith to lay the foundation and neither are there the kinds of national schools which existed in the silent film and made their general contribution—the Germans with their flair for light and angles, the Russians with montage, etc. The period of the silent film was one of common problems and common solutions, and, despite the rich variety of individual artists working in it, one tends to think naturally of *the silent film* as a medium which, by its very nature, defines the common boundaries (and I don't mean simply the silence) of the individuals working in it: how far the *medium*, irrespective of the individual artist, could go. Perhaps this wasn't strictly true but, as of 1927, the point became an academic one, and the fact is that *the sound film* in no such general way evokes a correspondingly homogeneous or sharply defined sense of medium as medium.

In saying this, one probably acknowledges the *cinéastes'* argument that the coming of sound did mean the medium's loss of "purity," though I would rather say it meant the replacing of one medium by another much less "pure." With the silent film, you always knew where you were at aesthetically, and knew you were not at the theater or reading a novel; the event of the silent film was a unique one, as were the criteria by which it might be discussed and judged. But in the sound film, at least the contemporary sound film, is one any longer sure that he's not at the theater while watching *Les Parents Terribles* or seeing a novel in *L'Avventura*? The "impurity" of the sound film consists not just in the adding of sound to silence but in the introduction to the film of the medium of language, and, with it, the opening up of all kinds of manifold possibilities for what the medium might now be able to do, or, to speak more strictly, what various artists could now do in it. Veneration of the silent film as aesthetically superior to the sound film is now, with the reconversion of Dwight Macdonald, no longer effectively with us except in our texts, but its legacy is to be found with those who continue to be convinced that the mark of a medium's merit resides in its "unique attributes"; including those who, like Dr. Siegfried Kracauer, have tried to redefine the medium's uniqueness in terms of its subject matter—in his case, physical reality. For those who wish to pursue a confrontation of the uniqueness argument head-on, I strongly urge a reading of the essay, "Style and Medium in the Motion Pictures," by Erwin Panofsky as it appears reprinted in *The Play*, an anthology edited by Eric Bentley, along with a dozen withering questions of Mr. Bentley's addressed to it. Here, I will content myself merely to declare a preference for pluralism, and to say that I believe the loss of purity or end of innocence, in art forms as in persons, tends to open the way for richer and larger orders of experience.

Given these distinctions about their respective mediums, one can say that, in a sense, there *is* a Griffith of the sound film; his name is Orson Welles, and his *The Birth of a Nation* was *Citizen Kane* in 1941. Far less than Griffith can Welles be said to have innovated those devices for which *Citizen Kane* has become famous; his prophetic masterpiece was nothing if not an eclectic one. And, unlike Griffith's, the influence of Welles in the area in which he genuinely innovated was scarcely to be felt for years afterward. For, beyond all the visual bravura and structural complexity of *Citizen Kane*—the deep focal lengths, involved tracking movements, low-angled setups—what is really important in it to the development of the medium was its discovery of a style in the use of sound, one in which image and language are imagined to work together in not simply an additive but truly integral combination. To what extent is our apprehension of the image of the burning sled, as of the film's entire structure, modified by the reporter's final speech; in effect, the speech becomes part of that image and all of the film's imagery; and, though this effect can be analyzed, its force cannot be felt short of its existence in the film. Neither language nor image fully exists without the other (which may explain why a good scenario is usually so agonizingly difficult to read). A play may fully materialize only in the theater, but its life is already in its language; it is a work of literature. But a scenario is merely a blueprint for a work which exists only on the screen.

In *Citizen Kane,* not for the first time but this time in a truly pervasive and exemplary way, one sees that language (and sound) in films can be an active collaborator with the visual image: that they might work together in complex ways in which each would radically affect our perception of the other. Now I am stressing complexity here, but manifestly a great work of art needn't be complex: greatness, to indulge in truism, may be achieved through simplicity as well. And, of course, there are other kinds of complexities besides those conveyed by language; to choose illustrations of this only from films (not, that is to say, from such obvious sources as painting, music, dance, etc.): *Un Chien Andalou, The Navigator, Nosferatu, Earth, City Lights.* But, in general, the kind of *intellectual* complexity of which language is the natural vehicle of expression doesn't appear as a pervasive characteristic of films until years after *Citizen Kane,* and perhaps not really pervasive until after the impact of Antonioni and Godard. In any event, without trying to fix any definite dates for this very gradual and uneven development, I think it clear that there are few of even the best films of the past—and I include films which I consider masterpieces and no less great than the films to come later— that have the kind of *intellectual complexity* one finds in works such as *Orpheus* or *The Diary of a Country Priest* or *Eroica* or *Le Petit Soldat* or *Eclipse.*

Again I am guilty of a notable omission for, in certain ways (for the film's audience, at any rate), the major transitional figure between the example of Orson Welles and a general consciousness of that example's implications is someone who is neither a great nor an innovating film-maker but nevertheless an important one: I mean Ingmar Bergman. It was Bergman, I think, who first made a sizable audience aware of the intellectual force language could exert in the film medium without diminishing a work's validity as a film; and, interestingly, his films gave rise to the first modern collection of scenarios intended to be read as literature, and since followed by those of Antonioni, Fellini, and Godard. Increasingly, one has come to feel the importance of the words which go into the making of a film, and, though I don't mean to say that these films have a prior existence on paper or that the words themselves can be any substitute for the film, neither can we really know or understand these modern films without knowing and understanding them in this aspect. Take Godard—surely as "cinematic" and revolutionary a film-maker as any there is—and yet notice how literary his films are—full of puns, riddles, epigrams, lines echoing lines, quotations from literature, interviews and monologues. As one who has written in considerable detail about Godard's first full-length film, I can attest to the desperation one can frequently feel trying to analyze such a work as *Breathless* without a script to refer to or a genius for shorthand. Of course, a film such as *Breathless* is noted first of all for its techniques: the jump cuts, hand-held camera, and the rest; but how can one isolate such things in the work of Godard as, of a Griffith or Pudovkin or Pabst, one could talk about innovations of close-ups or cutting or camera angles when these were merely devices to enhance the exposition of simple narrative? The innovations of Godard—and I refer to him here both as what he uniquely is and as a paradigmatic figure of the contemporary film-maker—the techniques and the style are too deeply implicated in the works' total meaning to be discussed apart from this. They are works no longer to be understood by the mentality which has dominated most of our writing about films until now; a mentality identifiable by the pedagogical label of "film appreciation"; but rather by the kinds of intelligent critical response one must make to the most serious drama and fiction—to a Beckett, to a Faulkner. Anyone for "novel appreciation"?

And that is why, while I agree with Pauline Kael that there is a vast area of the movies which can never be honestly legitimized for cultural consumption (though I'm aware that the day of Ph.D. theses on Humphrey Bogart is at hand, I can't but view it with horror), I believe there is also an expanding body of work within the film which demands the kind of serious and detailed attention that one associates with a first-rate criticism of literature and drama. And that is why, when a first-rate film critic comes along, he will write like Robert Warshow—and be damned for his insensitivity to "the medium"—and not like just another glibly knowledgeable contributor to our film periodicals; and why the film periodicals (and film histories) will continue to tell us so little about our films for all their cultivated expertise. I want to quote one last time from Robert Warshow in a review of a book still found on virtually every list of so-called "Basic Books on the Film" which is appended to the backs of film histories by those who write them so as to insure the complicity of such others who do as they perpetuate together those hoary untruths to which I have tried to address myself earlier.

> But there is a basic error in the idea of "appreciation" itself, an idea that presupposes a homogeneous culture in which a progressive refinement of taste will lead almost automatically from bad art to good art. . . . It is more than the development of taste that leads one to prefer Kafka to Somerset Maugham; indeed, the cultivated taste left to itself is perhaps a little more likely to choose Maugham. And in the films, though it is obviously desirable to respond as fully as possible to the aesthetic complexities of technique, these "pure" values are at least equalled in importance by the medium's immense power of communication, which always raises aesthetic problems that go beyond the boundaries implied by the idea of "appreciation"; the film "connoisseur" tends to go wrong in so far as his concern with the "cinematic" causes him to ignore these problems . . . one of the most sensitive of American critics has overvalued such trash as *The Best Years of Our Lives* and *Key Largo;* another critic, writing in one of the little magazines, has suggested that the films of Maya Deren are superior to Chaplin's *Monsieur Verdoux.* . . . These are contrary errors, but they come from the same source: a refusal to acknowledge the essential *aesthetic* importance of film content.[4]

This refusal—a refusal to come to grips aesthetically with the totality of a film, with its meaning, beyond its techniques and its form and its "place" in the institutionalized hierarchy—is really the source of virtually all of the "contrary" errors of film criticism and film history. It is a refusal without which there could be no "film appreciation." Without going beyond it, we will never free ourselves from the tyranny of our film "classics" and the inflated reputations of our Eisensteins and Griffiths. Nor will we ever understand what the films of Godard and most great films are all about.

4. "The Art of the Film," *Partisan Review*, October 1948.

III

I have reached the climax of my argument, but not quite its conclusion. For I find myself seemingly back where I began, and
sounding very much like the Mr. Y of my opening anecdote with
his advice to start with Godard—"That's art!" So I want to add a
short anticlimax by way of again saying No.

I have tried in this essay to formulate an argument about a
development in the medium toward a relatively new kind of serious film; a different, not superior, kind of film; one deeply involved in the kinds of complexity which the conjunction of image
and language can create. In making this general case about the
medium, I have explicitly excluded from consideration the work
of a number of the artists in it; people such as Renoir, Vigo,
Buñuel, Ford; they are, in a sense, irrelevant to my argument, or,
rather, I should say, my argument is irrelevant to them. Yet my
argument has a validity only insofar as its actuality and theirs are
seen to coexist. For among those my argument excludes are, in
fact, the artists I believe to be the greatest to have worked in
film; artists who, during a period about which I spoke of the
medium's withdrawal from language, were making such films as
L'Age d'Or, The Crime of Monsieur Lange, L'Atalante, and
Young Mr. Lincoln; were, that is to say, discovering for themselves
all the means that were necessary to create work as rich as any
their medium contains.

In every art form, there is discovery and consolidation, the
opening up of new territory and the inhabiting of it, and it is
the latter of each of these pairs of things with which my argument
was concerned: the ill-defined, sporadic transformation of a
medium which follows laggingly upon the impact of its greatest
artists' definitive achievements. I don't mean to suggest here
that the greatest artists are always innovators—every great artist
is a consolidator to some varying degree—but only that every
great artist, innovational or not, implies in his work a definition
of his medium which affects our sense of its boundaries and what
it can contain; he creates, in effect, the medium in which those
who follow him will work. Each artist starts with something given,
and a Bertolucci or Bellocchio starts now with, as given, a sense
of the capacities of his medium that the work of an Antonioni

and Godard (and Renoir, and Buñuel) has largely created—
though what these earlier artists created in the first place was not
their medium but their art; art which then extended the definition of their medium. For though one feels that the medium in
which Godard now works has come in general to suggest a different complex of possibilities from that in which Renoir once
did, of Renoir no less than Godard does one feel that the actuality
of his art springs from a complex of internal necessities in which
the medium as such plays no inhibiting part. For a Renoir (like
a Godard, Antonioni, Ford, Buñuel, Chaplin, Keaton, Vigo,
Satyajit Ray) is the kind of artist whose work seems not so much
to be contained within some definition of the nature of his
medium as rather to define that nature continually anew. Part
of what the nature of that medium is we know only because there
is *The Rules of the Game*. And that is part of what we mean
when we say that Renoir is great.

But this, and the rest of it, will never be known to us by the
criteria of film appreciation. And, if I have said previously that,
without freeing ourselves from such criteria, we will never understand what the films of Godard are about, it remains to be said
that, when one looks closely at those who now "start with
Godard," what one often finds is film appreciation in a newer,
more sophisticated guise. For the differences between Ernest
Lindgren sitting on the top floor of the British Film Institute
and waxing lyrical about the cream separator sequence in *The
General Line* and Richard Roud–Tom Milne panegyrizing the
plastic beauties of Godard and Susan Sontag calling for an erotics
of art are, finally, those of taste and intelligence (not much between the first two and lots between them and the third), not
essential character. Of course, Miss Sontag, at her best, is too good
a critic to put her theory into practice, but, where she declines,
there are a hundred with-it epigones to rush into the void, starting with Godard and ending with *2001*. Miss Sontag is right to
insist on that response to the sensuous aspect of film which has
been lacking in so much of its criticism; indeed, it is a deadness
to this sensuousness that has largely accounted, in the past, for
film appreciation's neglect of Renoir and elevation of Eisenstein;
that and the fact that Eisenstein's "contribution" to the medium
is so much easier pedagogically to isolate. But this failure doesn't

inhere in interpretive criticism, though all the English professor exegetes who "started with Bergman" may have made it appear so. And the newly ascendant dogma of film as a sensory medium is finally as stranglingly constrictive as that of the film as a visual medium ever was. They are equally evasions of a confrontation of the aesthetic ramifications of art's meaning, and, to the extent that they exclude our response to this, denials of part of what it is to be human. Our heightened sensitivity to the sensuousness of film is necessary to any whole response, but it will not suffice. No erotics of art will sufficiently enable us to grasp what is contained in such things as Octave's casual remark in *The Rules of the Game* that "The frightening thing about this world is that everyone has his reasons," or to fathom the power of that film's final image of moving shadows on a wall.

(1969)

INDEX

317

71 72 73 74 10 9 8 7 6 5 4 3 2 1